# First World War
## and Army of Occupation
# War Diary
## France, Belgium and Germany

15 DIVISION
45 Infantry Brigade,
Brigade Machine Gun Company
1 June 1916 - 28 February 1918

WO95/1947/3

The Naval & Military Press Ltd
www.nmarchive.com
**Published in association with The National Archives**

Published by

The Naval & Military Press Ltd

Unit 10 Ridgewood Industrial Park,

Uckfield, East Sussex,

TN22 5QE England

Tel: +44 (0) 1825 749494

www.naval-military-press.com

www.nmarchive.com

*This diary has been reprinted in facsimile from the original. Any imperfections are inevitably reproduced and the quality may fall short of modern type and cartographic standards.*

# Contents

| Document type | Place/Title | Date From | Date To |
|---|---|---|---|
| Heading | 1947/3 45th Brigade Machine Gun Company | | |
| Heading | 45th Machine Gun Coy. Jun 1916-Feb 1918 | | |
| Heading | 45th M.G. Coy. June 1916 | | |
| Miscellaneous | Memorandum. O.C. 45 Coy. Machine Gun Corps. D.A.G. 3rd. Echelon G.H.Q. | 02/07/1916 | 02/07/1916 |
| Heading | War Diary No 45 Coy Machine Gun Corps. June 1916. | | |
| War Diary | Aoyillo | 01/06/1916 | 19/06/1916 |
| War Diary | Vermelles | 26/06/1916 | 30/06/1916 |
| Heading | War Diary. 45th Machine Gun Company. 1st July 1916 to 31st July 1916. Volumn. | | |
| War Diary | Vermelles | 01/07/1916 | 05/07/1916 |
| War Diary | Aouille | 06/07/1916 | 21/07/1916 |
| War Diary | Moutesment | 22/07/1916 | 22/07/1916 |
| War Diary | Tangry | 23/07/1916 | 26/07/1916 |
| War Diary | Jashincourt | 27/07/1916 | 27/07/1916 |
| War Diary | Maininlablenol | 28/07/1916 | 28/07/1916 |
| War Diary | Le Meillard | 29/07/1916 | 31/07/1916 |
| Heading | 45th Brigade 15th Division Machine Gun Company August 1916 | | |
| Heading | Volume No. 3 No. 45 Company Machine Gun Corps. War Diary For August. 1916 | | |
| War Diary | Vignacourt | 01/08/1916 | 03/08/1916 |
| War Diary | Mollins Au Bois | 04/08/1916 | 04/08/1916 |
| War Diary | Bresle | 05/08/1916 | 07/08/1916 |
| War Diary | Contalmasng | 08/08/1916 | 13/08/1916 |
| War Diary | Beconstwood | 14/08/1916 | 14/08/1916 |
| War Diary | Albert | 15/08/1916 | 19/08/1916 |
| War Diary | Appendix. X 27a 9.4 | 20/08/1916 | 20/08/1916 |
| War Diary | X27a 9.4 | 21/08/1916 | 22/08/1916 |
| War Diary | Lower Wood | 23/08/1916 | 29/08/1916 |
| War Diary | X27a 9.7. | 30/08/1916 | 31/08/1916 |
| Heading | Summary for August Casualties | | |
| Heading | 45th M.G. Coy. September 1916 | | |
| Heading | 45th Machine Gun Company September 1916 | | |
| War Diary | Lonely. Trench X27a. 9.4 (App) | 01/09/1916 | 04/09/1916 |
| War Diary | E.8.A. | 04/09/1916 | 05/09/1916 |
| War Diary | Lavieville | 05/09/1916 | 12/09/1916 |
| War Diary | E.7. Anties | 12/09/1916 | 18/09/1916 |
| War Diary | Millencourt. | 18/09/1916 | 19/09/1916 |
| War Diary | Baizieux | 19/09/1916 | 30/09/1916 |
| Heading | Summary of Casualties for September Officers | | |
| Operation(al) Order(s) | No. 45 Machine Gun Coy. Operation Orders by Capt. H.V. Wilkinson Commanding No. 45 M.G. Coy. | 13/09/1916 | 13/09/1916 |
| Miscellaneous | No. 45 Machine Gun Coy. Supplement to O.O. dated 13-9-16 | 14/09/1916 | 14/09/1916 |
| Map | | | |
| Heading | 45th M.G. Coy. October 1916 | | |
| Heading | War Diary of No. 45 Company Machine Gun. Corps. from 1st October 1916 to 31st October 1916 Volume V | | |
| War Diary | Baizieux | 01/10/1916 | 05/10/1916 |

| | | | |
|---|---|---|---|
| War Diary | Bresle | 06/10/1916 | 10/10/1916 |
| War Diary | Martinpuich | 12/10/1916 | 14/10/1916 |
| War Diary | Lonely Tr | 15/10/1916 | 19/10/1916 |
| War Diary | Mill Martinpuich | 20/10/1916 | 31/10/1916 |
| Miscellaneous | Appendix I Movement Order by Capt. H.V. Wilkinson | 03/10/1916 | 03/10/1916 |
| Operation(al) Order(s) | Appendix II Operation Orders by Capt. H.V. Wilkinson | 24/10/1916 | 24/10/1916 |
| Miscellaneous | No. 45 Machine Gun Coy. Addendum to. O.O. dated 24-10-16 | 26/10/1916 | 26/10/1916 |
| Heading | 45th M.G. Corps. November 1916 | | |
| Heading | War Diary of 45 Coy Machine Gun Corps 1st to 30th November 1916 Volumn VI | | |
| War Diary | Mill Martinpuich | 01/11/1916 | 02/11/1916 |
| War Diary | Mill Lonely Trench | 03/11/1916 | 03/11/1916 |
| War Diary | Albert | 03/11/1916 | 05/11/1916 |
| War Diary | Franvillers | 06/11/1916 | 26/11/1916 |
| War Diary | Bazieux | 27/11/1916 | 30/11/1916 |
| Miscellaneous | Relief Orders to Captain H.V. Wilkinson Commanding 45th Coy M.G.C. in the field | | |
| Operation(al) Order(s) | Operation Orders by Capt. H.V. Wilkinson Comdg No 45 Machine Gun Coy | 04/11/1916 | 04/11/1916 |
| Heading | 45th M.G. Coy. December 1916 | | |
| Heading | War Diary of 45th Machine Gun Company M.G.C. 1st to 31st December 1916 Volumn VII | | |
| War Diary | Bazieux | 01/12/1916 | 01/12/1916 |
| War Diary | Millencourt. | 02/12/1916 | 15/12/1916 |
| War Diary | Shelterwood | 15/12/1916 | 16/12/1916 |
| War Diary | Middlewood | 16/12/1916 | 16/12/1916 |
| War Diary | Martinpuich | 16/12/1916 | 19/12/1916 |
| War Diary | Shelterwood | 20/12/1916 | 31/12/1916 |
| War Diary | Shelterwood Camp. | 31/12/1916 | 31/12/1916 |
| Miscellaneous | Relief Orders By Capt. H.V. Wilkinson Commanding No. 45 Machine Gun Coy. | 13/12/1916 | 13/12/1916 |
| Miscellaneous | Routine Orders By Capt. H.V. Wilkinson Commanding 45th Machine Gun Coy. | 13/12/1916 | 13/12/1916 |
| Miscellaneous | Relief Orders By Capt. H.V. Wilkinson. Commanding 45th Machine Gun Coy. | 22/12/1916 | 22/12/1916 |
| Heading | War Diary of 45th Company Machine Gun Corps. 1st To 31st January 1917. Volumn. VIII | | |
| War Diary | Shelter Wood Camp | 01/01/1917 | 04/01/1917 |
| War Diary | Martin Puich | 04/01/1917 | 12/01/1917 |
| War Diary | Aciddrop Camp South | 13/01/1917 | 16/01/1917 |
| War Diary | Pioneer Camp | 17/01/1917 | 24/01/1917 |
| War Diary | AcidDrop Camp South | 25/01/1917 | 28/01/1917 |
| War Diary | Martinpuich | 28/01/1917 | 31/01/1917 |
| Miscellaneous | Relief. Orders By Capt. H.V. Wilkinson Appendix No. I | 11/01/1917 | 11/01/1917 |
| Miscellaneous | Relief Orders By Capt. H.V. Wilkinson Commanding 45 Machine Gun Coy Appendix No II | 23/01/1917 | 23/01/1917 |
| Miscellaneous | Relief Orders By Major H.V. Wilkinson Commanding 45th Machine Gun Coy. Appendix No III | 27/01/1917 | 27/01/1917 |
| Miscellaneous | Relief Orders By Major H.V. Wilkinson Commanding 45th Machine Gun Coy Appendix No IV | 31/01/1917 | 31/01/1917 |
| Heading | War Diary of February 1917 1st To 28th February 1917 Volumn IX | | |
| War Diary | Martinpuich | 01/02/1917 | 01/02/1917 |
| War Diary | Fricourt | 02/02/1917 | 04/02/1917 |

| | | | |
|---|---|---|---|
| War Diary | Baizieux | 05/02/1917 | 16/02/1917 |
| War Diary | Barly | 17/02/1917 | 17/02/1917 |
| War Diary | Honval | 18/02/1917 | 18/02/1917 |
| War Diary | Foufflin Ricametz | 19/02/1917 | 24/02/1917 |
| War Diary | Noyellette | 25/02/1917 | 28/02/1917 |
| Miscellaneous | Movement Orders By Major H.V. Wilkinson Commanding 45th Machine Gun Coy | 03/02/1917 | 03/02/1917 |
| Heading | War Diary of 45th Machine Gun Company 1st To 31st March 1917 Volumn X | | |
| War Diary | Noyellette | 01/03/1917 | 02/03/1917 |
| War Diary | Arras | 03/03/1917 | 19/03/1917 |
| War Diary | Noyellette | 20/03/1917 | 30/03/1917 |
| War Diary | Arras | 31/03/1917 | 31/03/1917 |
| Operation(al) Order(s) | Operation Orders By Lieut F.C. Newton Commanding 45th Machine Gun Coy | 01/03/1917 | 01/03/1917 |
| Miscellaneous | Relief Orders Major H.V. Wilkinson Commanding 45th Machine Gun Coy. | 29/03/1917 | 29/03/1917 |
| Miscellaneous | Preliminary Instructions | 14/03/1917 | 14/03/1917 |
| Heading | War Diary of 45th Machine Gun Coy. 1st To 30th April 1917 Volume X.I. | | |
| War Diary | Arras | 01/04/1917 | 09/04/1917 |
| War Diary | Railway Triangle | 10/04/1917 | 10/04/1917 |
| War Diary | Feuchy | 10/04/1917 | 12/04/1917 |
| War Diary | Arras | 13/04/1917 | 20/04/1917 |
| War Diary | In The Line | 21/04/1917 | 29/04/1917 |
| War Diary | Berneville | 30/04/1917 | 30/04/1917 |
| Heading | 45th Company Machine Gun Corps War Diary For Month Of May 1917 Volume X.I.I. | | |
| War Diary | Berneville | 02/05/1917 | 07/05/1917 |
| War Diary | Wanquentin | 08/05/1917 | 08/05/1917 |
| War Diary | Beaudricourt | 09/05/1917 | 21/05/1917 |
| War Diary | Bonniers | 22/05/1917 | 22/05/1917 |
| War Diary | Quoeux | 23/05/1917 | 31/05/1917 |
| Miscellaneous | Tactical Scheme 28-5-17 | 26/05/1917 | 26/05/1917 |
| Heading | War Diary of 45th Machine Gun Company 1st to 30th June 1917 Volume XIII | | |
| War Diary | Quoeux | 01/06/1917 | 21/06/1917 |
| War Diary | Petit Houvin | 22/06/1917 | 22/06/1917 |
| War Diary | Conteville | 23/06/1917 | 23/06/1917 |
| War Diary | La Couture | 24/06/1917 | 25/06/1917 |
| War Diary | Neufpre | 26/06/1917 | 26/06/1917 |
| War Diary | Pradelles | 27/07/1917 | 27/07/1917 |
| War Diary | Watou Area | 28/06/1917 | 30/06/1917 |
| Heading | War Diary of 45th Machine Gun Company 1st to 31st July 1917 Volume XIV | | |
| War Diary | Broxeele Area. | 01/07/1917 | 09/07/1917 |
| War Diary | In The Line | 09/07/1917 | 19/07/1917 |
| War Diary | Forts Cont | 20/07/1917 | 22/07/1917 |
| War Diary | Watou Area | 22/07/1917 | 25/07/1917 |
| War Diary | In The line | 30/07/1917 | 31/07/1917 |
| War Diary | Forth Ant Area | 27/07/1917 | 29/07/1917 |
| War Diary | In The Line | 31/07/1917 | 31/07/1917 |
| Heading | War Diary of 45th Machine Gun Company 1st To 31st August 1917 Volumn XV | | |
| War Diary | In The Line | 01/08/1917 | 03/08/1917 |
| War Diary | Toronto Camp | 03/08/1917 | 03/08/1917 |

| | | | |
|---|---|---|---|
| War Diary | Winnezeele | 04/08/1917 | 19/08/1917 |
| War Diary | Upres | 19/08/1917 | 31/08/1917 |
| Heading | War Diary of 45th Machine Gun Company 1st To 30th September 1917 Volumn XVI | | |
| War Diary | Haggis Camp (Hpres) | 01/09/1917 | 01/09/1917 |
| War Diary | Wormhoudt | 01/09/1917 | 02/09/1917 |
| War Diary | Etrun | 03/09/1917 | 05/09/1917 |
| War Diary | Dingwall Camp (Blangy) | 05/09/1917 | 06/09/1917 |
| War Diary | In The Line | 07/09/1917 | 15/09/1917 |
| War Diary | Dingwall Camp | 15/09/1917 | 23/09/1917 |
| War Diary | In The Line | 24/09/1917 | 30/09/1917 |
| Heading | War Diary of 45th Machine Gun Corps Company 1st To 31st October 1917 Volumn XVII | | |
| War Diary | In The Line | 01/10/1917 | 07/10/1917 |
| War Diary | In The Line | 08/09/1917 | 09/09/1917 |
| War Diary | Dingwall Camp | 10/09/1917 | 11/09/1917 |
| War Diary | Dingwall Camp | 12/10/1917 | 12/10/1917 |
| War Diary | Arras | 13/10/1917 | 17/10/1917 |
| War Diary | In The Line | 18/10/1917 | 31/10/1917 |
| Heading | Subject. | | |
| Heading | War Diary of 45th Machine Gun Company 1st To 31st November 1917 Volumn XVIII | | |
| War Diary | In The Line | 01/11/1917 | 02/11/1917 |
| War Diary | Arras | 03/11/1917 | 12/11/1917 |
| War Diary | In The Line | 13/11/1917 | 26/11/1917 |
| War Diary | Arras | 27/11/1917 | 28/11/1917 |
| War Diary | In The Line | 29/11/1917 | 30/11/1917 |
| Miscellaneous | Addendum To W.D | 28/11/1917 | 28/11/1917 |
| War Diary | Famonchy | 24/04/1917 | 25/11/1917 |
| War Diary | Arras Beaudimont Barracks | 26/11/1917 | 30/11/1917 |
| Heading | War Diary of 45th Machine Gun Company 1st To 31st December 1917 Volume XIX | | |
| War Diary | In The Line | 01/12/1917 | 01/12/1917 |
| War Diary | Arras | 02/12/1917 | 08/12/1917 |
| War Diary | In The Line | 09/12/1917 | 23/12/1917 |
| War Diary | Arras | 24/12/1917 | 31/12/1917 |
| Heading | War Diary of 45th Machine Gun Company 1st To 31st January 1918. Volume XX | | |
| War Diary | Arras | 01/01/1918 | 01/01/1918 |
| War Diary | Warlus. | 02/01/1918 | 31/01/1918 |
| Heading | War Diary of 45th Machine Gun Company 1st To 28th January 1918. Volume XXI | | |
| War Diary | Warlus | 01/02/1918 | 05/02/1918 |
| War Diary | In The Line | 06/02/1918 | 28/02/1918 |

1947/3

45th Brigade Machine
Gun Company

15TH DIVISION
45TH INFY BDE

45TH MACHINE GUN COY.

JUN 1916 - FEB 1918

Index

**SUBJECT.**

45th M. G. Coy

| No. | Contents. | Date. |
|---|---|---|
| | June 1916 | |

(63,905). Wt.16,820—175. 2000. 9/21. Gp.164. A.&E.W.

[887] W13315 4182 5000.n 12/15a G & S 77 77 Forms 348 / 61

Army Form C. 348.

# MEMORANDUM.

| | |
|---|---|
| From O. C. 45 Coy. Machine Gun Corps. | From |
| To D. A. G. 3rd. Echelon. G. H. Q. | To |
| | ANSWER. |
| 2nd. July 1916 | 191 . |

Herewith War Diary of
45 Coy. Machine Gun Corps.
for the month of June 1916.

Cheslie Roberts
LIEUT:

O.C. No. 45 COY.
MACHINE GUN CORPS.

Instructions regarding War Diaries and Intelligence Summaries are contained in F. S. Regs., Part II. and the Staff Manual respectively. Title Pages will be prepared in manuscript.

# WAR DIARY

*or*

~~INTELLIGENCE SUMMARY~~

*(Erase heading not required.)*

XV

Army Form C. 2118

France

45 M G Coy

Vol 1

| Place | Date | Hour | Summary of Events and Information | Remarks and references to Appendices |
|---|---|---|---|---|
| | | | War Diary<br>No 45 Coy Machine Gun Corps.<br>June 1916.<br><br>Chas Roberts Lt. | |

No. 45 COMPANY
No.
Date 1 JUL 1916
MACHINE GUN CORPS.

O.C. No. 45 COY.
MACHINE GUN CORPS

1875 Wt. W593/826 1,000,000 4/15 J.B.C. & A. A.D.S.S./Forms/C. 2118.

Instructions regarding War Diaries and Intelligence Summaries are contained in F. S. Regs., Part II. and the Staff Manual respectively. Title Pages will be prepared in manuscript.

# WAR DIARY
*or*
~~INTELLIGENCE SUMMARY~~
*(Erase heading not required.)*

Army Form C. 2118

| Place | Date | Hour | Summary of Events and Information | Remarks and references to Appendices |
|---|---|---|---|---|
| Noyelles | 1/6/16 | | The Commanding Officer Major Macartney injured. One O.R. admitted into hospital. Major Macartney evacuated. One O.R. reinforcement joined from Base. | |
| " | 2/6/16 | | One OR evacuated. One OR proceeded on leave to UK. One OR returned from leave. | |
| " | 3/6/16 | | Two O.R. ~~to~~ returned from leave. One O.R. admitted to hospital. | |
| " | 4/6/16 | | Lieut J A McFerran proceeded on leave to U.K. One OR returned from leave. | |
| " | 5/6/16 | | Lieut A E Pescod returned from leave. Two OR admitted to hospital. | |
| " | 6/6/16 | | One OR evacuated. One OR proceeded on leave to UK. One OR returned from leave. | |
| " | 7/6/16 | | The OR reinforcement joined from base. One OR. evacuated | |
| " | 8/6/16 | | One OR proceeded on leave to UK. One OR returned from leave | |
| " | 9/6/16 | | One OR returned from leave | |
| " | 10/6/16 | | One OR rejoined company from hospital. One OR proceeded on leave to UK. One OR returned from leave | |
| " | 11/6/16 | | Eleven guns of No 45 Coy were relieved by eleven guns of No 44 Coy in the Quarries section. Five guns of No 45 Coy were left in the Village Line in position V4. V4a V5. V15 + V16. Relief was completed by 4-0 pm. Company billetted in huts at Noyelles. One OR proceeded on leave to UK | |

1875 Wt. W593/826 1,000,000 4/15 J.B.C. & A. A.D.S.S./Forms/C. 2118.

Instructions regarding War Diaries and Intelligence Summaries are contained in F. S. Regs., Part II. and the Staff Manual respectively. Title Pages will be prepared in manuscript.

# WAR DIARY
*or*
~~INTELLIGENCE SUMMARY~~
*(Erase heading not required.)*

Army Form C. 2118

| Place | Date | Hour | Summary of Events and Information | Remarks and references to Appendices |
|---|---|---|---|---|
| Noyelles | 12/6/16 | | One OR was granted leave to UK. One OR returned from leave | |
| " | 13/6/16 | | One OR admitted to hospital. One OR evacuated. Lieut J. A. McFerran returned from leave. One O.R proceeded on leave to UK. | |
| " | 14/6/16 | | One OR. rejoined from hospital | |
| " | 15/6/16 | | One O.R rejoined from hospital. One OR reinforcement joined from Base<br>One OR proceeded on leave to UK. | |
| " | 16/6/16 | | One officer reinforcement 2nd Lieut. Goddard RH joined from Base<br>One OR returned from leave | |
| " | 17/6/16 | | One O.R returned from leave | |
| " | 18/6/16 | | One OR admitted to hospital One OR returned from leave | |
| " | 19/6/16 | | The guns of No 45 Coy relieved the guns of No 46 Coy in the Hohenzollern section; the following gun positions were manned. S2. S5. S8. R1. R2. R3. R4. R5. R5-6. V6. V7. V8. V9. CK1. CK2 + J1. Relief was completed at 3·30 pm.<br>2nd Lieut E. P. Cartwright proceeded on leave to UK. One OR returned from leave. | |
| Vermelles | 20/6/16 | | Work in trenches proceeded with at all gun positions. Guns R4 + R5 each fired about 1000 rounds during the night on enemy's communication trenches. One OR returned from leave. | |

1875 Wt. W593/826 1,000,000 4/15 J.B.C. & A. A.D.S.S./Forms/C. 2118.

Instructions regarding War Diaries and Intelligence Summaries are contained in F. S. Regs., Part II. and the Staff Manual respectively. Title Pages will be prepared in manuscript.

# WAR DIARY
*or*
## ~~INTELLIGENCE SUMMARY~~
*(Erase heading not required.)*

Army Form C. 2118

| Place | Date | Hour | Summary of Events and Information | Remarks and references to Appendices |
|---|---|---|---|---|
| Vermelles | 21/6/16 | | All guns & emplacements completed with the necessary blankets for protection against gas. No night firing was done owing to large working parties being out in front of Reserve line | |
| " | 22/6/16 | | Situation normal during the last 24 hours. No night firing possible owing to working parties being out in front. One OR admitted to hospital. One OR rejoined from hospital. All ammunition in line was examined & all defective ammunition replaced. | |
| " | 23/6/16 | | Situation normal. 750 rounds fired at new trolley railway running from Potsdam trench to Fosse alley. One OR rejoined from hospital. One OR attached to the coy (cold shoes) One OR proceeded on leave to U.K. One OR returned from leave. | |
| " | 24/6/16 | | Intense Machine Gun Bombardment by No 45 Coy from 11-0 – 11-8 pm & 2-0 – 2-8 a.m. on enemies communication trenches & roads. Rounds expended 7900. Five Officers + 10 NCOs of No 120 Coy attached to No 45 Coy for training. Four Officers + 10 NCOs proceeded direct to trenches. O.C. stayed at HQ No 45 Coy. Two OR admitted to hospital | |
| " | 25/6/16 | | Raid by 45th IB arranged for the night was postponed as wind was unfavourable for using gas. Intense machine Gun bombardment from 12-55 am – 1-5 am (26th) by Guns R1, R2, R3, R4, R5 & R5b. Rounds fired 8650. Enemy aircraft was engaged by MG Fire, rounds expended 1510. Four attached officers + 10 attached NCOs returned to their unit. Four officers + 10 NCOs of No 120 MG Coy attached for training. They proceeded directly to the trenches. One OR slightly wounded shrapnel in leg. | |

1375 Wt. W593/826 1,000,000 4/15 J.B.C. & A. A.D.S.S./Forms/C. 2118.

Instructions regarding War Diaries and Intelligence Summaries are contained in F. S. Regs., Part II. and the Staff Manual respectively. Title Pages will be prepared in manuscript.

# WAR DIARY
*or*
~~INTELLIGENCE SUMMARY~~
*(Erase heading not required.)*

Army Form C. 2118

| Place | Date | Hour | Summary of Events and Information | Remarks and references to Appendices |
|---|---|---|---|---|
| Vermelles | 26/6/16 | | Raid by 45th IB postponed on account of unfavourable wind. Rounds fired during night by R1, R2, R3, R4 + R5 – 5400: Officers + NCOs of 120th IB MG Coy attached to No 45 Company returned to their own unit. One OR evacuated | |
| " | 27/6/16 | | The enemy was attacked by gas smoke + strong raiding patrols on the night of 27th-28th. Enemy's trenches were penetrated by the infantry of the 45th Brigade. Intense Machine Gun bombardment by 13 guns. (12 guns of No 45 Coy + 1 Gun of 11th Battery MMG) from 12-55 am to 1-5 am 28th. Rounds fired on to communication trenches, roads etc 11,657. 2nd Lieut E P Cartwright returned from leave. One OR admitted to hospital One OR evacuated. C + D Section No 45 Coy relieved A + B Section in the line. | |
| " | 28/6/16 | | Situation normal. Overhead fire during night onto enemy back system of trenches road junctions etc. Guns R1, R2, R3, R4 + R5 fired 2520 rounds. | |
| " | 29/6/16 | | A company of 6th Camerons raided the German trenches at 1-0 am. Machine Guns of No 45 Coy provided overhead fire for their support. Rounds fired 8100. The brewery Vermelles was bombarded during the night + one O.R. was wounded in the legs whilst lying in the cellar. | |
| " | 30/6/16 | | Situation normal. Night firing by four guns R.2, R3, R4 + R5. Rounds fired 3200. One OR admitted to hospital | |

1375 Wt. W593/826 1,000,000 4/15 J.B.C. & A. A.D.S.S./Forms/C. 2118.

15 July
45 M.G.C
Vol 2

CONFIDENTIAL.

WAR DIARY.

45TH MACHINE GUN COMPANY.

1st JULY 1916 to 31ST JULY 1916.

VOLUMN. ________

Instructions regarding War Diaries and Intelligence Summaries are contained in F. S. Regs., Part II. and the Staff Manual respectively. Title Pages will be prepared in manuscript.

# WAR DIARY
*or*
~~INTELLIGENCE SUMMARY~~
*(Erase heading not required.)*

No 45 COMPANY
MACHINE GUN CORPS

Army Form C. 2118

| Place | Date | Hour | Summary of Events and Information | Remarks and references to Appendices |
|---|---|---|---|---|
| Vermelles | 1/7/16 | | Situation normal during day. Intense bombardment on both sides of 45th IB. Overhead fire directed onto trenches in front of 33rd Division on our left. Five guns R1 R2 R3 R4 + R5 fired 7000 rounds. One OR admitted to hospital. | |
| " | 2/7/16 | | Situation normal during day. Artillery bombardment + attack with smoke bombs commenced at 10.0 pm. Hun retaliation on our front line. Gas attack cancelled owing to unfavourable wind. Machine Guns fired 6750 rounds on trenches in our own front. One OR evacuated. | |
| " | 3/7/16 | | Situation unchanged. Five guns R1. R2. R3, R4 + R5 fired 4850 rounds on to enemy communication trenches. One OR wounded. | |
| " | 4/7/16 | | Situation normal during day. Raid by 46th Infantry Brigade on German front line during night. Intense barrage by our artillery. No retaliation by Hun. Machine Gun long range fire from seven guns of No 45 Coy in support of raid. Rounds fired 10,000. | |
| " | 5/7/16 | | No 45 Company relieved in the trenches by No 44 Coy + Lewis Guns of 44th IB. Relief completed at 4.0 pm. Company moved to Noyelles + were billetted in huts | |
| Noyelles | 6/7/16 | | Noyelles was shelled at intervals during the day. Several civilians were amongst the casualties. One OR granted special leave to UK as per 1st Army 943/121a of 3/7/16 | [signature] |

1875 Wt. W593/826 1,000,000 4/15 J.B.C. & A. A.D.S.S./Forms/C. 2118.

Instructions regarding War Diaries and Intelligence Summaries are contained in F. S. Regs., Part II. and the Staff Manual respectively. Title Pages will be prepared in manuscript.

# WAR DIARY
*or*
# INTELLIGENCE SUMMARY
*(Erase heading not required.)*

Army Form C. 2118

| Place | Date | Hour | Summary of Events and Information | Remarks and references to Appendices |
|---|---|---|---|---|
| Noyelles | 7/7/16 | | Noyelles was again shelled during the afternoon. Situation Normal. | |
| " | 8/7/16 | 7-15pm | 45th Infantry Brigade placed in Army Reserve at 6 hours notice from 6-0 pm. German raid into our front trenches in Hohenzollern. Eleven prisoners taken by NLD. | |
| | | 10-30pm | Brigade warned to "Stand to" at half an hours notice to move. | |
| | | 11-30pm | Brigade "Stand down" Situation now normal. | |
| " | 9/7/16 | | Nothing to record | |
| " | 10/7/16 | | Situation normal. The 45th IB was removed from Army Reserve at 10-0 pm | |
| " | 11/7/16 | | One reinforcement Officer arrived 2nd Lieut. P.E Carr. | |
| " | 12/7/16 | | Nothing to record. 2nd Lieut V J H Brunt admitted to hospital. One OR evacuated | |
| " | 13/7/16 | | No 45 Company relieved No 46 Coy in GC in the Hulloch Section. Fifteen guns taken over as follows R1, R2, R3, R4, R5, R6, R7, R8, V3, V4, V4a, V5, V15, V16 & V17 Relief complete at 9-0 pm. Two OR admitted to hospital | |
| " | 14/7/16 | | 2nd Lieut P.E Carr admitted to hospital. Situation quiet, no firing done on account of wiring parties. | |
| | 15/7/16 | | Two OR evacuated. Noyelles shelled during the afternoon. Four casualties one OR killed A+SH One OR in 45 Coy slightly wounded. Indirect fire from eight guns in Reserve line on the back system of trenches. Rounds expended 10850. | [initials] |

1875 Wt. W593/826 1,000,000 4/15 J.B.C. & A. A.D.S.S./Forms/C. 2118.

Instructions regarding War Diaries and Intelligence Summaries are contained in F. S. Regs., Part II. and the Staff Manual respectively. Title Pages will be prepared in manuscript.

# WAR DIARY
*or*
# INTELLIGENCE SUMMARY
*(Erase heading not required.)*

Army Form C. 2118

| Place | Date | Hour | Summary of Events and Information | Remarks and references to Appendices |
|---|---|---|---|---|
| Noyelles | 16/7/16 | | One OR admitted to hospital from trenches. Indirect fire during night from eight guns in Reserve Line Rounds fired 10950 | |
| " | 17/7/16 | | Intense artillery bombardment on left of own front. Very little retaliation. Indirect fire during night from eight guns in reserve line. Rounds fired 11250. | |
| " | 18/7/16 | | During the afternoon an old gas cylinder at R8 commenced leaking. Whilst removing the gun from the emplacement one NCO + four men were gassed, the NCO + one man being detained in hospital. Raid by 47th Brigade (Leinsters) on our right commencing at 12.30am. Supporting fire from four guns was directed into Cite St Elie. During the night eight guns in Reserve Line engaged various targets behind enemy front line. Rounds expended 11750. Intense artillery bombardment afternoon + night. | |
| " | 19/7/16 | | Orders received as to action to be taken in case of a move. One OR admitted to hospital. Eight Guns in Reserve Line fired 8450 rounds on to enemy trenches + communications. | |
| " | 20/7/16 | | One OR reinforcement joined. One OR wounded. Officers of No 49 Coy MGC shown round gun positions in Hulluch Section. Rounds fired during night 5500. | |
| " | 21/7/16 | | One OR rejoined from hospital. No 45 Coy MGC relieved by No 49 Coy MGC in Hulluch Section. No 45 Coy moved to Noeux-les-Mines. One OR admitted to hospital. | [initials] |

1875 Wt. W593/826 1,000,000 4/15 J.B.C. & A. A.D.S.S./Forms/C. 2118.

Instructions regarding War Diaries and Intelligence Summaries are contained in F. S. Regs., Part II. and the Staff Manual respectively. Title Pages will be prepared in manuscript.

# WAR DIARY
*or*
# INTELLIGENCE SUMMARY
*(Erase heading not required.)*

Army Form C. 2118

| Place | Date | Hour | Summary of Events and Information | Remarks and references to Appendices |
|---|---|---|---|---|
| Noeux-les-Mines | 22/7/16 | | No 45 Coy moved to Tangry via Bruay & Pernes. Whilst passing through Bruay a Mills Hand Grenade exploded at the head of the company. Casualties Lt McZenan Coy Sergt Major & 6 other ranks wounded & admitted to hospital. Days march fifteen miles. | |
| Tangry | 23/7/16 | | 2nd Lieut G H Acton admitted to hospital. 2nd Lieut V J H Brunt rejoined from hospital. One OR admitted to hospital | |
| " | 24/7/16 | | Two OR admitted to hospital. Three OR evacuated | |
| " | 25/7/16 | | Two OR admitted to hospital | |
| " | 26/7/16 | | No 45 Coy marched to Tachincourt via Bryas, Ostreville & Roellecourt. Two OR admitted to hospital | |
| Tachincourt | 27/7/16 | | No 45 Coy marched to Maison Leblond via Sericourt & Frevent. | |
| Maison Leblond | 28/7/16 | | No 45 Coy marched to Le Meillard via Bonnieres, Villers l'Hopital, Frohen le Grand & Frohen le Petit. Two other ranks admitted to hospital. | |
| Le Meillard | 29/7/16 | | ~~One~~ Two OR admitted to hospital. Five NCOs & 63 men attached to No 45 Coy M G C from 45th I B. Six OR evacuated. Six OR struck off the strength authority 45 I B<br>A/688 | [signature] |

1875 Wt. W593/826 1,000,000 4/15 J.B.C. & A. A.D.S.S./Forms/C. 2118.

Instructions regarding War Diaries and Intelligence Summaries are contained in F. S. Regs., Part II. and the Staff Manual respectively. Title Pages will be prepared in manuscript.

# WAR DIARY
*or*
# INTELLIGENCE SUMMARY
*(Erase heading not required.)*

Army Form C. 2118

| Place | Date | Hour | Summary of Events and Information | Remarks and references to Appendices |
|---|---|---|---|---|
| Le Meillard | 30/7/16 | | Three OR evacuated. Five OR admitted to hospital. No 7025 Pte Kerr J W tried by F G Court-martial, charge When on Active Service Drunkenness whilst on duty. | |
| " | 31/7/16 | | No 45 Coy M G C marched to Vignacourt via Bernaville & Pernois. Ten OR admitted to hospital. Seven OR evacuated. One OR rejoined. Four Signallers & two reinforcements. No 7025 Pte J W Kerr 11th A & S Highlanders att No 45 Coy sentenced to 3 months F P No 1 | |

Alfred E Pescod Lieut

45 Coy. Machine Gun Corps.

1875 Wt. W593/826 1,000,000 4/15 J.B.C. & A. A.D.S.S./Forms/C. 2118.

45th Brigade .

15th Division.

---

45th BRIGADE

MACHINE GUN COMPANY

AUGUST 1 9 1 6

Instructions regarding War Diaries and Intelligence Summaries are contained in F. S. Regs., Part II. and the Staff Manual respectively. Title Pages will be prepared in manuscript.

# WAR DIARY
*or*
~~INTELLIGENCE SUMMARY~~
*(Erase heading not required.)*

~~Army~~ 45 Form C. 2118

45 M G C

| Place | Date | Hour | Summary of Events and Information | Remarks and references to Appendices |
|---|---|---|---|---|
| | | | Vol 3 | |

Volume No 3

No. 45 Company Machine Gun Corps

War Diary

for

August 1916.

A M Wilkinson
Captain
Commanding No 45 Coy
Machine Gun Corps.

1875 Wt. W593/826 1,000,000 4/15 J.B.C. & A. A.D.S.S./Forms/C. 2118.

Army Form C. 2118

# WAR DIARY
~~or~~
~~INTELLIGENCE SUMMARY~~
*(Erase heading not required.)*

Instructions regarding War Diaries and Intelligence Summaries are contained in F. S. Regs., Part II. and the Staff Manual respectively. Title Pages will be prepared in manuscript.

| Place | Date | Hour | Summary of Events and Information | Remarks and references to Appendices |
|---|---|---|---|---|
| Vignacourt | 1/8/16 | | Pte J W Kerr sentence Promulgated. | |
| " | 2/8/16 | | Three OR admitted to hospital. One man discharged from hospital. One OR rejoined. Interpreter attached to No 45 Coy MGC. O.C Coy visited trenches at Contalmaison | |
| " | 3/8/16 | | No 45 Coy MGC marched to Mollien-au-Bois via Flesselles & Villers Bocage. Two OR admitted to hospital. | |
| Mollien au Bois | 4/8/16 | | No 45 Coy MGC marched to Bresle via Behencourt & Baizieux. Two OR admitted to hospital. | |
| Bresle | 5/8/16 | | Six OR reinforcements joined from base depot. One OR rejoined. Three OR discharged from hospital. Two OR admitted to hospital | |
| " | 6/8/16 | | Four OR admitted to hospital. One OR rejoined | |
| " | 7/8/16 | | No 45 Company marched from Bresle to left sector of 15th Divn front. Transport parked in Becourt wood. No 45 Coy relieved No 69 Coy in the line. Dispositions of guns as follows Front line 5 guns. Contalmaison 7 guns. Horseshoe trench 4 Guns. HQ in dug out in Contalmaison. Relief complete at 3-20 pm. Intense bombardment during night. | |
| Contalmaison | 8/8/16 | | Guns in Front line relieved. One OR admitted to hospital. | |
| " | 9/8/16 | | Gun teams in front line relieved. The loop bombarded from 12-0 noon to 4-0 pm. Casualties Two OR Killed. Three OR wounded | |

1875 Wt. W593/826 1,000,000 4/15 J.B.C. & A. A.D.S.S./Forms/C. 2118.

Instructions regarding War Diaries and Intelligence Summaries are contained in F. S. Regs., Part II. and the Staff Manual respectively. Title Pages will be prepared in manuscript.

# WAR DIARY
*or*
# ~~INTELLIGENCE SUMMARY~~
*(Erase heading not required.)*

Army Form C. 2118

| Place | Date | Hour | Summary of Events and Information | Remarks and references to Appendices |
|---|---|---|---|---|
| Contalmaison | 10/8/16 | | Gun teams in front line relieved. Two OR killed. Switch patrolled during the day by 11th A+S Highlanders. | |
| " | 11/8/16 | | Gun teams in front line relieved. Two OR admitted to hospital. | |
| " | 12/8/16 | | Four additional guns & teams sent up to front line to man Strong Points which were formed by 45th IB after attack on the German Switch Line. 45th IB attack successful, No 46 Brigade on right was held up owing to machine Gun fire. 2nd Lieut. C. J. Cartwright + One OR killed during the operations. Two OR rejoined. Thirty five reinforcements joined from Base: Two OR admitted to hospital. One OR evacuated. One OR wounded One OR died of wounds. | |
| " | 13/8/16 | | No 45 Company relieved by No 44 Coy M.G.C. Nine guns in line taken over also two gun positions in front of Contalmaison. Relief complete at 10-15 pm. 2nd Lieut V J H Brent admitted to hospital sick. One OR admitted to hospital & evacuated. One OR discharged from hospital. Two OR rejoined. No 45 Coy marched to Becourt wood + bivouaced. | |
| Becourt Wood | 14/8/16 | | No 45 Coy marched to bivouac west of Albert. One OR evacuated. Three OR discharged from hospital | |
| Albert | 15/8/16 | | Ten reinforcements joined from Base. New C.O. Capt Williamson joined no 45 Company & took over command from Lieut C L Roberts. One OR discharged from hospital. | |

1875 Wt. W593/826 1,000,000 4/15 J.B.C. & A. A.D.S.S./Forms/C. 2118.

Army Form C. 2118

Instructions regarding War Diaries and Intelligence Summaries are contained in F. S. Regs., Part II. and the Staff Manual respectively. Title Pages will be prepared in manuscript.

# WAR DIARY
*or*
# INTELLIGENCE SUMMARY
*(Erase heading not required.)*

| Place | Date | Hour | Summary of Events and Information | Remarks and references to Appendices |
|---|---|---|---|---|
| ALBERT | 16/8/16 | | Two other ranks joined from Base, one other rank discharged from Hospital four other ranks admitted to hospital. Weather very changeable – occasional heavy showers. Instructional work and gun cleaning &c. | |
| | 17/8/16 | | Weather still changeable. One other rank joined. one other rank admitted to hospital. one other rank discharged from hospital. Warning order received that 45th Bde might have to relieve 46th Bde on 19th inst. OC 45 Coy visited OC No 46 Coy re relief. | |
| | | 5.0pm | Coy ordered to 'stand to' – all ready to move in ½ hour. | |
| | | 6.0pm | Ordered to 'Stand down'. | |
| | | 7.50pm | Coy again ordered to 'Stand to' and were ready to move in 25 mins. | |
| | | 9.30pm | 'Stand down' received. | |
| | 18/8/16 | | Instructional works continued and all limbers packed in readiness for relief. | |

1875 Wt. W593/826 1,000,000 4/15 J.B.C. & A. A.D.S.S./Forms/C. 2118.

Instructions regarding War Diaries and Intelligence Summaries are contained in F. S. Regs., Part II. and the Staff Manual respectively. Title Pages will be prepared in manuscript.

# WAR DIARY

*or*

~~INTELLIGENCE SUMMARY~~

*(Erase heading not required.)*

Army Form C. 2118

| Place | Date | Hour | Summary of Events and Information | Remarks and references to Appendices |
|---|---|---|---|---|
| ALBERT. | 19/8/16 | 5.30 am. | Company parade for Trenches – relief of No 46 Coy M.G.C. in the Right Section 15th DIV. | |
| | | | Disposition after relief:- | |
| | | | Lt. A.E. PESCOD and teams 5 & 6. Lt. R.R. NEILSON and team 9.10 & 11. in front line. | |
| | | | 2Lt. P. Wilson and teams 12.13.14.15 & 16 in Support. at KOYLI Trench & PIONEER REDOUBT. | |
| | | | Headquarters. X 27 a 9.4. approx. | |
| | | | Capt. H.V. Wilkinson. Lt. C.L. ROBERTS. 2Lt. J.D. MURRAY 2Lt. R.H. GODDARD and teams 1.2.3.4.7 & 8. Fighting limbers at H.Q. | |
| | | | Remainder of Transport under 2Lt. D. MANN at BLACK WOOD. | |
| | | | Relief completed 11.30 am. | |
| | | 3.0 pm. | Lt. A.E. PESCOD. L/Sgt. Holmes and 3 men admitted to Hospital suffering from shell shock. | |
| | | | 2Lt. J.D. MURRAY. and 4 other ranks sent up to replace casualties. | |
| approx. | | | Weather improving. | |
| X 27 a 9.4 | 20/8/16 | | Three other ranks kill by Shrapnel fire. One other rank wounded by Shrapnel one other rank admitted to Hospital – Shell Shock. four other Ranks admitted to hospital sick. one other rank evacuated. | |

1375 Wt. W593/826 1,000,000 4/15 J.B.C. & A. A.D.S.S./Forms/C. 2118.

Instructions regarding War Diaries and Intelligence Summaries are contained in F. S. Regs., Part II. and the Staff Manual respectively. Title Pages will be prepared in manuscript.

# WAR DIARY

*or*

~~INTELLIGENCE SUMMARY~~

*(Erase heading not required.)*

Army Form C. 2118

| Place | Date | Hour | Summary of Events and Information | Remarks and references to Appendices |
|---|---|---|---|---|
| X27 a 9.4. | 21/8/16 | | Weather fine.<br>Teams in the front line relieved by teams at PIONEER REDOUBT and returned to H.Q. Teams at H.Q. moved to PIONEER REDOUBT.<br>Two other ranks admitted to Hospital with Shell Shock. One other rank admitted to Hospital sick – one other rank rejoined. | |
| | 22/8/16 | | Weather still fine.<br>2nd Lt. R.H. GODDARD admitted to hospital Sick – one other rank admitted to hospital & evacuated with Shell Shock. Sgt. J. Smith and one other rank discharged from hospital – 2 other ranks evacuated. | |
| | | 8.30p | Headquarters removed to LOWERWOOD X18 a. 4. 9. | |
| LOWER WOOD | 23/8/16 | 9.0a. | Relief of teams in the front line by teams at Old H.Q. & PIONEER REDOUBT. Teams from front line returned to Old H.Q. | |
| | | 10.am | 2 Guns in PIONEER REDOUBT engaged enemy aeroplanes. S.A.A. expended 1000. | |

Army Form C. 2118

Instructions regarding War Diaries and Intelligence Summaries are contained in F. S. Regs., Part II. and the Staff Manual respectively. Title Pages will be prepared in manuscript.

# WAR DIARY

*or*

## ~~INTELLIGENCE SUMMARY~~

*(Erase heading not required.)*

| Place | Date | Hour | Summary of Events and Information | Remarks and references to Appendices |
|---|---|---|---|---|
| LOWER WOOD | 24/8/16 | | Weather, fine | |
| | | | Three other ranks admitted to hospital. three other ranks evacuated. One other rank reinforcement joined from Base. | |
| | | 3.45 pm | Bombardment of Intermediate line commenced prior to 1st DIV (on our right) attack. | |
| | | 5.45 pm | attack delivered. Guns in PIONEER REDOUBT brought overhead fire to bear on MARTINPUICH and enemy communications. | |
| | | | Guns in the line engaged enemy parties of varying numbers throughout the engagement. | |
| | | 9.15 pm | LOWERWOOD, MIDDLEWOOD and VILLAWOOD bombarded by enemy gas shells continuously for about 1 hour. Gas helmets had to be worn for about 1½ hours | |
| | | 10.45 pm. | Atmosphere again clear. helmets not necessary. | |
| | | 11.0 pm | Gas shell bombardment reopened - helmets again necessary. | |
| | | 12 midnight. | Atmosphere clear again. | |
| | | | During second bombardment three gas shells fell at Gun position in PIONEER REDOUBT and gassed one other rank. | |

1875 Wt. W593/826 1,000,000 4/15 J.B.C. & A. A.D.S.S./Forms/C. 2118.

Instructions regarding War Diaries and Intelligence Summaries are contained in F. S. Regs., Part II. and the Staff Manual respectively. Title Pages will be prepared in manuscript.

# WAR DIARY
or
~~INTELLIGENCE SUMMARY~~
*(Erase heading not required.)*

Army Form C. 2118

| Place | Date | Hour | Summary of Events and Information | Remarks and references to Appendices |
|---|---|---|---|---|
| LOWER WOOD | 25/8/16 | | Weather changeable but mostly fine – heavy showers late evening. | |
| | | | Warning order received to the effect that 44th Brigade on our ~~right~~ left might be extending their front to the left as far as WELCH ALLEY on 26th and that on the 27th we might have to take over portion of 1st DIV. front on our right as far as S 2 d 8.5. | |
| | | | Warned that 1st DIV mean to rush Intermediate Line which they failed to take last night – also warned that our M.G.'s must co-operate by firing across the 1st DIV. frontage and engage enemy communications; ZERO hr to be communicated later. Guns in the line warned and cautioned not to fire South of S.2.b.7.3. | |
| | | | Guns in pioneer redoubt laid on roads & communications in and around MARTINPUICH. | |
| | | 9.45. p.m. | ZERO hour received. | |
| | | 11.35. p.m. | M.G. opened fire as directed. S.A.A. expended during night. 5.000. | |
| | | 11.45. p.m. | ZERO hour. | |
| | | 11.50. p.m. | Order received from Div. through Brigade that as enemy prisoners report our M.G.'s could do more damage to their communication overhead fire must be commenced to-night | |

1875 Wt. W593/826 1,000,000 4/15 J.B.C. & A. A.D.S.S./Forms/C. 2118.

Army Form C. 2118

# WAR DIARY
*or*
# INTELLIGENCE SUMMARY
*(Erase heading not required.)*

Instructions regarding War Diaries and Intelligence Summaries are contained in F. S. Regs., Part II. and the Staff Manual respectively. Title Pages will be prepared in manuscript.

| Place | Date | Hour | Summary of Events and Information | Remarks and references to Appendices |
|---|---|---|---|---|
| LOWER WOOD | 26/8/16 | | Weather still Showery | |
| | | | 2nd Lt. C.R. WRIGHT joined. 11 Other ranks joined. Three O.R. discharged from Hospital. Sgt Pratt + one O.R. wounded Shell shock. one O.R. wounded Shrapnel. two O.R. evacuated. | |
| | | | Guns in PIONEER REDOUBT fired 3000 rounds S.A.A. indirect on Roads + Communication in + around MARTINPUICH. | |
| | 27/8/16 | | Showery all day - with short spells of sunshine. Trenches very muddy. | |
| | | 8 am | Guns in the line relieved as under:- | |
| | | | four guns from LONELY Trench relieved 4 guns in PIONEER REDOUBT who relieved 4 guns in front line Trenches. Guns from front line returned to LONELY Trench. | |
| | | | 2nd Lt. P. WILSON relieved Lt. R.R. NEILSON. | |
| | | 12 noon | LOWER WOOD, MIDDLE WOOD + Valley heavily bombarded by various types of shell including Gasshells. Gas of no effect in LOWER Wood. | |
| | | | Stokes mortar ammtn dump at MIDDLE WOOD blown up. | |
| | | 12.50 | Bombardment stopped. One O.R. PIONEER REDOUBT wounded Shellshock. | |

1875 Wt. W593/826 1,000,000 4/15 J.B.C. & A. A.D.S.S./Forms/C. 2118.

Army Form C. 2118

Instructions regarding War Diaries and Intelligence Summaries are contained in F. S. Regs., Part II. and the Staff Manual respectively. Title Pages will be prepared in manuscript.

# WAR DIARY
or
~~INTELLIGENCE SUMMARY~~
(Erase heading not required.)

| Place | Date | Hour | Summary of Events and Information | Remarks and references to Appendices |
|---|---|---|---|---|
| LOWER WOOD | 27/8/16 | 1.15pm | Bombardment reopened but not quite so bad at LOWER WOOD. a larger proportion of Gas Shells but again of no effect. | |
| | | 2.0pm | Bombardment stopped. NO Casualties. | |
| | | 6.0pm | Bombardment reopened again but heavier. Impossible to get either in or out of H.Q. Gas again of no effect. | |
| | | 6.30pm | Bombardment stopped. NO Casualties. | |
| | | | One other rank admitted to Hospital Sick. four other ranks rejoined. | |
| | | | During evening heavy bombardment heard on the left - this started when the bombardment of LOWERWOOD ceased (at 6.30pm) and continued for the greater portion of the night. | |
| | | 9.15pm | Notice received that the Bavarians who were opposite us at the HOHENZOLLERN were relieving the German troops opposite our present front to-night & to-morrow night. A warm reception asked for. This was communicated at once to 2nd Lt. P. WILSON in the line with orders | |

Instructions regarding War Diaries and Intelligence Summaries are contained in F. S. Regs., Part II. and the Staff Manual respectively. Title Pages will be prepared in manuscript.

# WAR DIARY
*or*
~~INTELLIGENCE SUMMARY~~
*(Erase heading not required.)*

Army Form C. 2118

| Place | Date | Hour | Summary of Events and Information | Remarks and references to Appendices |
|---|---|---|---|---|
| LOWER WOOD | 27/8/16 | 9.15 pm. | to keep a sharp look out especially at dawn. Guns in PIONEER REDOUBT fired 3000 rounds on Communications & Roads. | |
| | 28/8/16 | | 2nd Lt. C.R. WRIGHT taken around the trenches. | |
| | | | Weather still showery but with longer intervals of sunshine. | |
| | | | One O.R. slightly wounded by Shrapnel. | |
| | | 3.30 pm | A few enemy gas shells and a number of H.E. Shrapnel & Shrapnel burst between LOWER WOOD and THE CUTTING. Gas of no effect. | |
| | | 9.30 pm | LOWER WOOD, MIDDLE WOOD, and THE CUTTING heavily bombarded by shells of various calibre. and shrapnel. also a few Gas shells. Some very heavy shells were also used. Gas of no effect. | |
| | | 10.10 pm. | Bombardment stopped – but shelling continued intermittently and more scattered. | |
| | | | Guns in PIONEER REDOUBT kept up a fairly constant fire on Communications & Roads around MARTINPUICH. | |

1875 Wt. W593/826 1,000,000 4/15 J.B.C. & A. A.D.S.S./Forms/C. 2118.

Instructions regarding War Diaries and Intelligence Summaries are contained in F. S. Regs., Part II. and the Staff Manual respectively. Title Pages will be prepared in manuscript.

# WAR DIARY
*or*
~~INTELLIGENCE SUMMARY~~
*(Erase heading not required.)*

Army Form C. 2118

| Place | Date | Hour | Summary of Events and Information | Remarks and references to Appendices |
|---|---|---|---|---|
| LOWER WOOD | 29/8/16 | 4.15 am | Enemy reopened Bombardment around LOWERWOOD and valley. Not quite so bad as the previous barage being more distributed. Similar shells used but gas of no effect. | |
| | | | Heavy rain was falling at this time. | |
| | | 7.30 am | Weather cleared and promised a fine & sunshiny day. | |
| | | 8.30 am | Officer of NO 149 Coy M.G.C arrived to reconnoitre our front – was taken round the line by Capt H.V. WILKINSON. This officer was given all information required as NO 149 Coy may be relieving us, ~~on or about the 5th Sept~~. | |
| | | 9.0 am | Inter Company relief carried out to-day. | |
| | | | ~~Present~~ Disposition on Completion being:- | |
| | | | Front line System. Teams 2. 3. 4 and 12. under 2nd Lts. J. D. MURRAY and C.R. WRIGHT. | |
| | | | PIONEER REDOUBT. Teams. 6. 7. 10 & 11. | |
| | | | LONELY Trench. Teams. 1. 5. 13. 14. 8. 9. 15. & 16. Lt. R.R. NEILSON. & 2nd Lt. P. WILSON and Coy. Sgt. Maj. | |
| | | | BLACKWOOD ~~[illegible] Trench~~ Transport & 2 M. Stores under 2nd Lt. D. MANN. | |

1875 Wt. W593/826 1,000,000 4/15 J.B.C. & A. A.D.S.S./Forms/C. 2118.

Instructions regarding War Diaries and Intelligence Summaries are contained in F. S. Regs., Part II. and the Staff Manual respectively. Title Pages will be prepared in manuscript.

# WAR DIARY
*or*
~~INTELLIGENCE~~ SUMMARY

*(Erase heading not required.)*

Army Form C. 2118

| Place | Date | Hour | Summary of Events and Information | Remarks and references to Appendices |
|---|---|---|---|---|
| LOWER WOOD | 29/8/16 | | Disposition (cont). | |
| | | | LOWER WOOD – advanced Coy Headquarters – C.O. and Lt C.L. ROBERTS. 3 Signallers and orderly room Corporal (Cpl. Bishop) & servants | |
| | | 2 pm | Valley between LOWERWOOD and The CUTTING shelled slowly by heavy shells. | |
| | | 3. pm | Shelling becoming more intense. | |
| | | 3.30 pm | Bombardment intense and a great number of large calibre shells used 6 direct hits in LOWERWOOD. – 3 within 4 yds of H.Q dugout. | |
| | | 4:30. | rain commenced. | |
| | | 5.15 pm | Bombardment stopped – heavy thunderstorm started – all H.Q stores etc. packed up ready to move. | |
| | | 6.0 pm | H.Q partially packed on empty ration limber when Bombardment reopened thunderstorm over. | |
| | | 6.45. pm | Bombardment finished | |
| | | 7.0. pm. | H Q moved to LONELY TRENCH – X 27 a 9.4 approx. Heavy showers continued all night. 1 OR wounded Shell shock. 4 OR admitted to Hospital. 1 OR rejoined. | |

Army Form C. 2118

Instructions regarding War Diaries and Intelligence Summaries are contained in F. S. Regs., Part II. and the Staff Manual respectively. Title Pages will be prepared in manuscript.

# WAR DIARY
or
~~INTELLIGENCE SUMMARY~~
*(Erase heading not required.)*

| Place | Date | Hour | Summary of Events and Information | Remarks and references to Appendices |
|---|---|---|---|---|
| X27a97. | 30/8/16 | | Weather very bad trenches full of water and mud. Heavy rain<br>1. Other rank admitted to Hospital.<br>One mule wounded shrapnel, in ration limber | |
| | 31/8/16 | | Weather fine – sun shine most of the day – no rain.<br>Team in PIONEER REDOUBT relieved guns in the Front line<br>Four fresh teams sent to PIONEER REDOUBT. One more gun sent up to the Firing line. Lt NEILSON relieved 2Lt MURRAY & WRIGHT.<br>Present disposition. 5 guns FIRING LINE, 4 guns PIONEER REDOUBT<br>7 guns LONELY TRENCH. | |
| | | 7.55 am | Pte Smith C. wounded. S.I.W. after cleaning his rifle. at LONELY Trench. Wound serious in left forearm. Statements of witnesses taken.<br>Pte. Spindlow returned from [illegible] school 3. O.R. admitted to hospital – 2 O.R. discharged from hospital. 4 O.R. Reinforcements joined. | |

1875 Wt. W593/826 1,000,000 4/15 J.B.C. & A. A.D.S.S./Forms/C. 2118.

Army Form C. 2118

Instructions regarding War Diaries and Intelligence Summaries are contained in F. S. Regs., Part II. and the Staff Manual respectively. Title Pages will be prepared in manuscript.

# WAR DIARY
*or*
# INTELLIGENCE SUMMARY
*(Erase heading not required.)*

| Place | Date | Hour | Summary of Events and Information | Remarks and references to Appendices |
|---|---|---|---|---|
| | | | Position of Guns. | |
| | | | 4 in front Line | |
| | | | 2 -- Support Line | |
| | | | 1 -- KOYLI TRENCH | |
| | | | 2 -- PIONEER REDOUBT. | |
| | | | Summary for August. - Casualties. | |

| | Officers. | O. R. | |
|---|---|---|---|
| Killed | 1 | 9 | |
| Wounded | – | 9 | |
| -- Shell shock | 1 | 13 | (7 rejoined) |
| Sick. | 2 | 22 | |

H. Wilkinson
Capt
Comdg 45th M. G. Co

1875 Wt. W593/826 1,000,000 4/15 J.B.C. & A. A.D.S.S./Forms/C. 2118.

Index

# SUBJECT.

45th M. G. Coy

| No. | Contents. | Date. |
| --- | --- | --- |
| | September 1916 | |

(63,966). Wt.15,820—170. 2000. 9/21. Gp.164. A.&E.W.

Instructions regarding War Diaries and Intelligence Summaries are contained in F. S. Regs., Part II. and the Staff Manual respectively. Title Pages will be prepared in manuscript.

# WAR DIARY
*or*
# INTELLIGENCE SUMMARY
*(Erase heading not required.)*

Army Form C. 2118

| Place | Date | Hour | Summary of Events and Information | Remarks and references to Appendices |
|---|---|---|---|---|
| Original | | | 45th Machine Gun Company.<br>September 1916.<br>A. [illegible] Capt.<br>Cmdg. 45th M. G. Co | |

1875 Wt. W593/826 1,000,000 4/15 J.B.C. & A. A.D.S.S./Forms/C. 2118.

Army Form C. 2118

Instructions regarding War Diaries and Intelligence Summaries are contained in F. S. Regs., Part II. and the Staff Manual respectively. Title Pages will be prepared in manuscript.

# WAR DIARY
*or*
# INTELLIGENCE SUMMARY
*(Erase heading not required.)*

| Place | Date | Hour | Summary of Events and Information | Remarks and references to Appendices |
|---|---|---|---|---|
| LONELY. Trench. X 27 a. 9. 4 (approx) | 1/9/16 | | Weather fine but threatening. 6 Other ranks who had been sent from Battalion to a course of Machine Gunnery under III rd Corps Motor Machine Gun Battery join for duty. 1 Other Rank wounded shrapnel. 3 O.R. admitted hos. 4 O.R. discharged hos. Sergt Rooney P. rejoined from Base. | |
| | 2/9/16. | | Guns in the line relieved and 2 new positions taken up on the right. 2nd Lt. P. Wilson and P.R. Wright relieved Lt. R.R. NEILSON. Weather fine. Sergt Pratt rejoined from rest hospital. Sergt Ounsworth & 2 O.R. wound shellshock – 1 O.R. wounded shrapnel. Lt. F.C. NAWTON and 2nd Lt. G.V. Cox and 1 O.R. joined. | |
| | 3/9/16. | | Weather fine. Gun in elbow of INTERMEDIATE LINE badly shelled and brought back to Headquarters. 3 Other Ranks killed. 2 wounded shrapnel 1. wounded shell shock. 3. Other Ranks joined. | |

1875 Wt. W593/826 1,000,000 4/15 J.B.C. & A. A.D.S.S./Forms/C. 2118.

Army Form C. 2118

# WAR DIARY

*or*

~~INTELLIGENCE SUMMARY~~

*(Erase heading not required.)*

Instructions regarding War Diaries and Intelligence Summaries are contained in F. S. Regs., Part II. and the Staff Manual respectively. Title Pages will be prepared in manuscript.

| Place | Date | Hour | Summary of Events and Information | Remarks and references to Appendices |
|---|---|---|---|---|
| LONELY TRENCH X 27 a 9.4. (app) | 4/9/16 | 6. oam | Guns on the left relieved by No 103 Coy Machine Gun Corps: Guns on the right relieved by No 46 Coy M.G.C. On Completion of relief Headquarters & Company moved to Bivouac in E.8.a. taking over from No 44 Coy: No 44 Coy took over H.Q at LONELY. Trench. | |
| E.8.A. | | 12 noon | Weather bad heavy rain. Transport lines bad and dirty - report to this effect sent to Brigade. | |
| | | 5:30 pm | Bivouac & surrounding valley shelled - 8-10 shells fell in all - no casualties. | |
| | | 6.15 pm. | Shelled again this time 12-16 fell. | |
| E.8.A. | 5/9/16. | 3.0 am. | Reveille. Bivouac struck and evacuated at 6. oam. | |
| LAVIEVILLE | | 7. oam | Billets taken over - all men in barns. Officers in tents. Transport in the open - lines very muddy. 1 O.R. joined. 2 Discharged Hospital | |

1875 Wt. W593/826 1,000,000 4/15 J.B.C. & A. A.D.S.S./Forms/C. 2118.

Instructions regarding War Diaries and Intelligence Summaries are contained in F. S. Regs., Part II. and the Staff Manual respectively. Title Pages will be prepared in manuscript.

# WAR DIARY
*or*
# INTELLIGENCE SUMMARY
*(Erase heading not required.)*

Army Form C. 2118 3

| Place | Date | Hour | Summary of Events and Information | Remarks and references to Appendices |
|---|---|---|---|---|
| LAVIEVILLE. | 6/9/16. | | Weather fine.<br>4 other Ranks rejoined from Base. 1 O.R. reinforcement. 4 other Ranks rejoined from hospital.<br>2 hours gun cleaning only – remainder of day free. Company paid out. | |
| do | 7/9/16 | | Gun cleaning and instruction all day.<br>Weather fine<br>1. O.R. joined | |
| do. | 8/9/16 | | Weather fine. Gun cleaning & instructional work. Communication drill for Gun in N.C.O's<br>Sgt. Pratt and Private Cooper T. proceeded to rest camp at AULT for 7 days rest. 4 other R. admitted to Hospital. 7 Reinforcements joined. | |
| | 9/9/16 | | Weather fine. Advanced instruction to all Ranks. Coy. had baths & were issued with new socks and shirts. | |

1875 Wt. W593/826 1,000,000 4/15 J.B.C. & A. A.D.S.S./Forms/C. 2118.

Instructions regarding War Diaries and Intelligence Summaries are contained in F. S. Regs., Part II. and the Staff Manual respectively. Title Pages will be prepared in manuscript.

# WAR DIARY
*or*
~~INTELLIGENCE SUMMARY~~
*(Erase heading not required.)*

Army Form C. 2118 4

| Place | Date | Hour | Summary of Events and Information | Remarks and references to Appendices |
|---|---|---|---|---|
| LAVIEVILLE | 10/9/16 | | Weather still fine. Church parades for all Denominations. Promulgation of Field General Court Martial held on No 43945 Pte Smith C. at LAVIEVILLE on 9/9/16. Charge "When on active service Conduct to prejudice of good order & military discipline - self inflicting a wound." Sentence 35 days F.P. No 1. of which 7 days were remitted by Brigadier General Allgood 45th I.B. | |
| do. | 11/9/16 | | Weather still fine. Brigade field day rehearsal of an attack. 70/4 Private Stokar T.B. ordered to report to Base being under age. Warning order and final orders received for move into line. | |
| do. | 12/9/16 | 9.0 | Company left LAVIEVILLE by route march to Bivouac in E 7. central preparatory to moving into line. | |
| E.7. central | | 9.30 | Bivouac taken over. Orders issued for relief of No 44 Coy M.G.C in the line on the 13th. 3 reinforcement drivers joined. | |

1875 Wt. W593/826 1,000,000 4/15 J.B.C. & A. A.D.S.S./Forms/C. 2118.

Instructions regarding War Diaries and Intelligence Summaries are contained in F. S. Regs., Part II. and the Staff Manual respectively. Title Pages will be prepared in manuscript.

# WAR DIARY

or

~~INTELLIGENCE SUMMARY~~

(*Erase heading not required.*)

Army Form C. 2118 5

| Place | Date | Hour | Summary of Events and Information | Remarks and references to Appendices |
|---|---|---|---|---|
| E 7. Central | 13/9/16 | | Teams 5. 6. 7. and 8. relieved 4 Guns of No. 44 M. G. Coy in Front Line System and Team 15 relieved one Gun at PIONEER REDOUBT. | |
| " | " | | Remainder of Company moved to LONELY TRENCH as under<br>'A' Section moved off 7-45 a.m.<br>'C' " — " — 7-50 a.m<br>'D' " — " — 7.55 a.m | |
| " | | 9-30a.m. | All reliefs & moves completed by 9-30 a.m. | |
| " | | 10-30p.m. | Operation Orders received stating XV Division were to take part in an advance on 'Z' day. Final objective CUTTING M.32.d.2.7. (inclusive) along the railway to M.32.c.5.4. thence along road to road junction at M.32.c.4.8. thence to railway where it crosses FACTORY LINE M32.c.1.9. along Factory Line to a point 250 yards N.W. of the Railway.<br>45th INFANTRY BRIGADE'S objective:-<br>~~[illegible]~~<br>From right of Divisional objective to road junction M32.c.5.6. (Inclusive) | |

1875 Wt. W593/826 1,000,000 4/15 J.B.C. & A. A.D.S.S./Forms/C. 2118.

Instructions regarding War Diaries and Intelligence Summaries are contained in F. S. Regs., Part II. and the Staff Manual respectively. Title Pages will be prepared in manuscript.

# WAR DIARY
*or*
# INTELLIGENCE SUMMARY
*(Erase heading not required.)*

Army Form C. 2118 6

| Place | Date | Hour | Summary of Events and Information | Remarks and references to Appendices |
|---|---|---|---|---|
| | 13/9/16 | 10.30 p.M. | Operation Orders issued by CAPT. H.V. WILKINSON. Copy sent to Brigade and copies issued to all officers of 45 M. G. Coy. | |
| | | | 2nd LIEUT. R.H. GODDARD Rejoined | |
| | 14/9/16 | 11.0 a.m. | All Officers reconnoitred positions which guns had to take up. | |
| | " | 2.0 p.M. | Wire received saying that "Z" day would be the 15th and Zero hour 6.20 A.M. | |
| | | 5. p.m | LIEUT. R.R. NEILSON admitted to hospital Sick. | |
| | | 6.45 p.M | "D" Section under 2/Lts. P. Wilson and C.R. WRIGHT. moved off to take up positions | |
| | | 7.15 p.M | "A" Section under 2/Lts. J.D. MURRAY and R.H. GODDARD moved off | |
| | | 7-50 p.m. | Headquarters shifted to VILLA WOOD X 12. c. 4. 6. | |
| | | 8.15 p.M. | "C" Section under 2/Lts. MANN. & G.V. COX moved off. | |
| | | 9.00 p.m | Lt Roberts, adjutant, C.S.M + ammunition carriers moved up to 70th avenue | |

1875 Wt. W593/826 1,000,000 4/15 J.B.C. & A. A.D.S.S./Forms/C. 2118.

Instructions regarding War Diaries and Intelligence Summaries are contained in F. S. Regs., Part II. and the Staff Manual respectively. Title Pages will be prepared in manuscript.

# WAR DIARY
*or*
# INTELLIGENCE SUMMARY
*(Erase heading not required.)*

Army Form C. 2118

7

| Place | Date | Hour | Summary of Events and Information | Remarks and references to Appendices |
|---|---|---|---|---|
| | | | to the Company's main forward dump & advance Hd Quarters. | |
| | 4.9.16 | 11. p m | Lt Nawton returned with 2 teams to PIONEER REDOUBT to be in reserve. These guns carried on overhead fire as usual till 6. a m | |
| | | 11 pm | Went round guns in rear & up to 70th avenue, but could not get to forward guns owing to congestion of troops, returned to Hd Qts at 1·30 a m. Guns & teams were as follows:— | |
| | | | 2/Lt Wilson 2 Guns in sap off Welsh alley, forward of Sanderson Trench | |
| | | | 2/Lt Murray 2 — — — Lean alley | |
| | | | 2/Lt Wright 2 — in "T" heads on the right of Sanderson Trench. | |
| | | | 2/Lt Cox. 2 — in sap off Welsh alley aft Sanderson Trench. | |
| | | | 2/Lt Mann } 2/Lt Goddard } 6 — in O.G. 1 to do overhead fire. | |
| | | | Lieut. Nawton 2 — Pioneer Redoubt. in reserve. | |
| | | | Lieut. Roberts. with C.S.M. & ammunition carriers at 70th avenue | |
| | | | Capt Wilkinson with 3 runners at Brigade Battle Hd Quarters. | |
| | | | Orderley-room Cpl & 2 men Lonely Trench | |
| | | | C.Q.M.S. & store man at Transport Lines. | |

Instructions regarding War Diaries and Intelligence Summaries are contained in F. S. Regs., Part II. and the Staff Manual respectively. Title Pages will be prepared in manuscript.

# WAR DIARY
*or*
# INTELLIGENCE SUMMARY
*(Erase heading not required.)*

Army Form C. 2118 8

| Place | Date | Hour | Summary of Events and Information | Remarks and references to Appendices |
|---|---|---|---|---|
| | 15.9.16 | 6.20 a.m | Our troops launched their assault on the Enemy's Trenches S & S.W. of MARTIN PUICH. There was no preliminary intense bombardment, but the hostile positions had been subjected to a steady & ~~intense~~ continuous bombardment from guns of all calibres for several days before hand. The 8 leading guns went over with the Camerons, as per operation Order attached. | |
| | | | At ZERO opened up with 6 guns, indirect fire on objective for 5 minutes, then lifted to behind MARTIN PUICH & continued firing. These guns worked extremely well & fired 14,600 rounds in 1½ hours & from reports received gave considerable moral support & confidence to our Infantry. | |
| | | 7.a.m | Eased up fire. 8.30 Ceased fire on account of our Troops being reported in M 33. C. & D. | |
| | | 7.20 | First batch of German Prisoners passed down. about 50 in number looking very subdued. 8. a.m another batch of 50 or more. | |
| | | 7.25 | & 7.55 Received reports from Lt Roberts that he had seen all teams go over. & that Lieuts Wright & Murray were wounded. | |
| | | | The first objectives were taken without difficulty, the enemy | |

1875 Wt. W593/826 1,000,000 4/15 J.B.C. & A. A.D.S.S./Forms/C. 2118.

Instructions regarding War Diaries and Intelligence Summaries are contained in F. S. Regs., Part II. and the Staff Manual respectively. Title Pages will be prepared in manuscript.

# WAR DIARY
*or*
# INTELLIGENCE SUMMARY
*(Erase heading not required.)*

Army Form C. 2118 9

| Place | Date | Hour | Summary of Events and Information | Remarks and references to Appendices |
|---|---|---|---|---|
| | | | showing little inclination to fight, & being taken completely by surprise. | |
| | | | Our artillery barrage was not good, or else the Infantry advanced too close under it. it was a creeping barrage lifting 50 yards per minute. about 70% of our casualties reported to be from our own artillery. | |
| | | 7 30 | Wounded returning in fairly large numbers. but the R.A.M.C. arrangements were admirable. | |
| | | 12 15 | Received orders that at 3. p.m the Camerons – in support – would push through & capture MARTINPUICH. sent orders to Lt Mann. – who I had previously ordered up at 9.10 with 2 guns & teams to re-inforce 1 Gun destroyed & another put out of action. also Lieuts Wright & Murray had passed to the rear wounded. – to advance with them & get into action on the N.E corner of MARTINPUICH at the same time ordered Lt Wilson to take up one gun & get through the Village to cover the left of our Brigade. also sent to Lt Roberts warning him of the situation, so that he could be getting water & ammunition forward. | |
| | | 2 p.m | Went up to 70th Avenue and saw the assault on MARTINPUICH | |

Instructions regarding War Diaries and Intelligence Summaries are contained in F. S. Regs., Part II. and the Staff Manual respectively. Title Pages will be prepared in manuscript.

# WAR DIARY
*or*
# INTELLIGENCE SUMMARY
*(Erase heading not required.)*

Army Form C. 2118 10

| Place | Date | Hour | Summary of Events and Information | Remarks and references to Appendices |
|---|---|---|---|---|
| | 15.9.16 | | The Brigade swept through the N. E portion of the village, and after some bombing & sharp fighting, forced all the garrison to surrender capturing in this part along nearly 200 more prisoners. | |
| | | | Unfortunately whilst this was in progress the division on our right had had to retire somewhat. Thus leaving a nasty gap on our right, through which the Germans tried a feeble counter-attack. Lt Mann moved his 2 guns over to the right & mounted them in an excellent position, the enemy being within 40 yards before he opened fire, a part of the enemy were driven back, but he found others were creeping round & he was nearly surrounded. As no Infantry were near him at the time, he retired to the left rear, & got his guns & teams safely away. and again went forward when the Infantry did. | |
| | 16.9.16 | 2 am | Received word that water was badly wanted for the guns. after an hours search managed to send up 5 Petrol tins full. Raining nearly all night with intermittant heavy shelling. | |
| | | 6 30 a.m | Took up 6 teams from O.G.1 & Redoubt to relieve 6 teams forward. & Lt Nawton to relieve Lt Cox. Instructed Lt Wilson to return with | |

Instructions regarding War Diaries and Intelligence Summaries are contained in F. S. Regs., Part II. and the Staff Manual respectively. Title Pages will be prepared in manuscript.

# WAR DIARY
*or*
# INTELLIGENCE SUMMARY
*(Erase heading not required.)*

Army Form C. 2118 11

| Place | Date | Hour | Summary of Events and Information | Remarks and references to Appendices |
|---|---|---|---|---|
| | | | his teams, & Lt Mann to look after the 3 forward Guns. | |
| | 16.9.16 | 9. am | Went forward with Lt Nawton to relieve Lt Cox & despatched the other teams. went on alone to Lt Mann, but got caught in the barrage put up by the Germans when the Division on our right started to push forward again. so moved along to our left at the back of ~~the~~ village. to find our other two guns. Shelling all round was very heavy all this time. | |
| | | 4.P.M | Lt Wilson arrived back wounded. | |
| | | | Disposition of guns was now as follows:- | |
| | | | Lt Mann. 3 guns. in front of MARTINPUICH. | |
| | | | Lt Nawton. 2 -- in the TANGLE SOUTH. | |
| | | | 1 Gun in a shell hole about M. 32. c. 2. 2. | |
| | | | 1 Gun in a bit of a trench near the railway on the near side of the village. | |
| | | | 6 Guns in reserve & 3 guns knocked out. | |
| | | 7.pm | Ordered Lt Roberts to Hd 2rs for a meal & sleep, if possible as he had to go forward next morning to relieve Lt Mann. | |
| | 17.9.16 | 5 30 am | Went up with Lt Roberts who went on to relieve Lt Mann, then | |

Instructions regarding War Diaries and Intelligence Summaries are contained in F. S. Regs., Part II. and the Staff Manual respectively. Title Pages will be prepared in manuscript.

# WAR DIARY
*or*
# INTELLIGENCE SUMMARY
*(Erase heading not required.)*

Army Form C. 2118 /2

| Place | Date | Hour | Summary of Events and Information | Remarks and references to Appendices |
|---|---|---|---|---|
| | | | wait in round our positions. | |
| | 17.9.16 | 11. am | Returned to Hd Qrs & heard we were to be relieved by 44th Bdge at 2. p.m. Sent round to all Guns to have guides sent to lead the relieving teams in. | |
| | | 2 30 p.m | 44th M. G. Co arrived Hd Qrs but found they were only going to take over 4 forward guns out of the 7. saw the Brigadier who said the other 3 guns must wait until he handed over Command, before they returned. | |
| | | 6 p.m | Went up to 70th avenue. Germans putting up a Barrage all along that line & MARTINPUICH. having probably got wind of relief. | |
| | | 9. p.m | Four teams safely back | |
| | | 11. p.m | Heard relief was completed & sent to other 3 guns. | |
| | 18.9.16 | 2. am | I got back to CONTLEMAISON found everybody there. but 2 teams not yet in. | |
| | | noon. | Heard we were to be relieved from support. and going back. ordered up transport & made all arrangements. | |
| | | 2. 30 | Relief arrived. | |
| | | 3. 15. | Just got "A" Section away & were loading "B" limbers when the Germans started shelling heavily. first one dropped within about. | |

Instructions regarding War Diaries and Intelligence Summaries are contained in F. S. Regs., Part II. and the Staff Manual respectively. Title Pages will be prepared in manuscript.

# WAR DIARY
*or*
# INTELLIGENCE SUMMARY
*(Erase heading not required.)*

Army Form C. 2118 13

| Place | Date | Hour | Summary of Events and Information | Remarks and references to Appendices |
|---|---|---|---|---|
| | | | 10 yards of 40 of us. only 3 slightly wounded got off with wonderful luck. shelling was just round where we were & lasted one hour. | |
| | 18.9.16 | 5 30 p m | all clear and away. raining all the time. | |
| MILLEN COURT. | | 9.15. | arrived. gave the men a hot meal. had some our selves & turned in about midnight. | |
| | 19.9.16 | 11.30. | Left MILLEN COURT. | |
| BAIZIEUX | | 1. p.m. | arrived. but found another Brigade on our ground, so did not get settled in until 5. p.m., immediately set to work to clean guns & ammunition. but heavy rain & sodden round made this far from Easy. | |
| | 20.9.16 | | Weather very unsettled, all rank cleaning, guns, ammunition & equipment and themselves. checking loss, tracing missing men. Kit inspection, getting out indents for clothing. equipment. & spare parts etc. | |
| | | | Our losses during the advance were | |
| | | | Killed. 7. O. R. Wounded. { 3 Officers. 32. O. R. Missing. 3. O. R. | |
| | | | Guns. 1 destroyed. 5 damaged Tripods. 1 destroyed. 1 damaged. | |
| | | 4. p m | a draft of 30 other Ranks arrived recd 2 new guns from ordnance | |

Instructions regarding War Diaries and Intelligence Summaries are contained in F. S. Regs., Part II. and the Staff Manual respectively. Title Pages will be prepared in manuscript.

# WAR DIARY
*or*
# INTELLIGENCE SUMMARY
*(Erase heading not required.)*

Army Form C. 2118 16

| Place | Date | Hour | Summary of Events and Information | Remarks and references to Appendices |
|---|---|---|---|---|
| BAIZIEUX | 21/9/16 | | LIEUT R.R. NEILSON returned from Hospital. Two other ranks previously reported missing rejoined from 46th Coy. 2nd Lt. J.K. LIPSCOMB joined. Company continued reassortment of gunsets, gun cleaning, ammn cleaning etc carried on with | |
| | 22/9/16 | | New draft inspected by LIEUT R R NEILSON. NCO's received communication drill under adj. Remainder of Coy advanced gun drill & instruction. 2nd Lt. F MICHELMORE joined. | |
| | 23/9/16 | | 'C' Sect. went to range for grouping & swinging traverse. Remainder same as previous day | |
| | 24/9/16 | | 'B' Sect went to range. Remainder as before. 2nd Lieut A. ROBINSON joined. Two other ranks admitted to Hospital. | |
| | 25/9/16 | | LT ROBERTS, Sgt DUNSWORTH, Act Sgt LAFFERTY, & PTE GOLSON left to attend 33rd Vickers M.G. Course at CAMIERS. | |

1875 Wt. W593/826 1,000,000 4/15 J.B.C. & A. A.D.S.S./Forms/C. 2118.

Instructions regarding War Diaries and Intelligence Summaries are contained in F. S. Regs., Part II. and the Staff Manual respectively. Title Pages will be prepared in manuscript.

# WAR DIARY
*or*
# INTELLIGENCE SUMMARY
*(Erase heading not required.)*

Army Form C. 2118 / 15

| Place | Date | Hour | Summary of Events and Information | Remarks and references to Appendices |
|---|---|---|---|---|
| BAIZIEUX | 25/9/16 | | LIEUT R.R. NEILSON took over second in command during LT ROBERTS absence. | |
| | | | Three other ranks reinforcement joined from base. | |
| | | | One other rank admitted to Hospital. | |
| | | | 'B' Sec. proceeded to range for grouping & swinging traverse. | |
| | | | Remainder of company handling arms gun drill etc. | |
| | | | Weather for last five days Tropical. | |
| | | | F.G.C.M. assembled at H.Q. 5th Cameron Hg. for trial of No. 35784 Pte. D. GURNEY 45th M.G.Coy. Court was adjourned to future date owing to accused collapsing. | |
| — | 26.9.16 | | "A" Section on the range for the day, remainder of Coy carrying on with instructional work etc. C.O. 1 other Officer & 2 O.R to MONTIGNY for instruction in the new box respirator | |

Army Form C. 2118 16

Instructions regarding War Diaries and Intelligence Summaries are contained in F. S. Regs., Part II. and the Staff Manual respectively. Title Pages will be prepared in manuscript.

# WAR DIARY
*or*
# INTELLIGENCE SUMMARY
*(Erase heading not required.)*

| Place | Date | Hour | Summary of Events and Information | Remarks and references to Appendices |
|---|---|---|---|---|
| BAIZIEOX | 27.9.16 | | "D" Section on range. Dinner taken with them. Capt A. GARDNER gave an interesting lecture on "Esprit-de-Corps. 16th Division. Weather continues warm & fine. 100 men bathed 5 to 6. P.M. | |
| | 28.9.16 | | C.O inspected the whole Company morning. G.O.C's Inspection 2.15. satisfactory 199 on Parade. especially pleased with Transport. Rain evening. | |
| | 29.9.16 | | Wet day. Reveille 5. a.m. Route March 7. a.m to 10.30. remainder of Coy bathed. 11 to 12 noon. 2/Lt G. V. COX transferred back to his old Company no 151st. Lieut. F. C. NAWTON to PARIS for 3 days leave | |
| | 30.9.16 | | Fine again. 2nd Lieut D. MANN + 4 O.R proceeded to AULD, Corps Rest Camp, for 1 week. | |

H.W. Wilkinson
Capt

1875 Wt. W593/826 1,000,000 4/15 J.B.C. & A. A.D.S.S./Forms/C. 2118.

Instructions regarding War Diaries and Intelligence Summaries are contained in F. S. Regs., Part II. and the Staff Manual respectively. Title Pages will be prepared in manuscript.

# WAR DIARY
*or*
# INTELLIGENCE SUMMARY
*(Erase heading not required.)*

Army Form C. 2118

| Place | Date | Hour | Summary of Events and Information | Remarks and references to Appendices |
|---|---|---|---|---|
| | | | Summary of Casualties. for September. | |
| | | | | |

| | Officers | O. R | |
|---|---|---|---|
| Killed | - | 13 | |
| Wounded | 3 | 32 | |
| Sick. | 1 | 34. | (15 discharged from Hospital). |

[illegible] Capt.

1875 Wt. W593/826 1,000,000 4/15 J.B.C. & A. A.D.S.S./Forms/C. 2118.

Copy No 1

# No 45 Machine Gun Coy:

OPERATION ORDERS by CAPT: H. V. WILKINSON
Commanding No 45 M. G. Coy:

Reference 15th Division Special operation Map No: 4 A. 1: 5.000 and Sheets 57 D. S.E and 57 C. S.W. 1/20,000

The 15th Division is to take part in an attack on the Enemy's Trenches, on a date to be notified later, which will be indicated in these orders by the letter "Z"

1. OBJECTIVE

The final objective for the 45th Inf: Bde is CUTTING M. 32. D. 2. 7. (Inclusive along Railway to M. 32. C. 5. 4. thence along the road to junction M. 32. C. 5. 6

2. ASSAULT

(a). The assault will be carried out by the 11th Argyle & Sutherland Highlanders, on the right and the 13th Royal Scots on the left. The 6th Cameron Highlanders will move in support of the assaulting Battalions and the 6/7th Royal Scots Fusiliers and the 8th York & Lancs will be in Brigade reserve

(b) The assault will be delivered from HAM, EGG, POST, and SANDERSON TRENCHES The dividing line between the 11th Argyle and Sutherland Highrs. and 13th Royal Scots is shewn with a Red Line on the Special Map.

(C). The 45th Infantry Brigade will advance to the final objective in Two Bounds. The first bound will place them on a line from the right to the final objective of the Brigade to Road junction at M. 32. C. 2. 4.

The advance of the left of the Brigade (i.e.) that portion of the 13th Royal Scots from M. 32. C. 5. 5 to M. 32. C. 2. 4.) to the final objective will commence at ZERO plus 25 minutes.

3. <u>DISPOSITION OF GUNS</u>

2 Guns under 2/LT. P. WILSON will move with the leading wave of the 6th Bn. CAMERON HIGHLANDERS and take up positions on the Road between M. 32. C. 5. 4. and M. 32. C. 5. 6.

2 Guns under 2/LT. C. R. WRIGHT will go forward at the same time and come into action on the right of the final objective.

2 Guns under LT. R. R. NEILSON will move in rear of the 2nd wave of the 6th CAMERON HIGHLANDERS and will occupy THE TANGLE SOUTH.

2 Guns under 2/LT. J. D. MURRAY. will move at the same time and take up positions in TANGLE TRENCH to the left of BOTTOM ROAD.

The 6th CAMERONS will occupy prior to the assault SANDERSON TRENCH WEST OF WELCH ALLEY - H.L.I ALLEY - LANCS. TRENCH.

Small Saps to occupy these teams will be dug off WELCH ALLEY and from the Saps in front of SANDERSON TRENCH.

2 Guns under 2/LT. D. MANN
2 " " 2/LT. R.H. GODDARD
2 " " 2/LT. G.V. COX

will be in O.G.1 on either side of PEARL ALLEY and will bring Overhead fire to bear on the final objective in M. 32 C & D. at ZERO and after 5 minutes will lift to 32 A & B. also 25 D. on the Roads and Trenches leading into MARTINPUICH from the North East, North and North West.

2 Guns under LT. F.C. NAWTON in Reserve in PEARL ALLEY near VILLA WOOD.

4. HD. QTRS.

45th Infantry Bde HD. QTRS VILLA WOOD X.12.C.4.6

45th M.G. Coy — " — — " —

5. S.A.A.

N.C.O. to carry 1 Belt Box = 250

3.4.5.&6 — " — 2 " " = 2000

2250.

Separate Instructions will be issued regarding S.A.A. and Water Dumps

6 EQUIPMENT.

Fighting order. Haversack on Back.

The following will be carried by all Ranks.

Rations for Day
Iron Rations
Field Dressings
Identity Disc
Gas Helmets
2 Sandbags
Waterproof Sheet

In addition officers will also carry.

Revolver, Field Glasses and Note Book.

7 MEDICAL.

All troops are reminded that the care of the wounded is the duty of Regimental Stretcher Bearers and Field Ambulances, Fighting Troops are forbidden to accompany wounded men to the Dressing Stations

8. GAS.

Great care must be taken of Box Respirators and all Gas Helmets will be worn in the "ALERT" Position

9. IMPORTANCE OF THE ATTACK.

It is of the utmost importance for this attack to be successful and all officers, N.C.O's & Men must exercise their Maximum effort to push the attack home, and upon the energy and cheerfulness of all, depends the success of this engagement

10 WATER.

Commanders of Gun Teams must not be content with thinking they have suffecient water (also S.A.A. & oil). The carriers must keep on fetching up supplies and making Advance Dumps in the German Trenches. Teams should be cautioned about drinking water from the Wells etc. in the German Lines, until it has been tested to see if it is fit for drinking and cooking

11. DIARIES

All officers and N.C.O's will carry Note Books and pencils and must keep a Diary of the operation as it effects them, no small detail should be omitted

Put in:-
The Situation
How Guns are working
Casualties
Number of Rounds expended
Times should be noted of
any particular Incident
Changes and development of
Situation and any note useful
or Interesting.

12. OFFICERS KITS.

Will be packed up, marked clearly on the outside and left behind at LONELY TRENCH

| | | | |
|---|---|---|---|
| Copy No. 1 | War Diary | Copy No. 7 | 2/LT. D. MANN |
| 2 | office | 8 | " J.D. MURRAY |
| 3 | Brigade | 9 | " R.H. GODDARD |
| 4 | LT. C.L. ROBERTS | 10 | " C.R. WRIGHT. |
| 5 | LT. R.R. NEILSON | 11 | " G.V. COX |
| 6 | LT. F.C. NAWTON | 12 | " P. WILSON |

13th September 1916

# No 45 Machine Gun Coy.

## Supplement to O.O. dated 13-9-16.

S.A.A

The Company's main forward dump is in 70th AVENUE between WELCH ALLEY and the Railway (close to the gun emplacement there).

In addition Brigade Dumps are situated at

(1). In 4 Saps leading to 'T' Heads in SANDERSON TRENCH.

(2). In H.L.I TRENCH near junction with SANDERSON TRENCH.

(3). In WELCH ALLEY just before its junction with SANDERSON TRENCH

WATER

A small quantity of water can be obtained at each of these dumps

IRON RATIONS

Have also been placed in the 3 Brigade Dumps, in case of emergency only:-

Issues will be made on the signature of Officers Commanding Units and these dumps will not be drawn on until all ordinary means of getting rations have failed.

MESSAGES

Two special lines will be run forward from 2 points in HAM TRENCH, about midway between left and right boundaries of Brigade and the Railway

One will be known as No. 1 Report Centre and be in TANGLE TRENCH where the Railway crosses it and the other known as R.C. in TANGLE TRENCH also at M. 32. C. 8.0.

Messages will alway be sent by runners if possible, and all servants will act as runners to their officers

Distribubtition as for Operation order

14th September 1916

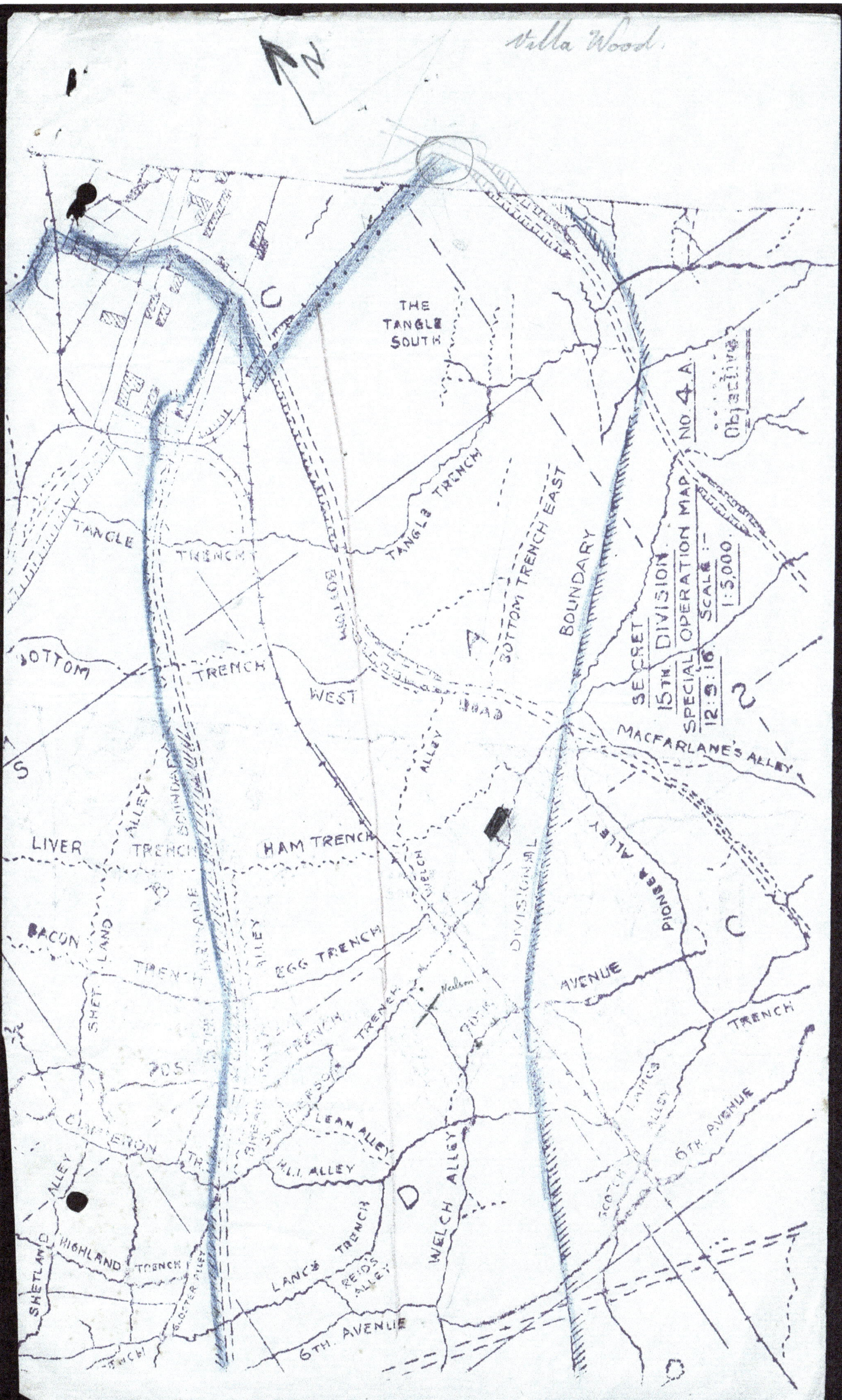

Villa Wood
N
THE TANGLE SOUTH
TANGLE TRENCH
TANGLE TRENCH
BOTTOM TRENCH
BOTTOM TRENCH EAST
BOTTOM TRENCH WEST
ROAD
BOUNDARY
DIVISIONAL
MACFARLANE'S ALLEY
ALLEY
LIVER TRENCH
HAM TRENCH
WELCH
BACON TRENCH
EGG TRENCH
SHETLAND ALLEY
PIONEER ALLEY
AVENUE
TRENCH
6TH. AVENUE
CAMERON TR
LEAN ALLEY
H.L.I. ALLEY
WELCH ALLEY
HIGHLAND TRENCH
LANCS TRENCH
REIDS ALLEY
SHETLAND
SCOTCH
Nelson
SECRET
15TH. DIVISION
SPECIAL OPERATION MAP NO. 4 A
12.9.16.
SCALE :- 1:5,000.
Objective

Index

# SUBJECT.

45th M. G. Coy

| No. | Contents. | Date. |
|---|---|---|
| | October 1916 | |

(63,965). Wt.15,820—176. 2000. 9/21. Gp.164. A.&E.W.

Instructions regarding War Diaries and Intelligence Summaries are contained in F. S. Regs., Part II. and the Staff Manual respectively. Title pages will be prepared in manuscript.

WAR DIARY

*or*

~~INTELLIGENCE SUMMARY.~~

*(Erase heading not required.)*

Army Form C. 2118.

Vol 5

| Place | Date | Hour | Summary of Events and Information | Remarks and references to Appendices |
|---|---|---|---|---|
| CONFIDENTIAL | | | WAR DIARY of No 45 Company Machine Gun Corps. from 1st October 1916 to 31st October 1916. Volume V. | |

[signature]
Capt
Comdg 45th M G Co

T2134. Wt. W708–776. 500000. 4/15. Sir J. C. & S.

Army Form C. 2118.

Instructions regarding War Diaries and Intelligence Summaries are contained in F. S. Regs., Part II. and the Staff Manual respectively. Title pages will be prepared in manuscript.

# WAR DIARY
or
# INTELLIGENCE SUMMARY.

(Erase heading not required.)

| Place | Date | Hour | Summary of Events and Information | Remarks and references to Appendices |
|---|---|---|---|---|
| BAIZIEUX | 1.10.16 | 10 a.m | Church Parade at noon Company Paraded for fitting new clothing weather fine. | |
| | 2.10.16 | | 6.45 a m all Tents struck re-pitched at 9 a m on account of rain. Gun cleaning morning. Physical Drill afternoon. | |
| | 3.10.16 | | Weather still very unsettled. Warning order received that the Brigade would probably move next day. Movement Order received 10. p.m. Brigadier's conference of C.Os at 5 p.m Company paid. | |
| | 4.10.16 | | Heavy rain morning. Company to move off, as per movement order attached. at the last minute this was cancelled on account of wet weather and Company marched straight to BRISLE. Left BAIZIEUX. all clear 10 a m arrived BRISLE. 11.15. all billeted in village. Gun & rifle inspection 5 p. m. | Appendix I |
| | 5.10.16 | | Weather fine. Brigade Field day in practice attack. 2 guns attached to each Battalion. 4 doing overhead fire & 4 in reserve, these last went forward when final objective was taken | |

2353 Wt. W2544/1454 700,000 5/15 D. D. & L. A.D.S.S./Forms/C. 2118.

Army Form C. 2118.

Instructions regarding War Diaries and Intelligence Summaries are contained in F. S. Regs., Part II. and the Staff Manual respectively. Title pages will be prepared in manuscript.

# WAR DIARY
*or*
# INTELLIGENCE SUMMARY.
*(Erase heading not required.)*

| Place | Date | Hour | Summary of Events and Information | Remarks and references to Appendices |
|---|---|---|---|---|
| BRESLE | 6.10.16 | | Weather fine Company cleaning billets, gun cleaning & instruction. | |
| | 7.10.16 | | Weather overcast. Gun instruction morning. Warning order received that we are to relieve the 23rd Division. Afternoon packing limbers. All ranks to carry great coats & W.P. sheets in their packs, all other belongings placed in sandbags & stored in Billet 12 B. BRESLE. | |
| | 8.10.16 | 7.20 | Left BRESLE Sections marched independly. "B" leading followed by "C" "D" & "A". arrived LONELY TRENCH 10.45. a.m. Pouring rain all day. Had to fall out on side of road. no shelter. Managed to serve tea to men. Conference at Brigade Hd 2rs at 1. p.m C.O went on to the MILL at MARTINPUICH to arrange relief with C.O 69th Machine Gun Company. | |
| | | | Company moved up to CONTLEMAISON at 2.30. PM arrived 3.15 unloaded fighting limbers & served a meal to all ranks | |
| | | | At 6.40. P.M. 10 Teams & Hd 2rs moved off to relieve 69th Machine Gun Company. Arrived CUTTING MARTINPUICH at 10.30 | |

2353 Wt. W2544/1454 700,000 5/15 D. D. & L. A.D.S.S./Forms/C. 2118.

Instructions regarding War Diaries and Intelligence Summaries are contained in F. S. Regs., Part II. and the Staff Manual respectively. Title pages will be prepared in manuscript.

# WAR DIARY
*or*
# INTELLIGENCE SUMMARY.
*(Erase heading not required.)*

Army Form C. 2118.

| Place | Date | Hour | Summary of Events and Information | Remarks and references to Appendices |
|---|---|---|---|---|
| | 8.10.16. | | where guides were waiting. All roads congested with traffic + troops, and going extremely heavy owing to the incessant rain. 5 Teams went on to the front line LE SARS arriving there about 1.15 a.m. | |
| | | | Disposition of guns as follows:- | |
| | | | Hd Qrs + 3 teams at the MILL, MARTINPUICH. | |
| | | | 3 Teams under 2/Lt MICHELMORE in front Line left of LE SARS. | |
| | | | 2 Teams under Lieut NAWTON ——— left of LE SARS. | |
| | | | 2 Teams at 70th AVENUE. | |
| | | | 2nd/Lts ROBINSON + LIPSCOMBE + 6 Teams remained at CONTLEMAISON. | |
| | | | 2nd Lt D. MANN + 5 O.R rejoined Company at LONLEY TRENCH from rest camp at ADLT. | |
| | 9.10.16. | 5.15 a.m | Lt MANN, Transport Officer arrived at MARTINPUICH with rations on Pack Mules. at 5.45 C.O went round the line and returned at 10. a.m. Head Quarters shelled at 9. a.m. 2nd/Lts ROBINSON + LIPSCOMBE with the 6 Teams from CONTLEMAISON | |

2353 Wt. W2544/1454 700,000 5/15 D. D. & L. A.D.S.S./Forms/C. 2118.

Instructions regarding War Diaries and Intelligence Summaries are contained in F. S. Regs., Part II. and the Staff Manual respectively. Title pages will be prepared in manuscript.

# WAR DIARY
*or*
# INTELLIGENCE SUMMARY.
*(Erase heading not required.)*

Army Form C. 2118.

| Place | Date | Hour | Summary of Events and Information | Remarks and references to Appendices |
|---|---|---|---|---|
| | 9.10.16 | | at 4. P.M. Officers to Hd Qrs, teams to trenches FACTORY LNES. | |
| | | | 5 30 P.M. Hd Qrs again heavily shelled, Weather fine. | |
| | 10.10.16 | 5. am | C. O. round the line, Weather fine, much improved, Rations arrived 6 a m and relief orders sent up by ration parties. | |
| | | 2.30 | 3 Teams under 2/Lt Robinson proceeded to relieve the 3 teams under 2nd/Lt Micklemore. | |
| | | | 2 Teams under Lieut Lipscombe to relieve 2 teams under Lt Naunton. | |
| | | | The 2 teams in 70th avenue were also relieved. | |
| | | | At 5 30. p. m Hd Qrs heavily shelled by 5 9's Teams just arriving back from Front Line. 2 men seriously wounded, wounds dressed & sent men to dressing station. | |
| | 11.10.16 | 5. a m | C. O went round the line and moved gun from the right of O G 1 to the left in O. G 2 about M 15 central. | |
| | | 4.P.M | Head Quarters shelled. Weather dull, more ammunition carried up to Brigade Dump during morning & afternoon. | |

Army Form C. 2118.

Instructions regarding War Diaries and Intelligence Summaries are contained in F. S. Regs., Part II. and the Staff Manual respectively. Title* pages will be prepared in manuscript.

# WAR DIARY
*or*
# INTELLIGENCE SUMMARY.
*(Erase heading not required.)*

| Place | Date | Hour | Summary of Events and Information | Remarks and references to Appendices |
|---|---|---|---|---|
| MARTINPUICH | 12.10.16. | | Lt NEILSON went round the line at 5. a m Gun on right of OG 2 was moved to about M. 15. D. 0.7. 2 O Rs wounded | |
| | | 2.5. | Division on our left assisted by this Division attacked Guns in 70th avenue fired 3,750 rounds on Trenches in back area. one of the front line guns caught a party of about 150 Germans retiring. and dropped 40 odd, the remainder scattering. | |
| | | 5 pm | 2 Teams of "A" relieved 2 teams of "B" in 70th avenue | |
| | | 5.30. | Lt NAWTON + 2 teams of "D" + 1 team of "B" proceed to relieve 2nd/Lt ROBINSON and one team of "A", "C" + "D" | |
| | | 8. P.M | Owing to guides being late 2nd/Lt Micklemore and 2 teams of "C" proceeded to relieve 2/Lt Lipscombe and 1 Team of "A" + 1 Team of "D". | |
| | | 1.30. | While 2 teams of "C" in FACTORY LINES were preparing Tea a buried "dud" shell exploded under the fire, wounding 7 men. Weather overcast. | |

2353 Wt. W2544/1454 700,000 5/15 D. D. & L. A.D.S.S./Forms/C. 2118.

Instructions regarding War Diaries and Intelligence Summaries are contained in F. S. Regs., Part II. and the Staff Manual respectively. Title pages will be prepared in manuscript.

# WAR DIARY
*or*
# INTELLIGENCE SUMMARY.
*(Erase heading not required.)*

Army Form C. 2118.

| Place | Date | Hour | Summary of Events and Information | Remarks and references to Appendices |
|---|---|---|---|---|
| | 13.10.16. | | C.O. round the line at 5. a.m. Head Quarters intermittently shelled during the day. Weather overcast. More ammunition carried up to both Brigade & Company dumps. 1 man wounded. | |
| | 14.10.16. | | C.O. round the line as usual. Warning order received to we may be relieved by 44th Company at 9. a.m. Lt Isaacs 44th Company arrived at the MILL 9.30 to arrange details They can only take over 4 positions in front line, owing to having to take over the whole Division front. | |
| | | 4.p.m. | Two teams in 70th Avenue & 1 Team in O.G.1. relieved by 3 teams from Factory lines. At 1.30 sent Lt Robinson & 3 men back to LONELY TRENCH to take over camp from 44th Company. & ordered up Transport, 2 limbers to be at MARTINPUICH at dusk & 2 at 10. p.m. | |
| | | | Lt. NEILSON left to go as 2nd in Command of No 8 Company | |
| | | | 2nd/Lt. J.R. STRANGE joined from Base | |

2353 Wt. W2544/1454 700,000 5/15 D. D. & L. A.D.S.S./Forms/C. 2118.

Army Form C. 2118

# WAR DIARY
*or*
# INTELLIGENCE SUMMARY.
*(Erase heading not required.)*

Instructions regarding War Diaries and Intelligence Summaries are contained in F. S. Regs., Part II. and the Staff Manual respectively. Title pages will be prepared in manuscript.

| Place | Date | Hour | Summary of Events and Information | Remarks and references to Appendices |
|---|---|---|---|---|
| MARTINPUICH | 14.10.16 | 5.45. | 2nd Lt STRANGE. C.S.M. and 8 Teams from Factory Lines returned to LONELY TRENCH. Guides from front lines arrived cutting at 6.30 p.m. 4 teams from 44th Company arrived at 7 p.m. & sent up to firing line with guides. Relief completed 11.30 p.m. and all returned to Lonely Trench, arriving there at 3 a.m. except:- 1 men from each of the 4 teams in front who remained behind with 44th Company for the night. Lt Lipscombe & 1 team at MILL. 2 teams in 70th AVENUE & 1 team ~~Factory Lines~~ Q.G.1. Divisional order being that 1 Section was to remain in support. Weather overcast. | |
| LONELY TR | 15.11.16 | | The 5th Team in front line i.e in O.G.1 relieved by 44th Coy. & returned to FACTORY LINES. also the 4 odd men came back. Weather fine but cold. 120 men bathed at BECOORT from 10 to 11 a.m. remainder of day gun cleaning & resting. ONE Blanket per man served out. | |

2353 Wt. W2544/1454 700,000 5/15 D. D. & L. A.D.S.S./Forms/C. 2118.

Instructions regarding War Diaries and Intelligence Summaries are contained in F. S. Regs., Part II. and the Staff Manual respectively. Title pages will be prepared in manuscript.

# WAR DIARY
*or*
# INTELLIGENCE SUMMARY.
*(Erase heading not required.)*

Army Form C. 2118.

| Place | Date | Hour | Summary of Events and Information | Remarks and references to Appendices |
|---|---|---|---|---|
| LONELY TR | 15.10.16 | | Lt ROBERTS and 4 O.R returned from CAMIERS. | |
| | 16.10.16 | | Fine bright weather, but cold. All teams cleaning guns making up shortages & repacking limbers. | |
| | | 1.30 | 2nd/Lt STRANGE, & 2 teams of "B" & 2 teams of "C" proceeded to relieve 2/Lt LIPSCOMBE & the 4 teams in support at MARTIN PUICH. | |
| | | | Decrease in strength during period in Line.<br>9 O.R. Wounded.<br>13 O.R. Admitted to Hospital. | |
| | 17.10.16 | | Weather fine & bright. Remainder of Company bathed at 7.30 a.m. Teams gun cleaning & drill all morning. Warning Order received that we may relieve tomorrow at 9.30 p.m. | |
| | 18.10.16 | | Operation order received 9.15 a.m that we are to relieve today sent an orderley up to MARTINPUICH to C.O. 46th M.G. Co. O.O. cancelled 11.30 a.m relief not to take place until 19th instant. at 1.30 p.m. 2nd/Lt Robinson and & 2 Teams of | |

2353 Wt. W2544/1454 700,000 5/15 D. D. & L. A.D.S.S./Forms/C. 2118.

Army Form C. 2118.

Instructions regarding War Diaries and Intelligence Summaries are contained in F. S. Regs., Part II. and the Staff Manual respectively. Title pages will be prepared in manuscript.

# WAR DIARY
or
# INTELLIGENCE SUMMARY.
(Erase heading not required.)

| Place | Date | Hour | Summary of Events and Information | Remarks and references to Appendices |
|---|---|---|---|---|
| | 18.10.16 | | "C" & 1 Team "A", 1 Team "D" relieved 2/Lt Strange and 2 Teams "C" & 2 Teams of "B". weather dull. rain early morning 7. O.R. joined from BASE | |
| | 19.10.16 | | Heavy rain early morning. Preparation for relief of 46 M G Coy. | |
| | | 1.45pm | Teams. 1.5.+6 under 2Lt F.C. NAWTON left for front line. | |
| | | 1.55pm | Teams 14+15 under 2Lt F. MICHELMORE left for front line | |
| | | 2.0pm | Remainder of Coy and Hd. 2trs moved off. | |
| MILL MARTINPUICH. | | 3.30pm | H.Q. arrived at MILL MARTINPUICH. Heavy rain fell all through relief. | |
| | | 4.30pm | Enemy barraged the front on right of LESARS and attacked - no result. | |
| | | 11.0pm | Relief complete. Lt. A.C ROBINSON reported his servant who had been sent on a message on the 18th. as missing. | |
| | 20 10/16 | 5am | C.O. visited the guns in the line, and moved 2 guns which had been pushed forward from 70th AVENUE by OC. 46 Coy back to 70th AVENUE weather fine and frosty. | |
| | 21 10/16 | 5am | C.O visited the guns in the line. | |

Instructions regarding War Diaries and Intelligence Summaries are contained in F. S. Regs., Part II. and the Staff Manual respectively. Title pages will be prepared in manuscript.

# WAR DIARY
*or*
~~INTELLIGENCE SUMMARY.~~
*(Erase heading not required.)*

Army Form C. 2118.

| Place | Date | Hour | Summary of Events and Information | Remarks and references to Appendices |
|---|---|---|---|---|
| MILL. MARTINPUICH. | 21/10/16 | 9.30am | Guns in forward position relieved: Present disposition | |
| | | | 2nd Lt. J R STRANGE and team 3 & 4. LE SARS. | |
| | | | 2nd Lt. J.K. LIPSCOMBE and team 7. 8 & 16 O.G.1. & GILBERT TRENCH. | |
| | | | Team 2 & 13. 70th AVENUE. Team 1, 5, 6, 9, 10, 11, 12, 14, 15 FACTORY LINE | |
| | | | C.O.: Lt. C.L. ROBERTS: 2Lts F.C. NAWTON. F. MICHELMORE: A.C. ROBINSON: C.S.M. and | |
| | | | H.Q. at MILL. MARTINPUICH. Transport Officer (2nd Lt D. MANN) C.Q.M.S. and | |
| | | | Transport at LONELY TRENCH X.27 c. 5.4 approx. | |
| | | 12 noon | Relief complete. | |
| | | 12.6 | Canadian attack on the left – successful. | |
| | | 5.30pm | 2nd Lt. R.S. MORDETH joined and came up to H.Q. | |
| | 22/10/16 | 5.0am | C.O. visited guns. Weather fine and frosty. | |
| | | | During the day MARTINPUICH was shelled. a few H.E. & shrapnel coming near H.Q but not damage done. | |
| | | | Teams in FACTORY LINE worked on improvements to the Trench. | |
| | 23/10/16 | 5.0am | 2nd in Command visited guns in the line. Weather fine but very misty. | |
| | | | Teams in the front system relieved. | |

2353 Wt. W2544/1454 700,000 5/15 D. D. & L. A.D.S.S./Forms/C. 2118.

Instructions regarding War Diaries and Intelligence Summaries are contained in F. S. Regs., Part II. and the Staff Manual respectively. Title pages will be prepared in manuscript.

# WAR DIARY
*or*
# INTELLIGENCE SUMMARY.
*(Erase heading not required.)*

Army Form C. 2118.

| Place | Date | Hour | Summary of Events and Information | Remarks and references to Appendices |
|---|---|---|---|---|
| MILL MARTINPUICH | 23/10/16 | 9.30 | Teams 9 & 10 under 2nd Lt A.C. ROBINSON relieved 2nd Lt J.R. STRANGE and teams 3 & 4. Teams 2, 11 & 12 under 2nd Lt R.S. MORDETH relieved teams 7, 8 & 16 under 2Lt J.K. LIPSCOMBE. Teams 14 & 15 relieved teams 2 & 13 in 70th AVENUE | |
| | | | Warning order that the Brigade will attack on 25th inst received. | |
| | | | Pte DUFF accidently wounded. He noticed a bandolier smouldering in a fire in a dugout in LE SARS and when he pulled it out a round exploded wounding him in the left hand & both legs. | |
| | | | Consider he saved a more serious accident. | |
| | 24/10/16 | 5.0am | Co. visited guns in the front system. | |
| | | | Two days rations received and one days ration dumped at H.Q. these are for use on the day of attack. | |
| | | 9.0am | 33 O.R. joined ~~as~~ attached from Brigade as carriers. One man for transport sent down to transport lines. | |
| | | 2.30pm | Pte Hobson of 11th A&SH who joined with above this morning was accidently shot and killed by Pte RAE 6th Cameron Hs who also joined this morning. Brigade informed and Court of Inquiry ordered to assemble at 10.am at Coy H.Q. on 25th inst. | |
| | | 3.0pm | Coy operation orders for attack issued to all officers and a copy sent to Brigade H.Q. | Appendix II |
| | | 4.0pm | 2nd Lt D. MANN arrived at H.Q. MILL & MARTINPUICH shelled for ½ hr no damage. | |

2353 Wt. W2544/1454 700,000 5/15 D. D. & L. A.D.S.S./Forms/C. 2118.

Army Form C. 2118.

Instructions regarding War Diaries and Intelligence Summaries are contained in F. S. Regs., Part II. and the Staff Manual respectively. Title pages will be prepared in manuscript.

# WAR DIARY
*or*
~~INTELLIGENCE SUMMARY.~~

*(Erase heading not required.)*

| Place | Date | Hour | Summary of Events and Information | Remarks and references to Appendices |
|---|---|---|---|---|
| MILL. MARTINPUICH | 24 10/16 | 11.30 pm | Orders received that attack of 26th is postponed till the 28th. Canadians on the left to attack at 7.0 am to-morrow 25th inst. | |
| | | | It has rained all day. Enemy communication fired on from 70th AVENUE & OG. 2 | |
| | 25 10/16 | 5.0 am | C.O visited guns in the line and took with him 2Lt. D. MANN. | |
| | | 7.0 am | Canadians attacked. guns cooperated with indirect fire on German communication. | |
| | | 10.0 am | Court of Inquiry into accidently death of Pte. Hobson 11th A&SH, attached, held at Coy H.Q. Company to find one member. | |
| | | 11.0 am | Guns in the line relieved & present disposition of guns. 2nd Lt F.C. NAWTON [redacted] and team 7 & 8, in LE SARS; 2nd Lt. D MANN and team, 1.14.115 in OG 2; Teams 5 & 13 in 70th AVENUE. Remaining officers at H.Q. and teams in FACTORY LINE. | |
| | | | Weather. Early morning fine but changed to rain with fine intervals. | |
| | | | Ground between MILL and THE CUTTING heavily shelled in the morning. | |
| | 26 10/16 | 5.0 am | C.O. and 2nd in Command visited guns in the line. Reconnoitred the CHALK PIT and the forward positions of LE SARS. | |
| | | | Orders received postponing attack from 28th to 30th addendum to Coy O.O. issued accordingly. | |

2353 Wt. W2544/1454 700,000 5/15 D. D. & L. A.D.S.S./Forms/C. 2118.

Instructions regarding War Diaries and Intelligence Summaries are contained in F. S. Regs., Part II. and the Staff Manual respectively. Title pages will be prepared in manuscript.

# WAR DIARY
*or*
~~INTELLIGENCE SUMMARY.~~

*(Erase heading not required.)*

Army Form C. 2118.

| Place | Date | Hour | Summary of Events and Information | Remarks and references to Appendices |
|---|---|---|---|---|
| MILL MARTINPUICH | 26/10/16 | | One O.R. wounded S.I.W. | |
| | | | 16 boxes S.A.A. sent up to Dugout in LESARS. The new attached men not giving satisfaction and grumbling one man refused to carry ammunition. Reported this to Brigade and the worst offenders returned to regiment. Court Martial proceedings applied for in the case of refusal. | |
| | 27/10/16 | 5.0am | C.O. visited guns in the line. Trenches becoming very much worse with mud & water. | |
| | | | One O.R. wounded in FACTORY LINES. Shrapnel. | |
| | | 9.30 | Guns in the line relieved. | |
| | | | Team 13 & 16 under 2nd Lt MICHELMORE relieved 2nd Lt F.C. NAWTON & teams 7 & 8. Teams 3.4 & 6 under 2nd Lt STRANGE relieved ~~...~~ 2nd Lt DMANN and teams 1.14 & 15. Teams 7.11 relieved 5 & 13 in 70th AVENUE | |
| | | | Whilst coming out team 8 suffered 5 casualties. | |
| | | | Orders received postponing attack from 30th to the 1st Nov. | |
| | 28/10/16 | 5.0am | C.O. visited all guns in the forward system. | |
| | | | 2nd Lt. DMANN returned to the Transport lines. | |
| | 29/10/16 | 5.0am | 2nd in Command visited all guns in the forward positions. | |
| | | | Guns in the line relieved. Present dispositions. | |

2353 Wt. W2544/1454 700,000 5/15 D. D. & L. A.D.S.S./Forms/C. 2118.

Instructions regarding War Diaries and Intelligence Summaries are contained in F. S. Regs., Part II. and the Staff Manual respectively. Title pages will be prepared in manuscript.

# WAR DIARY
*or*
# ~~INTELLIGENCE SUMMARY.~~
*(Erase heading not required.)*

Army Form C. 2118.

| Place | Date | Hour | Summary of Events and Information | Remarks and references to Appendices |
|---|---|---|---|---|
| MILL | 29/10/16 | 9.30 | Relief commenced and was complete by | |
| MARTINPUICH | | 1.0. | Teams 9 & 10 under 2nd Lt R.S. MORPETH in LE SARS. Teams 2. 11. 12 under 2nd Lt. LIPSCOMBE O.G. 2. Teams 1 & 16 in 70th AVENUE. Remainder of Coy: Officers at H.Q. except 2Lt. D MANN at Transport LINES. Teams in FACTORY LINES. | |
| | | | Both officers up the line are now in the one dug out in LE SARS as the one in O.G. 1 has been knocked in. | |
| | 30/10/16 | 5 am | C.O. visited all guns in the line. Guns carried out usual night firing. | |
| | | | Representatives of 143 Coy M.G.C. came to H.Q to arrange relief which is to take place after our attack. | |
| | | 12 noon | Orders received postponing attack till 3rd prox. 2nd Lt. MANN wired not to return to H.Q. yet. Brigade asked if we can be relieved for a day or two to get a change of dry clothes. Weather still bad with heavy rain, & strong wind. | |
| | | 10.30 pm | Message received that the enemy are carrying out a large relief. All guns warned to keep up fire on communication all night – 2000 rounds per gun. | |
| | 31/10/16 | 5.0 am | C.O. visited all guns in the line. Weather fine with sunshine. | |
| | | 9 am–12 noon | Guns in forward positions relieved. Present disposition being. Teams 14 & 15 under 2Lt J.R. STRANGE in LE SARS. Teams 5. 6 & 8 under 2Lt F.C. NAWTON in O.G. 2. Teams 3 & 4 in 70th Avenue. Remainder of Coy in FACTORY LINES. Officers at H.Q. 2nd Lt D MANN with Transport. | |

2353 Wt. W2544/1454 700,000 5/15 D. D. & L. A.D.S.S./Forms/C. 2118.

Instructions regarding War Diaries and Intelligence Summaries are contained in F. S. Regs., Part II. and the Staff Manual respectively. Title pages will be prepared in manuscript.

# WAR DIARY
*or*
# INTELLIGENCE SUMMARY.
*(Erase heading not required.)*

Army Form C. 2118.

| Place | Date | Hour | Summary of Events and Information | Remarks and references to Appendices |
|---|---|---|---|---|
| MILL MARTINPUICH | 31/10/16 | | Reported from transport lines that 2 O.R. drivers joined last night 30th inst | |
| | | | O.C. 143 Coy visited H.Q. for further particulars of the sector. | |
| | | | 2Lt A.C. ROBINSON sick with fever. (malaria) | |
| | | | One other rank wounded shrapnel at FACTORY LINES. | |
| | | | Headquarters shelled intermittently during the day. | |
| | | | 27 pairs of repaired boots were issued on exchange to the Company. | |
| | | | A.W. Atkinson Capt. 45th M. G. Coy | |

T2134. Wt. W708—776. 500000. 4/15. Sir J. C. & S.

Appendix I

MOVEMENT ORDER by CAPT. H.V. WILKINSON
Commanding No 45 Machine Gun Coy

BAIZIEUX 3rd October 1916

The 45th Inf Bde will move to BRESLE to the 4th inst in accordance with Special Training Scheme

2 Guns "A" Section under the senior N.C.O. will report to the C.O. 6/7th Royal Scots Fusiliers

2 Guns "B" Section will report to the C.O. 11th Argyle & Sutherland Highlanders

2 Guns "C" Section will report to the C.O. 13th Royal Scots

2 Guns "D" Section will report to the C.O 6th Cameron Highrs

All at 9-0 a.m

The remainder of the Coy will parade at 9-0 a.m. on the Coy Parade Ground

Dress for all :- Fighting order

The transport will move off at 9.15 a.m. and *must* be clear of the Eastern end of Village at 9.35 a.m. The brakesmen will act as billeting parties.

1. N.C.O. & 4 men will be left behind to clean up Camp and act as a loading party for the 2nd Journey of the Transport

Each team will carry Gun, Tripod, Spare Part Boxes, and 4 Belt Boxes

Christie Roberts. Lieut

2nd In Command

45 M. G. Coy.

Appendix II

OPERATION ORDERS by CAPT. H.V. WILKINSON
Commanding No 45 Machine Gun Company.

In the Field 24th Oct: 1916

1. The 4th and Reserve Armies will continue the attack on the 26th inst. the 50th Division on the right, the 15th Division in the centre and the 4th Canadian Division on the left

2. The 15th Division will attack the LITTLE WOOD front and support Lines, assaulting at ZERO hour from the line M.16. B.6.6. - M 9. D. 6.½. N.W. corner of CHALK PIT.

3. Brigade Boundaries
RIGHT. A line running N. & S. from M16 a. 2. 6½. to M. 10. c. 2½. 8. LITTLE WOOD inclusive.

4. LEFT. Divisional Line.
The attack of the 45th Infantry Brigade will be carried out by the 6/7th Royal SCOTS FUSILIERS on right and 11th A. & S. Highlanders on left and will be in four waves from SCOTLAND and CHALK TRENCHES.
The assaulting waves will move direct on to the objectives which will be consolidated.
Six strong points will be constructed

5. Disposition of Guns
2 Teams of 'D' Nos. 13 & 16 under 2/LT. LIPSCOMB will be in the CHALK PIT. and after

P.T.O

ZERO will push forward and come into action about M. 9. D. ½. 5. to cover our left front.

2. Teams of "A" Nos. 3 & 4 under 2/LT. MICHELMORE will also be in the CHALK PIT and as soon as the situation permits, move Guns forward to the CREST about M. 9. D. 4. 4.

2 ~~Guns~~ Teams of "C" Nos. 9 & 10 under 2/LT. ROBINSON will be in SUNKEN ROAD LE SARS and bring overhead fire to bear on Roads & Trenches in M 3. range about 2000 to 2,500 X

2 Teams of "C" Nos. 11 & 12 under 2/LT. MORPETH in O. G. 2 will bring overhead fire to bear on the roads & trenches in M. 4. A. & B. 2.500 X etc

2 Teams of "B" Nos. 5 & 6 under 2/LT. MANN will be in GILBERT ALLEY to bring overhead fire on M. 3. c. in particular.

2 Teams of "A" Nos. 1 & 2 under 2/LT. STRANGE will be in support in CABLE TRENCH CUTTING GILBERT ALLEY near DESTREMONT FARM.

4 Teams "B" & "D" Nos 7. 8. 14. & 15. under LT. NAWTON will be in reserve in 70th AVENUE.

C.S.M. & 2 Signallers will be at Advanced Hd. Qrs.

C. O. and Adjutant will be at Hd. Qrs.

6. There will be no increase of intensity of fire until ZERO HOUR.

At ZERO, the left group Divisional Artillery will place a barrage 150 yards in front of our line. It will lift at ZERO + 1 minute and creep forward at the rate of 50 yards a minute

P. T. O

At ZERO + 1 hour & 5 minutes the left Group will form a box barrage well ahead when patrols will be sent out

7. A Divisional O.P. has been established at about M 15. c. 6.6. This will be available for sending messages back to Brigade, but not forward.

8. MEDICAL

(1.) A collecting post for Stretcher cases will be established on the BAPAUME ROAD about 200 yards S.W. of DESTREMONT FARM

(2) Walking cases are to proceed direct to GUN PIT ROAD, and from there through MARTINPUICH following the route indicated to CONTALMAISON CHATEAU

9. PRISONERS

Prisoners will be handed over at DESTREMONT FARM to the A.P.M. 15th Division who will be responsible for conducting them to the Corps Cage in BAZENTIN LE PETIT.

10. BRIGADE Hd. QTS. will not move and are at M 32. c. 2.9.

Coy. Hd. QTS. will be at THE MILL

11. Ammunition

Each Gun in the Line must have 8 Belt Boxes and 5. 1,000 round boxes of S.A.A. Other teams will carry 8 Belt Boxes

Advance S.A.A. Dumps are in O.G.1 and Coy advance Dump in the dug-out in the SUNKEN ROAD LE SARS.

P.T.O

It is most important that this is pointed out to all men, particularly Ammunition Carriers

12 Officers and N.C.O's must keep control over their men and see that they do not wander away. There was too much of this in the last attack. and any man going to the rear without permission will be COURT MARTIALED and dealt with in the severest manner

13. Officers must watch their S.A.A. water. and Oil supplies very carefully. and take up as much of the latter as possible.

14. All Officers and N.C.O's will carry Note Books and report, casualties, the situation, stating time and Map references and anything of an interesting nature.

24.10.16.

A M Wilkinson
Capt
Comdg 45th M.G. Co

No. 45 Machine Gun Coy

ADDENDUM to O.O. dated 24-10-16

PARA I. For 26th read 30th inst.

PARA V. 2nd LT. MANN will be in charge of "A" teams 1 & 2 and 2nd LT. STRANGE in charge of "B" teams 5 & 6.

2nd LT. ROBINSON with teams 9 & 10 will be ready to move forward and occupy Strong Points 4 & 6 and 2nd LT. STRANGE with teams 5 & 6 to occupy S.P. 2 & 3 as soon as word is sent that the consolidation is complete

15. On the night of assembly complete silence will be observed forward of MARTINPUICH

16. Great care will be taken at dawn that there is no movement liable to cause suspicion. This is particularly important in view of hostile Aircraft observing our Lines. All ranks will be instructed not to look up at Enemy Aeroplanes.

17. When teams are in position on night 29/30th this will be reported to Advance Hd. Qrs. LE SARS ALLEY LE SARS and phoned back by code.

18 Any slightly wounded man moving to the rear without Arms and Equipment will be sent back to the Firing Line to fetch them.

19. These Operation Orders should be carefully explained to every N.C.O. & Man in the Unit

A.H. Wilkinson
Capt

26th October 1916

O.C. No 45 Machine Gun Coy.

Index

# SUBJECT.

45th M. G. Corps

| No. | Contents. | Date. |
|---|---|---|
| | November 1916 | |

(63,965). Wt.15,820—176. 2000. 9/21. Gp.164. A.&E.W.

Army Form C. 2118.

Instructions regarding War Diaries and Intelligence Summaries are contained in F. S. Regs., Part II. and the Staff Manual respectively. Title pages will be prepared in manuscript.

# WAR DIARY

*or*

~~INTELLIGENCE SUMMARY.~~

*(Erase heading not required.)*

Vol 6

| Place | Date | Hour | Summary of Events and Information | Remarks and references to Appendices |
|---|---|---|---|---|
| | | | CONFIDENTIAL. | |
| | | | WAR DIARY | |
| | | | OF | |
| | | | 45 Coy. MACHINE GUN CORPS | |
| | | | 1st to 30th NOVEMBER 1916 | |
| | | | VOLUMN VI | |
| | | | A.M. Wilkinson Capt | |
| | | | Comdg: 45th M.G. Co | |

2353 Wt. W2544/1454 700,000 5/15 D. D. & L. A.D.S.S./Forms/C. 2118.

1

Instructions regarding War Diaries and Intelligence Summaries are contained in F. S. Regs., Part II. and the Staff Manual respectively. Title pages will be prepared in manuscript.

# WAR DIARY

*or*

~~INTELLIGENCE SUMMARY.~~

*(Erase heading not required.)*

Army Form C. 2118.

| Place | Date | Hour | Summary of Events and Information | Remarks and references to Appendices |
|---|---|---|---|---|
| MILL | 1/11/16 | 5.am | C.O. visited the guns in the line. | |
| MARTINPUICH | | 10.am. | Court Martial held on No 21832 Pte Chesswell and No 21591 Pte Pae. G at CONTALMAISON. 2nd i Command prosecuted. | |
| | | | One O.R. wounded - sniped in the head. | |
| | | | 2nd Lt. F.R. KEITH joined from Base. | |
| | | 12 noon | Warning orders received re possible relief to-morrow. C.O. 145 Coy visited H.Q. to make arrangements. | |
| | | 5.0pm | Orders for relief confirmed. Coy orders issued accordingly. | 1. |
| | 2/11/16 | 5.am. | C.O. visited guns in the line. 2nd Lt. F.R. KEITH relieved 2nd Lt. F.C. NAWTON in the trenches. Orders received for move to ALBERT on 3rd inst. | |
| | | 5.pm | Relief commenced. | 1. |
| MILL. | 3/11/16 | 2.30am | H.Q at MILL MARTINPUICH closed; opened at LONELY TRENCH. | |
| LONELY | | 8.am | The last of the gunteams reported all correct at Headquarters. | 1. |
| TRench. | | 10.am | Coy moved off to Billets at ALBERT. | |
| | | 12.45 | H.Q. opened in RUE de BRAY ALBERT. | |
| ALBERT. | | | Small kit and Blankets arrived by lorry from BRESLE and issued to Coy | |

T2134. Wt. W708—776. 500000. 4/15. Sir J. C. & S.

Instructions regarding War Diaries and Intelligence Summaries are contained in F. S. Regs., Part II. and the Staff Manual respectively. Title pages will be prepared in manuscript.

# WAR DIARY
*or*
~~INTELLIGENCE SUMMARY.~~
(*Erase heading not required.*)

Army Form C. 2118.

| Place | Date | Hour | Summary of Events and Information | Remarks and references to Appendices |
|---|---|---|---|---|
| ALBERT. | 4/11/16. | 10 am | Coy parade for inspection of rifles kits &c followed by Gun Cleaning and repacking of limbers. Coy paid. | |
| | | 1.0 pm | Orders received as a warning that the Brigade might move tomorrow 5th inst. | |
| | | 5 pm | Warning Order confirmed. Coy Orders issued accordingly | 2. |
| | 5/11/16. | 10 am | Coy moved off in accordance with operation Orders. | 2 |
| FRANVILLERS | | 1 pm | Coy in Billets at FRANVILLERS. | |
| | 6/11/16. | | Coy parades for Physical Training, Inspections of Gun cleaning in the morning. | |
| | | 3 pm | New clothing issued as far as possible. | |
| | 7/11/16. | | Instructional parades for attached men. Heavy rain all day. | |
| | | 10.30 | 120 O.R parade for Baths at BAZIEUX. Remainder of Company paraded for P.T. drill & instructional parades. | |
| | 8.11.16 | | Parades & inspection as usual, Instructional classes for attached men started under 2nd Lieuts Morpath, Strange, & Keith & Sgt Rooney. Weather dull & overcast. Opened a small Canteen for the Company | |
| | | 4. P.M | Remainder of Company Paraded for Baths at BAISIEUX. | |
| | 9.11.16 | | Weather fine & much improved General Sir Douglas Haig | |

Instructions regarding War Diaries and Intelligence Summaries are contained in F. S. Regs., Part II. and the Staff Manual respectively. Title pages will be prepared in manuscript.

Army Form C. 2118.

# WAR DIARY
*or*
# INTELLIGENCE SUMMARY.
*(Erase heading not required.)*

| Place | Date | Hour | Summary of Events and Information | Remarks and references to Appendices |
|---|---|---|---|---|
| FRANVILLERS | 9.11.16 | | rode over & inspected the Brigade. The Company were carrying on the usual work. advance Gun Drill. Instructional class for new men. Range Taking. & Physical drill class for N.C.Os under 2nd Lt Michelmore | |
| | | 2.P.M | Lieut Roberts instructed to join no 48 Coy: as C.O. | |
| | 10.11.16 | | Weather fine & bright. Routine work as usual. 2nd Lieut Mann takes over the duties as 2nd in Command. | |
| | | 3.P.M | Lt Roberts left to take over Command of 48 Company | |
| | 11.11.16 | | Weather dull. Company Paraded for route March under C.O at 8.15. afternoon thoroughly cleaning & oiling limbers. | |
| | 12.11.6 | | Weather dull. Morning: Church parades. Afternoon: Company paid out. | |
| | 13.11.6 | | Weather dull. "A" Section on range. The remainder of the Company carried out Advanced Gundrill & attached men paraded for the instructional Classes. "D" section was inspected in full marching order by the C.O. 1. O.R to 45th F.A. for instruction in first aid | |

4

Army Form C. 2118.

Instructions regarding War Diaries and Intelligence Summaries are contained in F. S. Regs., Part II. and the Staff Manual respectively. Title pages will be prepared in manuscript.

# WAR DIARY
*or*
~~INTELLIGENCE SUMMARY~~.
*(Erase heading not required.)*

| Place | Date | Hour | Summary of Events and Information | Remarks and references to Appendices |
|---|---|---|---|---|
| Franvillers | 14-11-6 | 8.30 am | The C.O. proceeded to England on leave. 2nd Lt. D Mann took over the duties of Command and 2nd Lt. J.C. Newton took over the duties of 2nd in Command. "B" section on the Range. Remainder of Coy practised gun drill etc & there was classes for the attached men. "C" section inspected by the C.O. in the afternoon. Weather clearer. No 23265 Pte. B. Donaghy accidently shot himself in the left hand whilst cleaning his officers revolver. | |
| | 15-11-16 | | Weather very cold. Coy. paraded at 8.15 am. for route march. Notice received from Brigade that No 23765 Pte B. Donghy is to be tried by F.G.C.M. at ~~La Hou~~ LA HOUSSOYE at 9 am. 16th inst. All witnesses warned and escort arranged for prisoner. | |
| | 16-11-16 | | Weather cold. "II" section under 2nd Lt KEITH proceeded to LAVIÉVILLE to be attached to III Corps M.M.G. to undergo training in Anti-aircraft work. "C" section on Range. Remainder of Coy carried out gun drill & Coy drill. B sect. inspected in afternoon by C.O. F.G.C.M on Pte B. DONAGHY postponed until 17th. | |
| | 17-11-16 | | Weather Cold. Court Martial at LA HOUSSOYE at 13th R. SCOTS HQRS on | |

T2134. Wt. W708—776. 500000. 4/15. Sir J. C. & S.

5

Army Form C. 2118.

Instructions regarding War Diaries and Intelligence Summaries are contained in F. S. Regs., Part II. and the Staff Manual respectively. Title pages will be prepared in manuscript.

# WAR DIARY
*or*
# INTELLIGENCE SUMMARY.
*(Erase heading not required.)*

| Place | Date | Hour | Summary of Events and Information | Remarks and references to Appendices |
|---|---|---|---|---|
| FRANVILLERS | 17/11/16 | | Pte DONAGHY Morning: Physical Drill. Advanced Gun drill. Key drill. Afternoon 'A' Sect. inspected by C.O. Judging distance & visual training. Attached men on range. | |
| | 18/11/16 | | Coy paraded for Route March at 8-45. | |
| | | 11.45 | G.O.C. inspected billets. Promulgation of Court Martial proceedings on Pte DONAGHY. Weather: Sunny turning to rain later. | |
| | 19/11/16 | | Morning Church parade. Weather cold but fine. | |
| | 20/11/16 | | "A" Section on range. Remainder Physical drill. Guard mounting. Indication & recognition. Afternoon. 2.30. Inspection by Corps Commander. Advanced gun drill. | |
| | 21/11/16 | | B' section on range. Remainder. Physical Drill, Rifle drill & Advanced gun drill. Afternoon. Immediate action. | |
| | 22/11/16 | 8.45 am | Company paraded for route march. Afternoon. Mechanism. | |
| | 23/11/16 | 8.45 am. | Tactical training scheme. Afternoon. Company proceeded to BAZIEUX for baths. 2nd Lt. H. H. HENDERSON Joined from base. | |
| | 24/11/16 | | Morning Physical drill & Advanced gun drill. | |
| | | 11.45 | Company paraded in full marching order for inspection. | |
| | | 2 pm | Company Sports. | |

Instructions regarding War Diaries and Intelligence Summaries are contained in F. S. Regs., Part II. and the Staff Manual respectively. Title pages will be prepared in manuscript.

# WAR DIARY

*or*

~~INTELLIGENCE SUMMARY.~~

(*Erase heading not required.*)

Army Form C. 2118.

6

| Place | Date | Hour | Summary of Events and Information | Remarks and references to Appendices |
|---|---|---|---|---|
| FRANVILLERS | 25/11/16 | | Morning: Gun limbers cleaning. Court martial held at Coy headquarters on Pte SCARFF J. and Pte McCRANDLES J. Afternoon. Packing limbers. Weather for past few days cold & wet. | |
| | 26/11/16 | 10.15 am. | Company paraded in full marching order & proceeded to "B" Camp, BAZIEUX. Coy inspected by G.O.C. on line of march. 2nd Lt. LIPSCOMB and 1 O.R. proceeded to M.G. School CAMIERS. 1 O.R. proceeded to attend divisional signalling course at MOLLIENS-AU-BOIS. | |
| BAZIEUX | 27/11/16 | 7 am | All ranks cleaning Camp. | |
| | | 9 am. | Company drill. Instruction in recognition of targets. Afternoon cleaning clothing, equipment etc. in preparation of G.O.C. 15th Div. inspection. C.O. returned from leave. 2/Lt. A C ROBINSON admitted to Hospital. | |
| — | 28.11.16 | 7 am | Limbers cleaned & oiled. | |
| | | 11 am | Paraded for G.O.C. 15th Division Inspection. Coy drawn up in line with transport. "B" Section had to come into action. | |
| | | 2.15. | Coy cross country run. Weather very cold, but fine. | |
| | 29.11.16 | 8.45. | Company Route March in fighting order. C O's Conference at. | |

Army Form C. 2118.

Instructions regarding War Diaries and Intelligence Summaries are contained in F. S. Regs., Part II. and the Staff Manual respectively. Title pages will be prepared in manuscript.

# WAR DIARY
*or*
~~INTELLIGENCE SUMMARY.~~

*(Erase heading not required.)*

| Place | Date | Hour | Summary of Events and Information | Remarks and references to Appendices |
|---|---|---|---|---|
| BAZIEUX | 29-11-16 | | Brigade Hd Qrs CONTAY. Weather cold | |
| | 30-11-16 | 7.a.m | Physical Drill | |
| | | 9.am | Routine as usual. Lieut KEITH and "D" Section returned to Company from III Corps M. M. G. Battery | |
| | | 1.15pm | The whole Company Paraded & marched VADENCOURT for baths. | |
| | | 6pm | "D" Section paid. Lt Nawton took over the duties of 2nd in Command and Lt Mann Transport Officer. Weather very cold & foggy. | |

A. M. Wilkinson
Capt.
Cmdg 45th M. G. Co.

2353 Wt. W2544/1454 700,000 5/15 D. D. & L. A.D.S.S./Forms/C. 2118.

(2)

Relief Orders by Captain G. I. Atkinson
Commanding 145th Coy M-G-C
In the Field
1.11.16

No. 1. The 140th Coy will relieve the 145th M.G. Coy on the night of the 2/3rd inst.

No. 2. Two Guides per Gun from Factory Lanes to lead the relieving teams up to the forward positions to be at CONTALMAISON.VILLA. at 5 p.m.
Four more Guides from Factory Lanes to be at CONTALMAISON VILLA at 5.15 pm to bring up the remainder of the Companies nine teams to Factory Lanes and Head Qrs 2 teams to the MILL.

No. 3 The teams in the Front Lines will each hand over 8 Belt Boxes per gun and obtain a receipt for them and all trench stores handed over.

No. 4 Each team is to report at the Mill on its way down & will then be instructed where the limbers will be.

No. 5 On completion of relief the Company will move back by teams to LONELY TRENCH.

No. 6 __Transport__. Three, Six mule limbers to be at the Water Tanks culling at 6 pm to take away 9 Guns Tripods &c. & 90 Belt Boxes &c.
Two Six-mule limbers to be at the same place at 10.30 pm to load 7 guns, 16 boxes of ammunition & the mens packs from the line.

No. 7 Lieut MICHELMORE & 2 O.R will proceed to LONELY TRENCH at 10.30 am to take over there.

No. 8. The Coy. Cooks will have hot tea ready for the teams on arrival at LONELY TRENCH

No 9 On the 3rd inst the Coy will move on to ALBERT. time will be advised later. 2nd Lt MICHELMORE & 3 O.R. will report to the Town Major ALBERT at 9 a.m. to arrange billets.
The route to be followed by the Company on the 3rd inst will be: NORTH END of FRICOURT ROAD, through F 3 a - X. 26 D and C. E. 5. D & C.

No 10. All Ranks are reminded that there is equipment of all kinds lying about, and any man found deficient when we arrive back will be charged full value for same.

Chas Roberts
Lieut. 2nd in Command
45 Coy. L. G. Corps

(2)

Operation orders by
CAPT. H. V. WILKINSON
Comdg No. 45 Machine Gun Coy

Reference
ALBERT 1/40000
sheet 62D. 1/40000

ALBERT
4th Nov. 1916

1. No. 45 Coy Machine Gun Corps will move into Billets at FRANVILLERS to-morrow the 5th inst. in accordance with the 45th Infantry Brigade operation order No. 151 d. 4/11/16
Starting Point E. 5. Central.

2. Breakfast will be at 7.0 a.m.
Coy will parade in the RUE de BRAY at 10.0 am
Dress:- Marching order

"C" Section will lead followed by "D", "A" & "B"
A distance of 200 yards is to be maintained between Units and 100 yards between sections

Transport will join their Sections at the Transport Lines

Orderly officer to-morrow 2/LT. R.S. MORPETH

Next for duty:- " F.R KEITH

All Blankets to be rolled in bundles of ten and labelled. These will be stacked at Coy H.Qrs. by 9-0 a.m.

A lorry will be at the Church ALBERT at 1-0 P.M to convey blankets to the new area. 2nd LT. R.S. MORPETH and 3 Other Ranks will remain behind to conduct the lorry to the Billets and to assist in loading

4. All Billets will be thoroughly cleaned and inspected by Section officers by 9.30 PM

5. A Billetting party on Bicycles under LT. C.L. ROBERTS will proceed in advance and report to TOWN MAJOR FRANVILLERS at 9-0 am.

[illegible] Lieut.

for 2nd In Command

No 43 M. G. Coy

Index

## SUBJECT.

45th M G Coy

| No. | Contents. | Date. |
|---|---|---|
| | December 1916 | |

(63,965). Wt.15,820—176. 2000. 9/21. Gp.164. A.&E.W.

Army Form C. 2118.

Instructions regarding War Diaries and Intelligence Summaries are contained in F. S. Regs., Part II. and the Staff Manual respectively. Title pages will be prepared in manuscript.

# WAR DIARY

~~or~~

~~INTELLIGENCE SUMMARY.~~

(*Erase heading not required.*)

Vol 7

| Place | Date | Hour | Summary of Events and Information | Remarks and references to Appendices |
|---|---|---|---|---|
| | | | CONFIDENTIAL. | |
| | | | WAR DIARY OF 45th MACHINE GUN COMPANY M.G.C. | |
| | | | 1st to 31st DECEMBER 1916 | |
| | | | VOLUMN VII | |

[signature] Capt.

O.C. 45 Coy. Machine Gun Corps

2353 Wt. W2544/1454 700,000 5/15 D. D. & L. A.D.S.S./Forms/C. 2118.

Army Form C. 2118.

Instructions regarding War Diaries and Intelligence Summaries are contained in F. S. Regs., Part II. and the Staff Manual respectively. Title pages will be prepared in manuscript.

# WAR DIARY
*or*
# ~~INTELLIGENCE SUMMARY.~~
*(Erase heading not required.)*

| Place | Date | Hour | Summary of Events and Information | Remarks and references to Appendices |
|---|---|---|---|---|
| BAZIEUX | 1.12.16 | 7 a.m | All Company thoroughly cleaning camp & clearing out drains. 2/Lt Morpeth & 2 Signallers proceeded to MILLENCOURT to take over new camp. | |
| | | 9 a.m | Repacking Limbers & gun & ammunition cleaning. | |
| | | 12 50 | Company Paraded in full marching order & marched to MILLENCOURT via HENENCOURT, arrived 2. 30. Officers in 2 huts O R in tents. bitterly cold. | |
| MILLENCOURT | 2.12.16 | 7 a.m | Cleaning Camp | |
| | | 9 to 12 30 | Rifle drill, advance gun drill, afternoon inspection of Gas helmets, ammunition & Iron rations. Weather very cold, but fine. | |
| — " — | 3.12.16 | | Church Parade morning Football match afternoon. Very cold, | |
| — " — | 4.12.16 | 7 a.m | Running & rapid walking. | |
| | | 9-12.30 | Routine as usual. Attached men examined by C.O + 2/Lt Michelmore, in Test in Elementary Training. Lt Manton in mechanism, & 2/Lt Keith in Immediate action. | |
| | | 2 p.m | Parade, followed by footer match. Weather not quite so severe. | |
| — " — | 5.12.16 | 7 a.m | Physical Drill 9 a.m. Routine work as usual. Completion of | |

2353 Wt. W2544/1454 700,000 5/15 D. D. & L. A.D.S.S./Forms/C. 2118.

Army Form C. 2118.

Instructions regarding War Diaries and Intelligence Summaries are contained in F. S. Regs., Part II. and the Staff Manual respectively. Title pages will be prepared in manuscript.

# WAR DIARY
*or*
# INTELLIGENCE SUMMARY.

*(Erase heading not required.)*

| Place | Date | Hour | Summary of Events and Information | Remarks and references to Appendices |
|---|---|---|---|---|
| MILLENCOURT | 5.12.16 | | examination of attached men. 16 passed, 11 put back for further instruction. | |
| | | 2.30. | Whole company Paraded for cross country run. very heavy going. "D" Section first "C" second. Weather cold & dull. | |
| —"— | 6.12.16 | 8.45 | 10 mile Route march. only 1 man fell out & that after 7 miles. | |
| | | 2 pm | Parade | |
| | | 6 pm | Company Concert at Y.M.C.A. hut HENENCOURT. | |
| —"— | 7.12.16 | 7 am | Parade rapid walking & running. | |
| | | 9 am | attached men who passed on range, others further instruction, had to find 3 guards. one party of 20 and another of 5 for the Town Major, remainder of Company under 2/Lt Michelmore. | |
| | | 3 pm | 100 men of the Company bathed. Weather cold & dull | |
| —"— | 8.12.16. | 7 am | Physical Drill. | |
| | | 9 am | "A" & "B" Sections on range, attached men continued instruction as usual remainder of Company advance gun drill. Sgt WHITMORE & Pte DUNCAN accidently wounded, through Ptes ASHLEY & STIRLING negligently | |

Instructions regarding War Diaries and Intelligence Summaries are contained in F. S. Regs., Part II. and the Staff Manual respectively. Title pages will be prepared in manuscript.

# WAR DIARY
*or*
# ~~INTELLIGENCE~~ SUMMARY.
*(Erase heading not required.)*

Army Form C. 2118.

3

| Place | Date | Hour | Summary of Events and Information | Remarks and references to Appendices |
|---|---|---|---|---|
| MILLENCOURT | 8.12.16 | | Firing a Vickers Gun, a court of Enquiry at once assembled and statement of evidence taken. | |
| | | 3 P.M | All Company striping & drying belts. | |
| -- | 9.12.16 | 8.45am | Company Rcats march. | |
| | | 11 a.m | F. G. C. M on No 13132 Pte McCRANDLES. J. case took 3 hours & accused found guilty. | |
| | | 2.45 | Football match v Brigade Hd Qts. Weather cold & some rain. | |
| -- | 10.12.16 | | Church Parades morning. | |
| | | 2 p.m | Company Pay. Weather dull & cold Lieut Mann on leave. | |
| -- | 11.12.16 | 7 a.m. | Running & walking | |
| | | 9 am | "C" & "D" Sections on the Range remainder of Company on advance Gun drill. | |
| | | 10 a.m | C. O's Conference at Brigade Hd Qts. F. G. C. M on Ptes STIRLING & ASHLEY at ALBERT. | |
| | | 2 p.m | Promulgated Pte McCrandles F. G. C. M. followed by lecture by C. O. Weather overcast & cold | |

2353 Wt. W2544/1454 700,000 5/15 D. D. & L. A.D.S.S./Forms/C. 2118.

Army Form C. 2118. 4

Instructions regarding War Diaries and Intelligence Summaries are contained in F. S. Regs., Part II. and the Staff Manual respectively. Title pages will be prepared in manuscript.

# WAR DIARY
or
# INTELLIGENCE SUMMARY.
(Erase heading not required.)

| Place | Date | Hour | Summary of Events and Information | Remarks and references to Appendices |
|---|---|---|---|---|
| MILLENCOURT | 12.12.16 | 7 a.m | Physical Drill. | |
| | | 9 am | Company Drill. The whole Company bathed between 10.30 and 12.30. C.O proceeded up to VILLA WOOD to discuss relief with C.O 145th Coy: F.G.C.M. on Ptes Stirling & Ashley promulgated. L/Cpl Duncan proceeded on leave | |
| | | 2 pm | Inspection of Company in full marching order. Rain & cold | |
| — | 13.12.16 | 7 a.m | Running & walking. | |
| | | 9 a.m | Gun cleaning. repacking limbers, going through Belt Boxes and general preparations for going into the line. III Corps M G Officer came to talk things over with C.O. | |
| | | 2 pm | Inspection of Sections by Section Officers. Relief orders issued Pte Forbes J. proceeded on leave | 1 |
| — | 14.12.16 | 8 a.m | 2/Lts Strangs & Morpeth & teams 5, 6, 7, 8, 10, 11, & 12. proceeded to ACID DROP COPSE SOUTH as per relief order attached | 1 |
| | | 9 a.m | 2nd in Command to Divisional Gas school. for a 1 days course Company thoroughly cleaning Camp & Transport Lines, Clearing drains. | |
| | | 2 pm | Remainder of Company putting small kit in sandbags. Final clearing up | 2 |

Instructions regarding War Diaries and Intelligence Summaries are contained in F. S. Regs., Part II. and the Staff Manual respectively. Title pages will be prepared in manuscript.

# WAR DIARY
*or*
# INTELLIGENCE SUMMARY.
*(Erase heading not required.)*

Army Form C. 2118. 5

| Place | Date | Hour | Summary of Events and Information | Remarks and references to Appendices |
|---|---|---|---|---|
| MILLENCOURT | 15.12.16 | 9.15 | Company (less 7 Guns) Paraded in marching Order, and proceeded to SHELTER WOOD. Relief of 7 Guns 145th Company completed by 5.30 a.m | |
| SHELTERWOOD | | 12.15 | arrived. Cooks had been sent on ahead and men's dinners nearly ready. | |
| | | 2.30 | C.O. and 2nd in Command – Lieut Mawton walked up to the MILL MARTINPUICH. and obtained particulars from C.O. 144th Coy. Weather rain & dull | |
| — | 16.12.16 | 8.15 | Remainder of Company Paraded, and proceeded to MIDDLE WOOD CAMP. accommodation for men not good, only gipsy shelters. | |
| MIDDLE WOOD | | 9.30 | Arrived. Company carrying up stores rations etc. | |
| | | 2.30 | Head Quarters moved on to the MILL. MARTINPUICH. arrived | |
| MARTINPUICH | | | Mill, and C.O went on up to LE SARS. Weather very unsettled, snow & rain. | |
| | | 6.pm | 2nd Lt LIPSCOMBE & 2 other ranks, returned from course at CAMIERS. C.Q.M.S returned from leave. | |
| — | 17.12.16 | 3.30am | 2nd Lt KEITH and 4 teams proceeded to LE SARS to relieve | |

2353 Wt. W2544/1454 700,000 5/15 D. D. & L. A.D.S.S./Forms/C. 2118.

Army Form C. 2118. 6

Instructions regarding War Diaries and Intelligence Summaries are contained in F. S. Regs., Part II. and the Staff Manual respectively. Title pages will be prepared in manuscript.

# WAR DIARY
*or*
# INTELLIGENCE SUMMARY.
*(Erase heading not required.)*

| Place | Date | Hour | Summary of Events and Information | Remarks and references to Appendices |
|---|---|---|---|---|
| MARTINPUICH | 17.12.16 | | 2nd Lt STRANGE & 4 teams. 2nd Lt HENDERSON & 3 teams to relieve 2nd Lt MORPETH & 3 teams, relief completed 6. a.m. | |
| | | 9.30. | C.O and 2nd in Command went all round the line. all so called trenches are in the same condition, nothing could be worse. movement being only possible over the top, either after dark or when foggy. Weather foggy all day. thank goodness. | |
| | | | Disposition of Company:- | |
| | | | 2/Lt Keith & 4 Guns LE SARS. (1 in cutting, 2 in O.G 2 & 1 in O.G 1.) | |
| | | | 2/Lt Henderson & 3 Guns Hd Qrs. (1 in 26 avenue & 2 near DESTRAMONT FM:) | |
| | | | G. & H. Positions. | |
| | | | C.O 2nd in Command signallers & 7 Runners etc, at Hd Qrs. THE MILL. 2nd Lts Lipscombe, Mickelmore, Morpeth & Strange. C.S.M and remainder of Company at MIDDLE WOOD CAMP. | |
| | | 3.30. | Met the Brigadier General & talked over the Intermediate Line defence scheme. | |
| | | | Cpl Beatson proceeded on leave | |

2353 Wt W2544/1454 700,000 5/15 D. D. & L. A.D.S.S./Forms/C. 2118.

Instructions regarding War Diaries and Intelligence Summaries are contained in F. S. Regs., Part II. and the Staff Manual respectively. Title pages will be prepared in manuscript.

# WAR DIARY
*or*
# INTELLIGENCE SUMMARY.
*(Erase heading not required.)*

Army Form C. 2118. 7

| Place | Date | Hour | Summary of Events and Information | Remarks and references to Appendices |
|---|---|---|---|---|
| MARTINPUICH | 18.12.16 | 9 a.m | Sent more ammunition up to the gun positions. Guns in the Intermediate line fired 1,900 rounds during the night on Enemy's communications and back positions. C.O. 44th Coy came to Hd Qrs re relief | |
| | | 10 a.m | C.O. round the Intermediate line, with the C.O. Engineers. | |
| | | 3.30 pm | 2/Lt Michelmore & 4 Teams relieved 2/Lt Keith & 4 Teams in LE SARS etc. 2/Lt Lipscombe & 3 Teams relieved 2/Lt Henderson & 3 Teams in the Intermediate Line. | |
| | | | Weather fine & clear. Enemy shelling considerably increased in consequence | |
| — | 19.12.16 | 6 a.m | 2nd in Command round the line. C.O. round the Intermediate Line | |
| | | 3 pm | Seven teams of 44th Coy arrived and sent off with guides, relief all complete by 5.45. without a casuality. Snowing all the time. Could not bring guns back by Transport on account of the slipperyness of the roads, some carried, others brought up on the light railway. All back at SHELTER WOOD CAMP by 8.40 p.m. the remainder of the Company having moved from MIDDLE WOOD during afternoon. | |

2353 Wt. W2544/1454 700,000 5/15 D. D. & L. A.D.S.S./Forms/C. 2118.

Instructions regarding War Diaries and Intelligence Summaries are contained in F. S. Regs., Part II. and the Staff Manual respectively. Title pages will be prepared in manuscript.

# WAR DIARY
*or*
# INTELLIGENCE SUMMARY.
*(Erase heading not required.)*

Army Form C. 2118. 8

| Place | Date | Hour | Summary of Events and Information | Remarks and references to Appendices |
|---|---|---|---|---|
| SHELTER WOOD | 20.12.16 | 8.45. | 100 O.R. Paraded for bathing. remainder of Coy cleaning camp. | |
| | | 11.30. | All men who originally came out from England with Company, balloted for leave places. | |
| | | 1.30 | Rifle inspection followed by Gun & ammunition cleaning. C.O and 2nd in Command rode over to transport lines. Lovely sunny day. - first for weeks, cold, dry with snow on the ground | |
| —"— | 21.12.16 | 7.15 | Running & walking | |
| | | 9.30 | C.O's Conference at Brigade Hd Qrs. The Company marched to Transport Lines to clear limbers & bring back more ammunition. | |
| | | 1 pm | C.O. to MARTINPUICH to see 46th Coy with regard to relief. | |
| | | 2 pm | Feet inspection & rubbing, & inspection of gas helmets & equipment. Weather rain & milder again. much mud. | |
| —"— | 22.12.16 | 7.15 | Walking & doubling | |
| | | 9 am | Clearing & cutting new drains & generally improving camp. Weather dull & showery. | |
| | | 2.15 | Lecture by C.O to all Officers and N.C.O's | |

2353 Wt. W2344/1454 700,000 5/15 D. D. & L. A.D.S.S./Forms/C. 2118.

Army Form C. 2118. 9

Instructions regarding War Diaries and Intelligence Summaries are contained in F. S. Regs., Part II. and the Staff Manual respectively. Title pages will be prepared in manuscript.

# WAR DIARY
*or*
# INTELLIGENCE SUMMARY.
*(Erase heading not required.)*

| Place | Date | Hour | Summary of Events and Information | Remarks and references to Appendices |
|---|---|---|---|---|
| MARTINPUICH | 23.12.16 | | Weather fine. Coy relieved the 46th M G Co on the right Sector all relief completed by 6 p.m. remainder of Coy moved from SHELTER WOOD to PIONEER CAMP. | III |
| | | | Disposition of Coy:— | |
| | | | Left. Lt Lipscombe with 3 guns. two in posts at top of LE SARS TRENCH SOUTH and one at the MILL. | |
| | | | Right 2/Lt Michelmore 3 guns. MAXWELL SUPPORT, THE SNAG & the PIMPLE. | |
| | | | Intermediate Line 2/Lt Henderson & four guns D.E & F nests & outside Officers dug out | |
| | | | C.O. & Signallers stopping at TRENCH MORTAR Hd Qrs MARTINPUICH, one gun team & eleven carriers in dugouts at MARTINPUICH | |
| | | | Lt Nawton, 2/Lt Morpeth, Strange & Keith C.S.M. & remainder of Coy at PIONEER CAMP | |
| | 24.12.16 | 3.30pm | 2/Lt Morpeth & 2 O.R. to CAMIERS for M.G. course. | |
| | | | C.O. all round the line visited every gun back 9.15 am mud very bad weather cold unsettled | |
| | | 2.30pm | Lt Nawton came up to Hd Qrs | |

2353 Wt. W2544/1454 700,000 5/15 D. D. & L. A.D.S.S./Forms/C. 2118.

Instructions regarding War Diaries and Intelligence Summaries are contained in F. S. Regs., Part II. and the Staff Manual respectively. Title pages will be prepared in manuscript.

# WAR DIARY
*or*
# INTELLIGENCE SUMMARY.
*(Erase heading not required.)*

Army Form C. 2118.

| Place | Date | Hour | Summary of Events and Information | Remarks and references to Appendices |
|---|---|---|---|---|
| MARTINPUICH | 25.12.16 | 10AM | C.O. round Intermediate Line | |
| | | 4 pm | 2/Lt Strange & two teams relieved Lt Lipscombe & two teams on the right. The gun in MAXWELL SUPPORT withdrawn to BARRIER about M 22. B. 5. 8 Lt Lipscombe then relieved 2/Lt Michelmore at the SNAG, PIMPLE, MILL & NEW POSITION being reinforced by two teams & in his turn took over the INTERMEDIATE LINE from 2/Lt Henderson & four teams who retired to PIONEER CAMP | |
| | | 10-30pm | Relief complete. 1 O.R. slightly wounded. Weather fine in morning, rain later C.O. up the line from 4 pm. to 8-30 pm | |
| " | 26.12.16 | 4 pm | Lt Nawton went on leave C.O. visited guns on left & looked for new positions further left back 8 pm raining & a very dark night Hostile shelling more active. Intermediate Line heavily shelled at midnight | |
| | 27.12.16 | 4 pm | 2/Lt. Henderson & two teams relieved 2/Lt Strange & two teams on the left who with those teams plus one from MARTINPUICH relieved three teams under Lt Lipscombe on the right who in turn took over the Intermediate Line from 2/Lt Michelmore who then retired to PIONEER CAMP. One team from PIONEER CAMP proceeded to MARTINPUICH leaving one section only at PIONEER CAMP | |

Army Form C. 2118. 11

Instructions regarding War Diaries and Intelligence Summaries are contained in F. S. Regs., Part II. and the Staff Manual respectively. Title pages will be prepared in manuscript.

# WAR DIARY
*or*
# INTELLIGENCE SUMMARY.
*(Erase heading not required.)*

| Place | Date | Hour | Summary of Events and Information | Remarks and references to Appendices |
|---|---|---|---|---|
| MARTINPUICH | 27.12.16 | 11.55 P.M | Ptes Preston & Pearce whilst on Sentry go were accidently wounded. Pte Pearce was digging when he struck a Mills Bomb, which exploded wounding both. | |
| | 28.12.16 | | Weather unsettled rain. | |
| | | 4 a.m | C.O. round the right Sector and Intermediate Line. | |
| | 29.12.16 | 4.30 am | C.O round left sector. Heavy rain and unsettled weather. Hostile Artillery more active | |
| | | 4. P.M | Usual 48 hours relief. not complete until after midnight. very dark night. | |
| | | | Disposition of guns & Teams | |
| | | | Left. 2 Guns in Post on right from LE SARS. under 2/Lt Mickelmore | |
| | | | Right 4 Guns The Snag, Pimple, Mill and Barrier under 2/Lt Henderson | |
| | | | Intermediate Line 4 Guns in Nests "D". "E" & "F" & adv Hd Qrs under 2/Lt Strange. | |
| | | | MARTINPUICH. 2 Guns in reserve, Carriers & C.O etc. | |
| | | | PIONEER CAMP 4 Guns. Lt Lipscombe & Keith and remainder of Coy. | |
| | 30.12.16 | 10.30 | 2nd Lt Keith, & C.S.M came up to Hd Qrs. 2nd in Command 44th Company came up to arrange about relief. | |

Instructions regarding War Diaries and Intelligence Summaries are contained in F. S. Regs., Part II. and the Staff Manual respectively. Title pages will be prepared in manuscript.

# WAR DIARY
or
# ~~INTELLIGENCE~~ SUMMARY.
(*Erase heading not required.*)

Army Form C. 2118. 12

| Place | Date | Hour | Summary of Events and Information | Remarks and references to Appendices |
|---|---|---|---|---|
| MARTINPUICH | 30.12.16 | 2.P.M | MARTINPUICH heavily shelled with 5"9" & 8". | |
| | | 3.P.M | C.O. all round the line Intermediate, right & left sectors. back | |
| | | | 8.30. P.M. Weather better. Ammunition carriers brought back 38 Belt boxes. | |
| | | 11.P.M | Pte Heeble wounded shrapnel 2/Lt THOMSON joined from BASE | |
| — | 31.12.16 | | Weather dull but fine. | |
| | | 10.am | Excess belt boxes Trench boots etc. pushed up the light railway on | |
| | | | Trucks to Villa Station thence by transport to SHELTER WOOD | |
| | | 3.30. | 44th Company arrived to relieve us. all teams away by 4.20 P.M | |
| | | 7.30. | Relief complete and Hd 2rs in Martinpuich closed | |
| | | 3.P.M | Lt Lipscombe & 2/Lts Keith & Thomson & remainder of company moved | |
| | | | from PIONEER CAMP to SHELTER WOOD CAMP. | |
| SHELTERWOOD CAMP. | | 9.30 pm | all back & Hd 2rs opened here. hot tea served out to men | |

A W Wilkinson
Capt.

O.C. No. 125 COY.
MACHINE GUN CORPS.

2353 Wt. W2544/1454 700,000 5/15 D. D. & L. A.D.S.S./Forms/C. 2118.

RELIEF ORDERS BY CAPT: H. V. WILKINSON.
Commanding No. 45. Machine Gun Coy.

13th December 1916

1. The 15th Division will relieve the 48th Division in the left sector III Corps on the 14th, 15th & 16th December 1916

2. The 45th Machine Gun Coy will relieve as follows:

(a). On the 14th inst: 2/LT. J. R. STRANGE with teams 5. & 6. and 2/LT. R. S. MORPETH with teams 10. 11. 12. and teams 7. & 8. will proceed by lorry from MILLENCOURT at 8.30 a.m. to ACID DROP COPS CAMP. SOUTH and report to the C.O. 145th Company. There they will rest and have a hot meal and be ready to move up to the front line at 2.0 am. on the 15th inst. The C.O. 145th Company will provide guides

The Guns will be taken over on the early morning of the 15th inst: as at present in the line.

2/LT. J. R. STRANGE will proceed to the dug-out in the Sunken Road LE SARS. 1 Team in the Orchard and 1 in O. G. 2.

2/LT: R. S. MORPETH will have 3 Guns in the Corps Line. 1 in 26th AVENUE and 2 in nests between DESTREMONT FARM. and 26th AVENUE. and 2 guns in reserve FACTORY LINES His Head Quarters will be at THE MILL.

Two days rations will be taken by all

(b). On the 15th inst. the Company less of Guns will proceed at 9-30 a.m. VIA. ALBERT - LA BOISSELLE - CONTALMAISON to SHELTER WOOD

P.T.O.

2.

(X. 21. D.) An advance party of 2/LT. H. H. HENDERSON and 2. O.R. to report there and take over the Camp by 10.30 a.m.

(c). On the 16th inst the Company less 7 Guns will move at 8.40 a.m. to MIDDLE WOOD

3. Transport will accompany Units and will be accommodated at CHAPES SPUR, Units taking over the same lines as when the Brigade was last in the line. The Entrance to these transport lines is near the Cross Road at X 13. D. 3. 0.

A.W. Wilkinson
Capt.

O.C. No. 45 COY.
MACHINE GUN CORPS.

ROUTINE ORDERS by CAPT. H. V. WILKINSON
Commanding 45th Machine Gun Coy

MILLENCOURT
13th Dec. 1916

1. DUTIES
Orderly officer to-morrow 2/LT. F. MICHELMORE
Next for Duty:- 2/LT. J. R. STRANGE

2. MOVE
"B" & "C" Sections (less No 9 team) will parade to-morrow at 8-15 a.m. as per relief orders. Dress:- Fighting order. Overcoats will be worn Leather Jerkin, 1 Blanket, Waterproof Sheet, towel, 2 pairs of socks, etc. will be carried in the pack. The remainder of the Kit will be placed in Sandbags bearing the No: and name of the owner.
No blankets will be taken into the line, one per man will be stored with the kit in ALBERT and one per man will be in BOTTOM WOOD CAMP available for the men that are resting there.
Remainder of Company thoroughly Cleaning Camp, Transport

Lines and Drains
On going into the Line Section officers must always bear in mind the following:-
Water (and Glycerine)
Ammunition
Rations
Sanitation
Personally examine the mens feet once a day, thereby seeing that boots are removed and socks changed, and they must always see that a small supply of Whale oil is kept with each section.

3. SICK.
In future anyone reporting sick and on examination being shown as "DUTY" will be Court Martialed.

4. GERMAN SERUM.
The Germans are using a serum labelled "RAUSCHBRAUCH SERUM" in bottles. It is thought that this is for use as a preventative against Gas. Should any be

found or captured it is to be at once sent in to Hd. Qrs.

6. WATER SUPPLY and SANITATION

Cases of dysentry have recently occurred and it is reported that men have been seen filling water bottles from shell holes and also using the water for washing.

As many of these shell holes have formerly been used as latrines this practice is extremely dangerous to health.

After the publication of this order disciplinary action is to be taken if men are found using water in shell holls for any purpose.

(Authority III Corps R.O. No. 307. d. 11/12/16)

H.C. Mawdor
Lieut
2nd In Command
45 M.G. Coy.

RELIEF ORDERS by Capt: H.V.WILKINSON.
Commanding 45th Machine Gun Coy.

In the Field.
22nd. Dec. 1916.

The 45th. Machine Gun Coy. will relieve the 46th. Machine Gun Coy. to-morrow the 23rd. inst.

3 teams of "B" Section under LT. LIPSCOMB will be on the left, 3 teams of "A" Section under 2/LT.MICHELMORE on the right, with the 4th. team in MARTINPUICH. 4 teams of "D" under 2/LT.H.H.HENDERSON in the INTERMEDIATE LINE.

"C" Section & the 4th. team of "B" will be at PIONEER CAMP

Guides will be at the 46th. Bde. Hdqrs. at 4.0.p.m.

2/LT. MORPETH & "C" Section will take the guns up to Hdqtrs. at 10.0a.m. to-morrow.

The remainder of the Coy. will move to PIONEER CAMP at 2.0p.m.

100 blankets will be taken to PIONEER CAMP. Remainder will be taken to Storeroom at ALBERT.

All teams will take one days rations in the line.

Guns, Tripods, & spare parts will be taken up; but belt boxes, and Gum Boots will be exchanged.

Headquarters will be in MARTINPUICH. ( T.M.Bttry. Hdqrs.)

3 Telephone Operators will be there and 2 in the INTERMEDIATE LINE.

LT.F.C.NAWTON and advance party will proceed to PIONEER CAMP to take over there at 9.30 a.m.

[signature]

CAPT:

Commanding 45th. M.G.Coy.

Instructions regarding War Diaries and Intelligence Summaries are contained in F. S. Regs., Part II. and the Staff Manual respectively. Title pages will be prepared in manuscript.

# WAR DIARY
*or*
# INTELLIGENCE SUMMARY.
*(Erase heading not required.)*

Army Form C. 2118.

Vol 8

| Place | Date | Hour | Summary of Events and Information | Remarks and references to Appendices |
|---|---|---|---|---|
| | | | CONFIDENTIAL.<br>War Diary<br>of<br>45th Company Machine Gun Corps.<br>1st to 31st January 1917.<br>Volumn. VIII<br>[signature]<br>Major | |

2353 Wt. W2544/1454 700,000 5/15 D. D. & L. A.D.S.S./Forms/C. 2118.

Instructions regarding War Diaries and Intelligence Summaries are contained in F. S. Regs., Part II. and the Staff Manual respectively. Title pages will be prepared in manuscript.

# WAR DIARY
*or*
~~INTELLIGENCE SUMMARY.~~
*(Erase heading not required.)*

Army Form C. 2118. 1

| Place | Date | Hour | Summary of Events and Information | Remarks and references to Appendices |
|---|---|---|---|---|
| SHELTER WOOD CAMP | 1.1.17 | 9 am | Parade Rifle inspection & gun cleaning. | |
| | | 11.30 | Company Paid out. | |
| | | 3 P.M | Company Dinner. C.O's Conference at Brigade Head Quarters. Weather fine but dull. | |
| — | 2.1.17 | 9 am | 2 O.R to MONTIGNY for Bayonet & musketry instruction. Draining and cleaning camp. going through Belt boxes. and spare parts. | |
| | | 11.15. | 100 O.R Paraded for bath & clothing inspection. | |
| | | 3 P.M | Officers Conference. No 8560 Pte (L/Cpl) Green. to Base for Home Establishment, authority A G's 6864 dated 29.12.16. Weather overcast. | |
| — | 3.1.17 | 8.30. | Working Party of 1 Officer & 30. O.R. on road at Transport Lines. | |
| | | 9 am | Preparation for going into Line. Lieut Lipscomb to see O.C. 46th Coy at Martinpuich. Building new cook house and re-boarding interior of huts where required. | |
| | | 2. P.M | Cleaning Camp. 15 O.R to the Boot shop at ALBERT to be refitted. | |
| | | 5.30 | No 3165 Cpl (A/Sgt) Baker & 3219. L/Cpl Golsen to Base for Home | |

2353 Wt. W2544/1454 700,000 5/15 D. D. & L. A.D.S.S./Forms/C. 2118.

2

Instructions regarding War Diaries and Intelligence Summaries are contained in F. S. Regs., Part II. and the Staff Manual respectively. Title pages will be prepared in manuscript.

# WAR DIARY
*or*
# ~~INTELLIGENCE SUMMARY.~~
*(Erase heading not required.)*

Army Form C. 2118.

| Place | Date | Hour | Summary of Events and Information | Remarks and references to Appendices |
|---|---|---|---|---|
| SHELTER | 3.1.17 | | Establishment. one O.R on leave | |
| WOOD | 4.1.17 | 9 am | Cleaning Camp & preparations for going into the line. | |
| CAMP | | 2 P.M | Company Paraded as per relief orders attached, arrived MARTINPUICH 3.30 all teams away with guides by 4.15. P.M | I |
| MARTINPUICH | | 6.05 P.M | Relief complete. | |
| | | | Disposition of Company:- | |
| | | | 4 Guns forward under 2/Lts Keith & Thomson. (1 at top of JOCK ALLEY. 1 in CHALK PIT TRENCH. 1 in O.G.1 & 1 in O.G.2. | |
| | | | 1 Gun in "H" nest & 2 in "G" nest. 1 in reserve in MARTINPUICH. | |
| | | | C.O. Lieut Lipscomb, signallers & 8 carriers at the MILL Head Quarters, | |
| | | | 2nd Lts Michelmore, Strange & Henderson, C.S.M & remainder at ACID DROP CAMP SOUTH. Weather dull but fair. | |
| | 5.1.17. | 5 am | C.O all round the line. visited each gun & team, back 8.30 a.m | |
| | | 6 am. | Lieut Lipscomb round intermediate line! Weather fine & bright sunshine nearly all day. many aeroplanes up. | |
| | | 7 pm | a pit for Anti-aircraft dug about M. 16. a. 6½. 3½ gun from JOCK | |

2353 Wt. W2544/1454 700,000 5/15 D. D. & L. A.D.S.S./Forms/C. 2118.

3

Army Form C. 2118.

Instructions regarding War Diaries and Intelligence Summaries are contained in F. S. Regs., Part II. and the Staff Manual respectively. Title pages will be prepared in manuscript.

# WAR DIARY
*or*
# INTELLIGENCE SUMMARY.
*(Erase heading not required.)*

| Place | Date | Hour | Summary of Events and Information | Remarks and references to Appendices |
|---|---|---|---|---|
| MARTINPUICH | 5.1.17 | | ALLEY brought back & new position made there, for night time, to be mounted for anti-aircraft day. Hd Qrs tear shelled 6.30 to 7.30 P.M. | |
| — " — | 6.1.17 | 5 am | C.O. round all positions. over 4,000 rounds fired from Intermediate Line during the night on Enemy tracks & communications. Weather snow early morning. improving later on. | |
| | | 4.30 PM | The 3 guns at Nests & 1 in reserve changed places with the four guns forward. 1 O.R. on leave. Heard from W.O. that Lieut D. MANN had been granted sick leave, while on leave in England, struck off strength from 22nd December 1916 | |
| — " — | 7.1.17 | 5 am | Lt Lipscomb round front line. C.O round Intermediate Line, 5,500 rounds fired on Enemy tracks during night. Weather fine & clear | |
| | | 11 30 | 2/Lts Michelmore & Henderson came up to Hd Qrs. | |
| | 8.1.17. | 5 am | C.O round all positions. | |
| | | 3 30 | Head Quarters heavily shelled with 5'9" for ½ hour. | |
| | | 4.PM | 2/Lts Strange & Henderson & 4 teams of "A" section, relieved 2/Lts Keith & Thomson & 4 teams of "C" section in front positions | |

2353 Wt. W2544/1454 700,000 5/15 D. D. & L. A.D.S.S./Forms/C. 2118.

Army Form C. 2118. 4

Instructions regarding War Diaries and Intelligence Summaries are contained in F. S. Regs., Part II. and the Staff Manual respectively. Title pages will be prepared in manuscript.

# WAR DIARY
*or*
## ~~INTELLIGENCE SUMMARY.~~
*(Erase heading not required.)*

| Place | Date | Hour | Summary of Events and Information | Remarks and references to Appendices |
|---|---|---|---|---|
| MARTINPUICH | 8.1.17 | | 4 Teams of "D" relieved 4 teams of "B". 3 guns in "Nests" and 1 in reserve in Martinpuich. Carried up expanding metal angle iron, & pit prop etc for forward anti aircraft gun position. | |
| — " — | 9.1.17 | 5 a.m | C.O. round all guns. 2 inches of snow on ground, and snowing then, but improved later. Usual indirect Machine Gun fire during night. Commenced 2nd anti aircraft pit about M. 21. c. 8 9. | |
| — " — | 10.1.17 | 5 a.m | Lieut Lipscomb round all guns. weather dull. | |
| | | 4 pm | "A" Section & "D" section changed over positions. forward anti-aircraft pit finished | |
| — " — | 11.1.17 | 5 a.m | C.O. round all guns. Heavy enemy barrage on Chalk Pit Road from 6.45 to 7.15 a.m. Weather foggy morning, clearing afternoon snowing 10 to 12 noon. 2nd anti-aircraft pit finished | |
| | | 2 pm | Brigade relief orders received, and Company orders issued. | ~~II~~ I |
| | | 3 pm | C.O. round Intermediate Line, more snow. | |
| — " — | 12.1.17 | 5.30 a.m | Lt ~~Lipscombe~~ round gun positions. Lieut Nawton returned | |

Army Form C. 2118. 5

Instructions regarding War Diaries and Intelligence Summaries are contained in F. S. Regs., Part II. and the Staff Manual respectively. Title pages will be prepared in manuscript.

# WAR DIARY
*or*
~~INTELLIGENCE SUMMARY.~~
*(Erase heading not required.)*

| Place | Date | Hour | Summary of Events and Information | Remarks and references to Appendices |
|---|---|---|---|---|
| MARTINPUICH | 12.1.17. | | from leave. | |
| | | 4.30. | 44th Company arrived to relieve this Company. all teams away by 5. p.m. Relief complete 7. p.m. Head Quarters closed Martinpuich 8 P.M. opened Shelter Wood Camp 9.30 P.M remainder of Coy: left Acid Drop Camp South at 2 P.M | |
| ACID DROP CAMP SOUTH | 13.1.17 | 9 am | Rifle inspection, followed by Gun & ammunition cleaning, feet inspection, and troops cleaning themselves & the camp. which was left in a filthy condition. | |
| | | | 2nd Lieut Michelmore & 3 O.R proceed to CAMIERS. | |
| | | 10.30 | C.O. & 2nd Lt Strange to Transport Lines. the latter taking over the duties of Transport Officer temporary. | |
| | | 3 P.M | C.O's Conference at Brigade Hd Qrs. 1 O.R. on leave | |
| — " — | 14.1.17 | 10 a.m | Brigadier took C.O. to Division to discuss M.G positions in the Divisional front. Church Parades morning. | |
| | | 2 p.m | Company paid out. Weather, cold, dull & raw. | |
| | | 6 p.m | Lieut Lipscomb. proceeded on leave | |

2353 Wt. W2344/1454 700,000 5/15 D. D. & L. A.D.S.S./Forms/C. 2118.

Instructions regarding War Diaries and Intelligence Summaries are contained in F. S. Regs., Part II. and the Staff Manual respectively. Title pages will be prepared in manuscript.

# WAR DIARY
*or*
# INTELLIGENCE SUMMARY.
(*Erase heading not required.*)

Army Form C. 2118. 6

| Place | Date | Hour | Summary of Events and Information | Remarks and references to Appendices |
|---|---|---|---|---|
| ACID DROP CAMP SOUTH. | 15.1.17 | 9. a.m | Rifle inspection, gun & ammunition cleaning. & usual routine. | |
| | | 4.15. | All the Company Paraded for bathing. Whale oil taken, and feet well rubbed afterwards. Camp shelled 10.30 & midnight. | |
| — | 16.1.17 | | 45th M.G. Co relieving the 46th M.G. Co in the line. Guns sent up to Martinpuich by rail morning. and stores etc moved to Pioneer Camp. Weather fine. but cold and dull. | |
| | | 2.45. | "A" Section Paraded, followed by "B" & "C." all away by 3.30 Guides for teams at Hd Qts Martinpuich, all teams away 5. P.M. relief complete 8 p.m. | |
| | | | Disposition of guns:- | |
| | | | Left. 2nd/Lt Thomson & 3 Guns. - 2 in Posts in front of Le Sars, & 1 in cutting. | |
| | | | Right. 2nd/Lt Keith & 3 Guns. - 2 in Mill & 1 at the Pimple | |
| | | | Intermediate line 2/Lt Henderson & 4 Guns. in "D" "E" & "F" nests & adv Hd Qts. | |
| | | | Lt Nawton, 2 Guns & teams. 10 Carriers & signallers at Martinpuich. | |
| | | | C.O. and remainder of Company at PIONEER CAMP. | |
| | | | 2nd Lt Morpath & 2 O.Rs returned from CAMIERS. | |

2353 Wt. W2544/1454 700,000 5/15 D. D. & L. A.D.S.S./Forms/C. 2118.

Army Form C. 2118. 7

Instructions regarding War Diaries and Intelligence Summaries are contained in F. S. Regs., Part II. and the Staff Manual respectively. Title pages will be prepared in manuscript.

# WAR DIARY
*or*
# INTELLIGENCE SUMMARY.
*(Erase heading not required.)*

| Place | Date | Hour | Summary of Events and Information | Remarks and references to Appendices |
|---|---|---|---|---|
| PIONEER CAMP | 17.1.17 | 5 am | Lt Nawton round all gun positions. Heavy snow storm all night. 3 feet deep in parts, and impossible to see shell holes. | |
| | | | 1. O.R on leave. Pte Waddell wounded by Bomb explosion, in Transport Lines | |
| | | 9 pm | 9 O.R joined from Base. Pioneer Camp shelled. | |
| — | 18.1.17 | 9.30 am | New draft inspected by C.O. | |
| | | 3 pm | 2nd Lt Morpath & "D" Section relieved 2nd Lt Thomson & "A" Section on the left who in turn took over from 2nd Lt Keith & "B" Section on the right. On complitition 2nd Lt Keith & "B" Sect: relieved 2nd Lt Henderson & "C" Section in the Intermediate Line, when the latter returned to PIONEER CAMP. all back by 11.30 P.M | |
| | | 2 pm | C.O. up to Martinpuich. Weather bright & fine | |
| — | 19.1.17 | 9 am | 4 O.R sent to Base in accordance with DO 245/1 dated 10.9.1915. | |
| | | 10 am | Rifle & Gun inspection & and general cleaning up. Fine but very cold wind & snow on ground. | |
| | | 5 am | Lt Nawton round all gun positions | |
| — | 20.1.17 | 3 P.M | 2/Lt Henderson & "C" Section proceed to relieve on left then | |

2353 Wt. W2544/1454 700,000 5/15 D. D. & L. A.D.S.S./Forms/C. 2118.

8

Army Form C. 2118.

Instructions regarding War Diaries and Intelligence Summaries are contained in F. S. Regs., Part II. and the Staff Manual respectively. Title pages will be prepared in manuscript.

# WAR DIARY
*or*
# ~~INTELLIGENCE SUMMARY.~~
*(Erase heading not required.)*

| Place | Date | Hour | Summary of Events and Information | Remarks and references to Appendices |
|---|---|---|---|---|
| PIONEER CAMP | 20.1.17 | ~~20~~ | all changed as on the 18th 2nd Lt Keith & "B" section returned to Pioneer Camp. all back by midnight. Camp shelled about this time. | |
| — | 21.1.17 | | Section cleaning themselves morning. Rifle & gun inspection 2. P.M | |
| | | 2.30 | C.O to Transport Lines. advance Hd 2/3 heavily shelled, 5 hits. 1 on gun emplacement 1 on latrine. 1 in Trench & 2 mouth of dug-out. No one hurt, but the sentry had a thin time. | |
| — | 22.1.17 | 9.a.m | C.O up to Martinpuich. | |
| | | 3 P.M | 2nd Lt Keith & "B" section to relieve on left. all sections changed round & 2/Lt Thomson & "A" section returned to Camp. 10.30 P.M. Weather still very cold and more snow. | |
| — | 23.1.17 | 5.a.m | Lt Nawton round all Gun positions. | |
| | | 2.P.M | Rifle and Gun Inspection. Brigade relief orders received, and Coy. relief orders issued. Weather Bitterly cold | ~~III~~ II |
| — | 24.1.17 | 11.a.m | Commenced moving stores etc from Pioneer to Shelter Wood camp. | |
| | | 10.31 PM | Relief Complete and all back at SHELTER WOOD CAMP except No I | |

2353 Wt. W2544/1454 700,000 5/15 D. D. & L. A.D.S.S./Forms/C. 2118.

Instructions regarding War Diaries and Intelligence Summaries are contained in F. S. Regs., Part II. and the Staff Manual respectively. Title pages will be prepared in manuscript.

# WAR DIARY
*or*
# INTELLIGENCE SUMMARY
*(Erase heading not required.)*

Army Form C. 2118. 9

| Place | Date | Hour | Summary of Events and Information | Remarks and references to Appendices |
|---|---|---|---|---|
| ACID DROP CAMP SOUTH. | 25.1.17 | 10 am | 13 O. R. joined from Base Company cleaning themselves morning. | |
| | | 2 pm | Rifle inspection, followed by Gun & ammunition cleaning | |
| | | 3 pm | C.O's conference at Brigade Hd Qrs. Weather bitterly cold | |
| — " — | 26.1.17 | 9 am | Nos 1 & 2 gun cleaning. remainder of Company to Transport Lines to clean & oil limbers. C.O & Lt Nawton visited Transport Lines. | |
| | | 2.30 pm | Company Pay. No72207. Pte Elder brought back from leave under escort. | |
| — " — | 27.1.17 | 9 am | Pte Elder brought before C.O. remanded for F.G.C.M. and summary of evidence taken | |
| | | 10 am | C.O. to Martinpuich to see C.O. 46th M.G.Co. Company usual routine | |
| | | 2 pm | Gas Helmet & ammunition inspection. relief orders issued Weather still terribly cold. | ~~IV~~ III |
| | 28.1.17 | 9 am | Guns tripods etc sent up to Martinpuich by light railway remainder of Company moving Camp. | |
| | | 3 pm | Company Paraded to relieve 46 Coy according to orders. Relief | ~~III~~ III |

2353 Wt. W2544/1454 700,000 5/15 D. D. & L. A.D.S.S./Forms/C. 2118.

10

Instructions regarding War Diaries and Intelligence Summaries are contained in F. S. Regs., Part II. and the Staff Manual respectively. Title pages will be prepared in manuscript.

Army Form C. 2118.

# WAR DIARY
*or*
# INTELLIGENCE SUMMARY.
*(Erase heading not required.)*

| Place | Date | Hour | Summary of Events and Information | Remarks and references to Appendices |
|---|---|---|---|---|
| MARTINPUICH | 28.1.17 | | Completed by 8. p.m somewhat heavy shelling at Martinpuich. 3 O.R wounded, and a fourth wounded at LE SARS. | |
| | | | Disposition of Guns as follows:- | |
| | | | LE SARS 2nd Lt Keith. 2 Guns at head of JOCK ALLEY. 1 in SUNKEN RD | |
| | | | — 2nd Lt Morpath. 2 Guns. one O.G. 1 and one O.G. 2. | |
| | | | Intermediate Line 2/Lt Henderson. 3 Guns. two in "H" and one in "G" Nests. | |
| | | | Head Qrs. C.O. Lt Mawdon. Signallers and 8 carriers. | |
| | | | 2 Teams, with guns etc in reserve in Cellars at Martinpuich. | |
| | | | 2nd Lt Thomson C.S.M and remainder of Company at ACID DROP CAMP. | |
| — | 29.1.17 | 5.a.m | C.O round all gun positions. | |
| | | 9.a.m | Orders received that the 44th Brigade - on our right - would raid the BUTTE. | |
| | 30.1.17 | 1.45a.m | Zero, all guns opened fire, on Enemy's back areas & tracks facing our front & left. Raid quite successful. all dug-out bombed. 17 prisoners taken, many killed. our casualties slight. We fired 15,500 rounds. | |
| | | 5 a.m | C.O. all round all positions. weather still very cold snow about 9. a.m. Hd Qrs rather heavily shelled about 5. P.M | |

2353 Wt. W2544/1454 700,000 5/15 D. D. & L. A.D.S.S./Forms/C. 2118.

11

Army Form C. 2118.

Instructions regarding War Diaries and Intelligence Summaries are contained in F. S. Regs., Part II. and the Staff Manual respectively. Title pages will be prepared in manuscript.

# WAR DIARY
*or*
# ~~INTELLIGENCE SUMMARY.~~
*(Erase heading not required.)*

| Place | Date | Hour | Summary of Events and Information | Remarks and references to Appendices |
|---|---|---|---|---|
| MARTINPUICH | 31.1.17 | 5.am | Lt Mawton round all guns, Weather still very cold and under snow. | |
| | | 3 P.M | C.O & 2 Officers No 7. Australian M.G.Co. arrived at Hd Qrs to arrange relief | |
| | | 5.15.PM | Lt Henderson took one Officer round all Intermediate guns. C.O took C.O Australian Coy: & one Officers to see forward guns also did the "Nests" on the way back, returned 7.45. Quiet going round<br>Relief orders issued | IV |

[illegible]
Major.

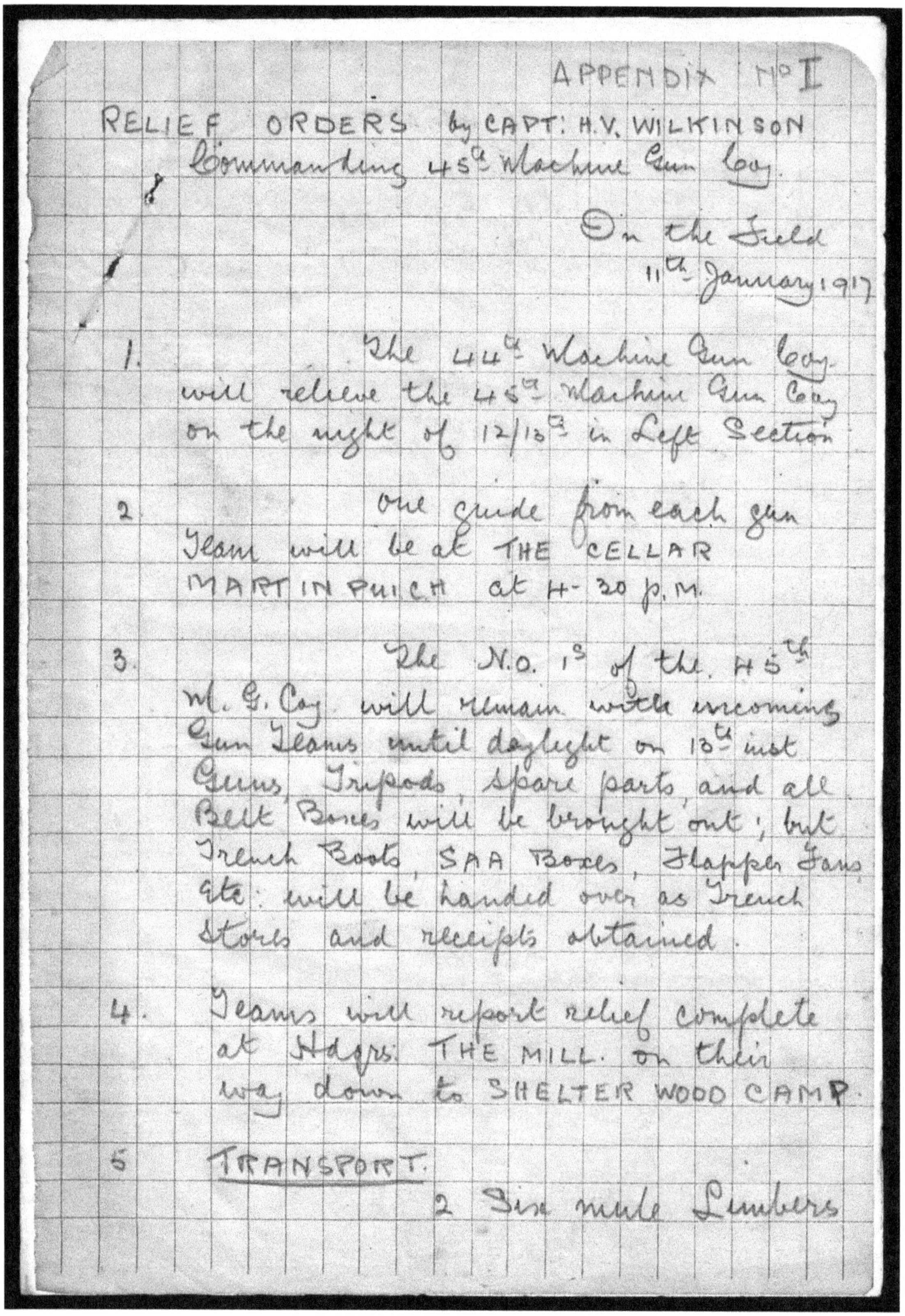

APPENDIX No I

RELIEF ORDERS by CAPT: H.V. WILKINSON
Commanding 45th Machine Gun Coy.

On the Field
11th January 1917

1. The 44th Machine Gun Coy. will relieve the 45th Machine Gun Coy on the night of 12/13th in Left Section

2. One guide from each gun Team will be at THE CELLAR MARTINPUICH at 4-30 p.m.

3. The No. 1s of the 45th M.G. Coy will remain with incoming Gun Teams until daylight on 13th inst Guns, Tripods, Spare parts, and all Belt Boxes will be brought out; but Trench Boots, SAA Boxes, Flapper Fans etc. will be handed over as Trench Stores and receipts obtained.

4. Teams will report relief complete at Hdqrs. THE MILL. on their way down to SHELTER WOOD CAMP.

5. TRANSPORT.

2 Six mule Limbers

will be at the WATER TANKS MARTINPUICH at 7-30 p.M.

1 Limber will be at VILLA STATION at 11-0 am. for extra Belt Boxes etc:

6. 2/LT. THOMSON and 2 O.R. will proceed to SHELTER WOOD CAMP at 11-30 a.m. to take over camp.

Remainder of Coy: will move at 2-0 p.M.

H.M. Wilkinson Capt

Commanding 45th M.G. Coy.

APPENDIX No II

RELIEF ORDERS by CAPT: H.V. WILKINSON
Commanding 45th Machine Gun Coy.

On the Field
23rd Jan: 1917

1. The 44th Machine Gun Coy will relieve the 45th Machine Gun Coy in the Right Section to-morrow the 24th inst:

2. 1 Guide from each Gun Team will be at THE CELLAR MARTINPUICH at 4-30 p.m.

3. All Guns, Tripods, Spare Parts etc. Belt Boxes and Gum Boots will be brought out

4. A party will be detailed to bring back extra stores etc: from MARTINPUICH at 8-30 a.m. to-morrow to VILLA STATION

5. TRANSPORT

1 Limber to be at VILLA STATION at 10-30 a.m. and 2 Six mule limbers to be at The WATER TANKS, MARTINPUICH, 1 at 6-00 p.m. and 1 at 7-30 p.M

2 Limbers to be at PIONEER CAMP at 10-30 a.m

6. On completition of relief all teams will go straight to the WATER TANKS MARTINPUICH. Team Commanders must see there is no delay there as the Transport must not be kept waiting.

7. Section officers will report relief complete to LIEUT: NAWTON at MARTINPUICH.

8. 2/LIEUT: THOMSON and 2. O.R. will proceed to SHELTER WOOD CAMP at 1-30 p.m to take over Camp.

Remainder of Company will move off at 3-0 p.m

[signature]

Capt

Commanding 45th M. G. Coy.

APPENDIX No III

RELIEF ORDERS by MAJOR H.V. WILKINSON
Commanding 45th Machine Gun Coy

In the Field
27th Jan: 1917

1. The 45th Machine Gun Coy will relieve the 46th Machine Gun Coy in the left Section to-morrow the 28th inst:

2. 2/LTS: KEITH and MORPETH and "A" Section and 1 team of "D" will parade at 3-0 p.M and proceed to MARTINPUICH where guides from Front Line teams will meet them.

3. 2/LT: HENDERSON and the remaining 3 teams of "D" will parade at 3-10 p.M and proceed to MARTINPUICH where guides from "G" and "H" Nests will meet them.

4. 1 Team of "B", 1 team of "C" and the Ration Carriers will parade at 3-15 p.M. and proceed to MARTINPUICH. They will be stationed in THE CELLAR.

2/LT: THOMSON and 1 team of "B" and 1 team of "C" will take Guns and equipment and 36 boxes of ammunition and be at VILLA STATION at 10-0 a.m. where Push Trucks have been arranged to take the Guns etc: on to MARTINPUICH.

6. TRANSPORT

2 Limbers to be at SHELTER WOOD CAMP at 9-0 am to take guns etc to VILLA STATION after which they will return to SHELTER WOOD CAMP to move stores etc:
2 other Limbers to be at SHELTER WOOD CAMP at 10-0 a.m. to shift stores to ACID DROP SOUTH.

Cookes Cart to be at SHELTER WOOD CAMP at 1-30 P.M.

7. Sergt. Bishop and 2 O. Ranks will proceed to ACID DROP SOUTH at 2-0 P.M to take over Camp.

Remainder of Company will move off at 3-30 P.M

8. Section officers are reminded that they must have plenty of glycerine and whale oil

9. Receipts of all Trench Stores taken over will be sent to Hdqrs: THE MILL MARTINPUICH by 8-0 p.M. the 29th inst.

J.C. Maurton
Lieut
2nd In Command
43rd M.G. Coy

APPENDIX No IV

RELIEF ORDERS by MAJOR H.V. WILKINSON
Commanding 45th Machine Gun Coy.

In the Field
31st January 1917

1. The 7th AUSTRALIAN Machine Gun Coy. will relieve the 45th Machine Gun Coy. in left Section on night 1/2nd Feb.

2. Guides will be at VILLA STATION at 4-30 p.m. These will be supplied from Hdqrs. and need not be sent down from FRONT LINE

3. The No. 1s. of outgoing M.G. teams, will remain with incoming Detachments for 24 hours after which they will join the 45th M.G. Coy at FRICOURT CAMP.
The infantry attached from the 46th Brigade in the INTERMEDIATE LINE (NESTS) will go with the 45th M.G. Coy. on relief to FRICOURT CAMP.

4. Incoming Units will retain the right of way on Trench Board Tracks over Outgoing Units

5 All Trench Maps, Sketches, programmes of work in progress, and Defence Schemes, will

be handed over and receipts obtained
All Trench stores, camps and camp
Equipment will be handed over and
receipts obtained

6. 2/LT. THOMSON and 2 O.R. will proceed to FRICOURT CAMP to take over from the 7th AUSTRALIAN M.G. Coy. at 12.0 noon on 1st Feb:

7. Guns, [redacted] and spare Parts etc. [redacted] will be brought out of the Line. [redacted]

8. <u>TRANSPORT</u>

[redacted];

1 Six mule limber to be at the "WATER TANKS" MARTINPUIC at 7.0 p.m. and another to be there at 7.30 p.m.

9. On completition of relief gun Team commanders will take their teams direct to the Water Tanks and they must get them there with as little delay

as possible, as the transport must not be kept waiting. They will then march
off to FRICOURT CAMP.
Officers will report "Relief complete" at
H.Qrs. THE MILL.
Transport will also be required to
move Coy. Stores etc: from ACID
DROP SOUTH to FRICOURT CAMP.

10. Receipts for all Trench stores handed over are to be sent to the ORDERLY ROOM by 9.0 a.m on 2nd inst.

A.M. Wilkinson
Major
Commanding 45th M.G. Coy.

Copy No. 1. War Diary
2 do
3 45th Inf. Bde
4 File
5 2/Lts. KEITH & MORPETH
6 C.O. 7th AUSTRALIAN M.G. Coy
7 C. S. M.
8 TRANSPORT OFFICER.

**NOTE**

Tripods, All Belt Boxes and Gum Boots will be handed over

Instructions regarding War Diaries and Intelligence Summaries are contained in F. S. Regs., Part II. and the Staff Manual respectively. Title pages will be prepared in manuscript.

# WAR DIARY
*or*
# INTELLIGENCE SUMMARY.
*(Erase heading not required.)*

Army Form C. 2118.

45 M G Coy

Vol 9

| Place | Date | Hour | Summary of Events and Information | Remarks and references to Appendices |
|---|---|---|---|---|
| | | | CONFIDENTIAL<br>WAR DIARY<br>OF<br>FEBRUARY 1917<br>1st to 28th FEBRUARY 1917<br>VOLUMN IX | |

[signature] Lieut

O.C. No 45 COY. MACHINE GUN CORPS.

2353 Wt. W2544/1454 700,000 5/15 D. D. & L. A.D.S.S./Forms/C. 2118.

Instructions regarding War Diaries and Intelligence Summaries are contained in F.S. Regs., Part II. and the Staff Manual respectively. Title pages will be prepared in manuscript.

# WAR DIARY
*or*
# ~~INTELLIGENCE SUMMARY.~~
*(Erase heading not required.)*

Army Form C. 2118.

| Place | Date | Hour | Summary of Events and Information | Remarks and references to Appendices |
|---|---|---|---|---|
| MARTINPUICH | 1.2.17. | 2 P.M | Remainder of Company moved from ACID DROP CAMP to FRICOURT CAMP. | |
| | | 3 P.M | Guides sent to VILLA STATION, CONTLEMAISON to lead in teams from no 7 Australian Company M.G. Corps. all teams away from the MILL 5. p.m. | |
| | | 8.15 pm | Relief complete, Head Quarters closed. all back at FRICOURT CAMP 10.30 Hot Soup served to all. Bitterly cold & ground very slippery. Lt Lipscomb returned from leave | |
| FRICOURT | 2.2.17. | 9. a.m | Cleaning Clothing & equipment. | |
| | | 10 30. | F.G.C.M on no: 72206 Pte McCrandles, for desertion | |
| | | 2 pm. | Rifle inspection, followed by Gun cleaning etc. | |
| — | 3.2.17 | 9 a.m | Physical drill, 10 a.m. Washing & oiling limbers. | |
| | | 12 noon | C.O's Conference at Brigade Hd Qts. | |
| | | 2 p.m | Inspection of Company in full marching order. Weather still very cold 1. O.R. to CAMIERS for advanced training. Movement orders issued. | I |
| — | 4.2.17 | 9. a.m | Repacking limbers & preparing for move | |
| | | 12 noon | Company paraded for inspection. & F.G.C.M on no 72206 Pte McCrandles promulgated | |
| | | 2.45 | Company Paraded for move to BAIZIEUX according to programme. | I |
| | | 7 30. | Arrived BAIZIEUX. very comfortable billets. Bitterly cold coming along | |

2353 Wt. W2544/1454 700,000 5/15 D. D. & L. A.D.S.S./Forms/C. 2118.

Instructions regarding War Diaries and Intelligence Summaries are contained in F. S. Regs., Part II. and the Staff Manual respectively. Title pages will be prepared in manuscript.

# WAR DIARY
*or*
# ~~INTELLIGENCE SUMMARY.~~
(*Erase heading not required.*)

Army Form C. 2118.

| Place | Date | Hour | Summary of Events and Information | Remarks and references to Appendices |
|---|---|---|---|---|
| | | | hot tea and rum issued on arrival. | |
| BAIZIEUX | 5.2.17 | 9.a.m | Rifle drill under C.S.M 10.15. Cleaning arms. | |
| | | 2 P.M | Kit and Clothing Inspection. | |
| — | 6.2.17. | 7.15 am | Running. 9. a.m. Rifle drill under C.S.M. | |
| | | 10 a.m | Inspection of all Gun Parts & limbers. | |
| | | 2.p.m | Equipment cleaning & checking deficiencies 2/Lt macpeth to Hospital | |
| | | 10 a.m | Divisional Sports Committee at A.P.M's Office. | |
| | | 2.30 p.m | C.O. to Conference of C O's at FRANVILLERS. | |
| — | 7.2.17 | 7.15 am | Running. 9. a.m Gun instruction. | |
| | | 2.p.m | Company Pay out. Weather still bitterly cold. | |
| — | 8.2.17 | 9.a.m | Company Paraded for Route march. fighting order about 10. miles and only 1 man fell out. 2/Lt mitchelmore & 3 other ranks, returned from CAMIERS. | |
| | | 2.p.m. | Sections working independently. Draft of 15 arrived from Base, & 9 attached men from Battalions | |
| — | 9.2.17. | 7.15 am | Running 9 am. Squad Drill | |
| | | 10 am | Gun Instruction | |
| | | | 6 teams under 2Lt Thomson paraded & took over duties und anti-aircraft | |

Instructions regarding War Diaries and Intelligence Summaries are contained in F. S. Regs., Part II. and the Staff Manual respectively. Title pages will be prepared in manuscript.

# WAR DIARY
*or*
# INTELLIGENCE SUMMARY.
*(Erase heading not required.)*

Army Form C. 2118.

| Place | Date | Hour | Summary of Events and Information | Remarks and references to Appendices |
|---|---|---|---|---|
| | 9.2.17 | | Battery (P) at Meaulte Defences. | |
| | | 2 PM | Lecture by 2 Lt F. Michelmore to NCOS No 1 & 2 | |
| | | | 2nd Lt E J BRUNSDEN & 2 Lt W C DICKINSON joined from Base. Weather cold. | |
| | 10.2.17 | 7.15 am | Physical Drill 9 am Rifle Drill | |
| | | 10 am | Gun Drill | |
| | | 2.30 PM | Company Football Team played 46 Machine Gun Co at Warloy | |
| | | | Score 46 Company 2 goals 45 Company nil. | |
| | | | Weather still very cold & ground covered with snow. | |
| | 11.2.17 | | Company paraded for usual Church Parades | |
| | | 2. PM | Company paraded for Fatigue to strike Baizieux Camp | |
| | | | One riding horse shot as unfit for active Service. | |
| | | | Weather bright & cold The 6 gun teams & personal returned from "P" anti aircraft Battery. | |
| | | 6 PM | C.O's Conference at Brigade Head Quarters. FRANVILLERS. | |
| | 12.2.17 | | Usual routine during day. Weather not quite so cold. Football match against 44th M G Co afternoon. draw. 2 goals all. | |

2353 Wt. W2544/1454 700,000 5/15 D. D. & L. A.D.S.S./Forms/C. 2118.

Instructions regarding War Diaries and Intelligence Summaries are contained in F. S. Regs., Part II. and the Staff Manual respectively. Title pages will be prepared in manuscript.

# WAR DIARY
*or*
# ~~INTELLIGENCE SUMMARY.~~
*(Erase heading not required.)*

Army Form C. 2118.

| Place | Date | Hour | Summary of Events and Information | Remarks and references to Appendices |
|---|---|---|---|---|
| BAIZIEUX. | 13.2.17 | 7.15. | Company Parade. Points before firing. | |
| | | 9 - | All Company on Range. every gun tested, and all fired, including new + attached men. F.G.C.M. on no. 18457 L/Cpl DUNCAN. | |
| | | 2 pm | Gun cleaning + packing limbers. Marching Orders received, and Company Movement orders issued | II |
| — | 14.2.17. | 7.15. | Packing all limbers. | |
| | | 9.15. | Parade in full marching Order for C.O's Inspection at 9.45. | |
| | | 10.15. | The whole Company rehearsed for move tomorrow. everything packed on limbers and every man paraded except the Guard. Road space allowed 311 x actual 240 x. Time allowed for passing a point 4 mi 21 secs. actual 3 minutes 42. seconds. Weather beautifully fine. freezing at nights, but thawing during the day. | |
| | | 2 p | Limbers packed ready for the move. | |
| | 15.2.17. | 10.25 | Company paraded + marched to BEAUVAL arrived at 4.30 pm. 3 men fell out on march, two of whom were admitted to hospital | |
| | 16.2.17 | | Company moved off at 9 AM + marched to BARLY + arrived | |

2353 Wt. W2544/1454 700,000 5/15 D. D. & L. A.D.S.S./Forms/C. 2118.

Army Form C. 2118.

Instructions regarding War Diaries and Intelligence Summaries are contained in F. S. Regs., Part II. and the Staff Manual respectively. Title pages will be prepared in manuscript.

# WAR DIARY
*or*
# INTELLIGENCE SUMMARY.

(*Erase heading not required.*)

| Place | Date | Hour | Summary of Events and Information | Remarks and references to Appendices |
|---|---|---|---|---|
| | 16.2.17 | | at 1.15 P.M weather fine & roads in good condition. No one fell out on march | |
| BARLY. | | 2.30p | Company paraded & cleaned guns &c. | |
| BARLY | 17.2.17 | 8 a | Company paraded 8 o clock & marched off at 8.15 to HONVAL via S of ABBRES & REBREUVE & arrived at 11.45 weather wet & misty & poor billets | |
| HONVAL | 18.2.17 | 8.15a | Company paraded & marched to FOUFFLIN-RICAMETZ via HOUVIGNEUL, MONCHEAUX, BUNEVILLE & TERNAS & arrived at 11.40. weather wet & roads in a poor state | |
| FOUFFLIN-RICAMETZ | 19.2.17 | 9 a | Cleaning guns & ammunition | |
| | | 2 a | Inspection of Sections in fighting order | |
| | | | C.O unwell & confined to bed. | |
| – – | 20.2.17 | 7.15 | Running | |
| – – | | 9.0 | Rifle Drill | |
| – – | | 10.0 | Gun instruction | |
| – – | | | Instructional Classes commenced for all attached men who had | |

Instructions regarding War Diaries and Intelligence Summaries are contained in F. S. Regs., Part II. and the Staff Manual respectively. Title pages will be prepared in manuscript.

# WAR DIARY
*or*
# INTELLIGENCE SUMMARY.
*(Erase heading not required.)*

Army Form C. 2118.

| Place | Date | Hour | Summary of Events and Information | Remarks and references to Appendices |
|---|---|---|---|---|
| FOUFFLIN-RICAMETZ | 20.2.17 | | not previously done a MG Course. | |
| | | | Class in Rifle & Musketry Instruction commenced for men of the last two drafts. | |
| | | | MAJOR H.V. WILKINSON admitted to Hospital. Weather damp. | |
| | | 2.PM | Gas Helmet drill & inspection | |
| — " — | 21.2.17 | 7.15 | Running | |
| — " — | | 9- | Rifle Drill | |
| — " — | | 10 | Gun Cleaning & Immediate Action | |
| — " — | | 11.30 | Rifle & Musketry instruction continued | |
| — " — | | 2.30 | Company paraded for medical inspection | |
| | | | Company Football Team played 45 TMB & lost 1-3. | |
| | | | weather wet & misty | |
| " | 22.2.17 | 7.15 | Inspection of gas helmets | |
| | | 9- | Company paraded in marching order for CO's inspection | |
| " | | 10am | advanced gun drill & gun cleaning. | |
| | | | Instructional Classes continued as usual. | |
| " | | 3.30pm | Company pay. Weather still wet & miserable. | |

Army Form C. 2118.

Instructions regarding War Diaries and Intelligence Summaries are contained in F. S. Regs., Part II. and the Staff Manual respectively. Title pages will be prepared in manuscript.

# WAR DIARY
*or*
# INTELLIGENCE SUMMARY.
*(Erase heading not required.)*

| Place | Date | Hour | Summary of Events and Information | Remarks and references to Appendices |
|---|---|---|---|---|
| FOUFFLIN RICAMETZ | 23.2.17 | 7.15 | A & B Sections Points before firing C & D Sections running | |
| | | 9am | A & B on range Remainder of Company advanced drill & Rifle drill | |
| | | 2 pm | Medical Inspection of Company. | |
| | | 3 | 1st Round of Company Football Competition C Section 4. B Section 0. Weather dull but dry. | |
| | ~~24.2.17~~ | | Operation Orders received that Company was to march to NOYELLETTE next day. | |
| | 24.2.17 | 9 am | Medical Inspection of Company. | |
| | | 7.30 | Company marched to NOYELLETTE via AMBRINES. NOYELLE-VION arrived 2.15 pm. Weather dull & misty | |
| NOYELLETTE | 25.2.17 | 6.30 am | 100 men under 2 Lts MICHELMORE & KEITH paraded & proceeded to join Brigade Working Party on railway. | |
| | | 1.30 pm | 2/Lt MICHELMORE proceeded on compassionate leave to UNITED KINGDOM. | |
| | 26.2.17 | 9 am | Company paraded & cleaned guns, ammunition & limbers. | |
| | | 2 | Football Competition:- Head Quarters 10. Transport 0. | |

2353 Wt. W2544/1454 700,000 5/15 D. D. & L. A.D.S.S./Forms/C. 2118.

Army Form C. 2118.

Instructions regarding War Diaries and Intelligence Summaries are contained in F. S. Regs., Part II. and the Staff Manual respectively. Title pages will be prepared in manuscript.

# WAR DIARY
*or*
# INTELLIGENCE SUMMARY.
*(Erase heading not required.)*

| Place | Date | Hour | Summary of Events and Information | Remarks and references to Appendices |
|---|---|---|---|---|
| NOYELLETTE | 26.2.17 | | 2nd Lt STRANGE returned from Transport Course. | |
| | | | Pte PARK returned from MG School CAMIERS. | |
| | | | Pte CHEATLE proceeded to Course at MG School CAMIERS | |
| | 27.2.17 | 9 am | All ranks washing & cleaning their equipment | |
| | | 11.45 | Inspection of Company by CO | |
| | | | The G.O.C also inspected the Company on this parade. | |
| | | 2 o'c | Inspection of gas helmets by Section officers. | |
| | | 2 o'c | CO & Second in Command visited 35th Coy at LOUEZ re taking over two anti-aircraft guns in accordance with instructions received from Division. | |
| | 28.2.17 | 6.30 | 2Lt KEITH and fifty other Ranks proceeded to join Brigade working party on railway line. | |
| | | 10 AM | 9 2 Officers & Men fitted & tested in new Box Respirators. | |
| | | 1.15 PM | ~~2Lt DICKIN~~ 2Lt. DICKINSON and two teams of "C" Section proceeded to LOUEZ for Anti Aircraft Defence. | |
| | | 3.0 PM | 2Lt. H. H. HENDERSON and 21 O.R. proceeded to join Brigade working | |

Army Form C. 2118.

Instructions regarding War Diaries and Intelligence Summaries are contained in F. S. Regs., Part II. and the Staff Manual respectively. Title pages will be prepared in manuscript.

# WAR DIARY
*or*
# INTELLIGENCE SUMMARY.
*(Erase heading not required.)*

| Place | Date | Hour | Summary of Events and Information | Remarks and references to Appendices |
|---|---|---|---|---|
| NOYELLETTE | 28.2.17 | 30 P.M. | party or Railway line<br>Rest of Company on cleaning guns & ammunition.<br>PTE KNIGHT returned from Transport course at ABBEVILLE.<br>Warning order that Brigade will move into line on night of 3rd-4th March received<br>Weather cloudy, but fine till evening when it commenced to rain | |

2353 Wt. W2544/1454 700,000 5/15 D. D. & L. A.D.S.S./Forms/C. 2118.

MOVEMENT ORDERS by MAJOR H.V. WILKINSON

– Commanding 45th Machine Gun Coy.

In the Field
3rd February 1917

1. The 45th Machine Gun Coy will march to BAIZIEUX to-morrow the 4th inst.

2. STARTING POINT F. 9. a. 6. 5. thence to ALBERT along the main ALBERT – AMIENS RD. to Road Junction D. 20. B. 6. 2.

3. Company will parade in full marching order at 2.45 P.M

4. Distances of 200 yards will be maintained between Units and 100 yards between Sections

5. LIEUT: J.K. LIPSCOMB and 1 Signaller will report to the TOWN MAJOR BAIZIEUX at 10-0 a.m. to arrange billets

6. On arrival in Billets Section officers will immediately report the number of men falling out on the march

7. A Motor Lorry will call for all blankets and officers Valises at 9-0a

All Blankets to be rolled in bundles of 10 and labelled by 8.30 a.m.

J C Hawkins
Lieut
2nd In Command
45th M. G. Coy

Army Form C. 2118.

Instructions regarding War Diaries and Intelligence Summaries are contained in F. S. Regs., Part II. and the Staff Manual respectively. Title pages will be prepared in manuscript.

# WAR DIARY
~~or~~
~~INTELLIGENCE SUMMARY.~~
*(Erase heading not required.)*

| Place | Date | Hour | Summary of Events and Information | Remarks and references to Appendices |
|---|---|---|---|---|
| | | | CONFIDENTIAL. | Vol 10 |
| | | | WAR DIARY | |
| | | | OF | |
| | | | 45th MACHINE GUN COMPANY | |
| | | | 1st to 31st MARCH 1917 | |
| | | | VOLUMN X | |
| | | | A.M. Wilkinson Major. | |
| | | | O.C. No. 45 COY. MACHINE GUN CORPS. | |

A5834 Wt. W4973/M687 750,000 8/16 D. D. & L. Ltd. Forms/C.2118/13.

1

Army Form C. 2118.

Instructions regarding War Diaries and Intelligence Summaries are contained in F. S. Regs., Part II. and the Staff Manual respectively. Title pages will be prepared in manuscript.

# WAR DIARY
*or*
# INTELLIGENCE SUMMARY.
*(Erase heading not required.)*

| Place | Date | Hour | Summary of Events and Information | Remarks and references to Appendices |
|---|---|---|---|---|
| NOYELLETTE | 1.3.17 | 9.a | Gun & ammunition cleaning & packing limbers | |
| | | | 65 Officers & OR issued & fitted with small box respirator | |
| | | 2 p. | Medical inspection of Company followed by respirator drill | |
| | | 10.30 | COs Conference at Brigade Headquarters | |
| | | | CO afterwards proceeded to ARRAS to 46 Company re relief to take place next day. | |
| | | | Operation orders received from Brigade & Company Orders issued | I |
| | 2.3.17 | 9 am | Company paraded for Baths at HABARCQ | |
| | | 4.45 | Company paraded in full marching order & moved off at 5 pm & proceeded to Headquarters of 46 Company in ARRAS | |
| | | | Weather dull but dry. | |
| ARRAS. | 3.3.17 | 10 a | 4 Teams of A & 2 teams of C relieved 6 teams of 46 Coy in I 3 Sector. Relief complete by 1.45 pm. | |
| | | | CO round line in morning & again in afternoon. 10 R. joined. | |
| | 4.3.17 | | CO went round all guns in morning weather fine but turned to heavy snow at night. Sector very quiet & the change from | |

2353 Wt. W2544/1454 700,000 5/15 D. D. & L. A.D.S.S./Forms/C. 2118.

Instructions regarding War Diaries and Intelligence Summaries are contained in F. S. Regs., Part II. and the Staff Manual respectively. Title pages will be prepared in manuscript.

# WAR DIARY
*or*
# INTELLIGENCE SUMMARY.
*(Erase heading not required.)*

Army Form C. 2118.

| Place | Date | Hour | Summary of Events and Information | Remarks and references to Appendices |
|---|---|---|---|---|
| | | | late Sector much appreciated | |
| ARRAS. | 5 3 17 | | Took over two guns from 35 Company in cemetery defences relief complete by 5.30 pm. | |
| | | | CO round line in afternoon. Weather dull & dry. | |
| | | | One gun did indirect fire on RAILWAY SWITCH. | |
| | 6 3 17 | | Co. round all guns in morning. Weather fine. | |
| | 7 3 17 | | Headquarters shelled about 2 pm. | |
| | | | Co. round all guns. Weather cold & some snow. 5 guns did indirect fire. | |
| | 8 3 17 | | Brigadier went round all guns in morning with CO. | |
| | | | MAJOR H.V. WILKINSON rejoined Company from Hospital | |
| | | | Weather cold & snow in morning. 3 guns did indirect fire at night. | |
| | 9 3 17 | | C.O. & Second in Command went round all guns in morning. | |
| | | 4 pm | Teams at positions R6. R7. R8. R9 & B4 relieved. Weather dull & dry. | |
| | 10 3 17 | | C.O. & 2/i/C round all guns in morning. ~~Front guns fired 6.000 rounds at dawn during artillery barrage on expected Bosch raid~~ | |

Army Form C. 2118.

Instructions regarding War Diaries and Intelligence Summaries are contained in F. S. Regs., Part II. and the Staff Manual respectively. Title pages will be prepared in manuscript.

# WAR DIARY
*or*
# INTELLIGENCE SUMMARY.
(*Erase heading not required.*)

| Place | Date | Hour | Summary of Events and Information | Remarks and references to Appendices |
|---|---|---|---|---|
| ARRAS | 10.3.17 | | ARRAS fairly heavily shelled during short periods. | |
| | | | 8 O.R joined from the BASE | |
| " | 11.3.17 | | CO. & 2/i/c round all guns in morning. Front guns fired *6000 rounds at dawn during Artillery barrage on suspected Bosch raid. 2Lt MICHELMORE reported his arrival at NOYELLETTE from leave to UNITED KINGDOM. | |
| | | | Pte WYLIE left for compassionate leave to UNITED KINGDOM. | |
| " | 12.3.17 | | CO. & 2/i/C round all guns & front line | |
| | | | Company paid | |
| | | | Headquarters & billets heavily shelled one billet blown in & B5 gun position also badly damaged. Pte HAWKYARD badly wounded. | |
| | | | 2Lt MICHELMORE returned to Company from leave to UNITED KINGDOM. | |
| | | | Working party continued work at night on barrage emplacements. | |
| " | 13.3.17 | | CO. attended Conference at Brigade Headquarters DUISANS. | |
| | | | 2/i/command round all guns. | |

4

Instructions regarding War Diaries and Intelligence Summaries are contained in F. S. Regs., Part II. and the Staff Manual respectively. Title pages will be prepared in manuscript.

# WAR DIARY
*or*
# INTELLIGENCE SUMMARY.
*(Erase heading not required.)*

Army Form C. 2118.

| Place | Date | Hour | Summary of Events and Information | Remarks and references to Appendices |
|---|---|---|---|---|
| ARRAS | 13.3.17 | | Work commenced on Battle Headquarters RUE de DOUAI one O.R. (driver) joined Company. Part of Company attended Baths. | |
| | 14.3.17 | | CO. & 2/c/command round guns & front line. Weather fine but trenches very dirty. Two A.A. teams at LOUEZ relieved by 46 M.G.C. Preliminary Instrs issued | II |
| | 15.3.17 | | CO. & 2/c/command round all guns. Guns R6 & R8 cooperated with heavy artillery in a 20 minutes shoot from 1.50 pm to 2.10 pm. Work commenced at night on barrage emplacements for right sector. Weather fine & Huns fairly quiet. Sgt PRATT left to take up appointment as QMS of 86 M.G.C | |
| | 16.3.17 | | Co & 2/c/command round all guns. All teams relieved in morning. Weather fine & dry much colder. Good progress being made with Battle Headquarters | |
| | 17.3.17 | | Co & 2/i/C round all guns & front line. R6 & R8 guns fired in conjunction with 12th DIVISION raid on right of our Sector. Beautiful day & much aerial activity | |
| | 18.3.17 | | CO. round all guns. 8 teams of 46 Company arrived in Arras. | |

Instructions regarding War Diaries and Intelligence Summaries are contained in F. S. Regs., Part II. and the Staff Manual respectively. Title pages will be prepared in manuscript.

# WAR DIARY
*or*
# INTELLIGENCE SUMMARY.
*(Erase heading not required.)*

Army Form C. 2118.

| Place | Date | Hour | Summary of Events and Information | Remarks and references to Appendices |
|---|---|---|---|---|
| ARRAS. | 18.3.17 | | SGT ROONEY left for Gas Course at Divisional Gas School. | |
| | | | 2 LT F.R. KEITH & L/SGT. SHERWOOD left for Machine Gun School CAMIERS. | |
| " | 19.3.17 | | Co & 2/i/c of 46 Coy round all guns. | |
| | | 2.30 pm | 8 teams of 46 M.G.C relieved 8 teams of 45 M.G.C in line. | |
| | | | ARRAS heavily shelled during afternoon | |
| | | 8.30 pm | Company left ARRAS & marched to NOYELLETTE & arrived about midnight. Weather very wet & stormy. | |
| NOYELLETTE | 20.3.17 | 10 am | Company paraded to march to GOUY-en-TERNOIS but were stopped on road & returned to NOYELLETTE under Brigade Orders. | |
| | | | Weather very stormy. Company standing by to move at short notice | |
| " | 21.3.17 | 9 am | Checking deficiencies, gun cleaning & packing limbers. | |
| | | 2 pm | Parade under Section officers arrangements. | |
| | | | Co attended conference at AMBRINES | |
| | | | Fall of snow at night & weather very cold. | |
| | 22.3.17 | 7 am | Physical training | |
| | | 9.10 am | Rifle & Company Drill under C.S.M. | |

2353 Wt. W2544/1454 700,000 5/15 D. D. & L. A.D.S.S./Forms/C. 2118.

6

Army Form C. 2118.

Instructions regarding War Diaries and Intelligence Summaries are contained in F. S. Regs., Part II. and the Staff Manual respectively. Title pages will be prepared in manuscript.

# WAR DIARY
*or*
# INTELLIGENCE SUMMARY.
*(Erase heading not required.)*

| Place | Date | Hour | Summary of Events and Information | Remarks and references to Appendices |
|---|---|---|---|---|
| NOYELLETTE | 22.3.17 | 10.15 a | Advanced Gun Drill | |
| | | 3.15 | Inspection of Company in fighting order by C.O. | |
| | | | L/C ROBERTS left for DIVISIONAL. GAS. SCHOOL | |
| | | 5 pm. | Football A Section 2. Headquarters 1 | |
| " | 23.3.17 | 7 am | Physical Drill | |
| | | 9–10 | Rifle & Company Drill under C.S.M. | |
| | | 10.15. | Advanced Gun Drill | |
| | | 2 pm | Box Respirator Instruction & Drill | |
| | | | Sgt ROONEY returned from Gas Course | |
| | | | Weather fine but bitterly cold. | |
| " | 24.3.17 | 9.30 am | Tactical Scheme. | |
| | | 2 pm | Washing limbers | |
| | | 3.15. | Final Company Football Competition D Section 3 A Section 0. | |
| | | | Weather very windy & cold. | |
| " | 25.3.17 | 10 am. | Voluntary Church Service at HABARCQ | |
| " | | 3 pm. | Co. went to Brigade Conference at AMBRINES. Weather fine & warmer. | |

2353 Wt. W2544/1454 700,000 5/15 D. D. & L. A.D.S.S./Forms/C. 2118.

Instructions regarding War Diaries and Intelligence Summaries are contained in F. S. Regs., Part II. and the Staff Manual respectively. Title pages will be prepared in manuscript.

# WAR DIARY
*or*
# INTELLIGENCE SUMMARY.
*(Erase heading not required.)*

Army Form C. 2118. 7

| Place | Date | Hour | Summary of Events and Information | Remarks and references to Appendices |
|---|---|---|---|---|
| NOYELLETTE | 26.3.17 | 7-7.30 am | Physical Drill | |
| | | 9-10 | Cleaning equipment | |
| | | 10.15-12.30 | Gun cleaning & advanced drill | |
| | | 2pm | Sections paraded under Section Officers' arrangements | |
| | | | Weather very wet & stormy. | |
| | 27.3.17 | 7am | Physical drill | |
| | | 9.30 | Inspection of Company in Battle order by C.O. | |
| | | 10.15 | Advanced Gun Drill | |
| | | 2pm | Rifle & Company Drill | |
| | 28.3.17 | 7am | Physical drill | |
| | | 9.30 | C.O's parade in fighting order. | |
| | | 2pm | Gas helmet & Box respirator drill & inspection. Weather cold & windy. | |
| | 29.3.17 | 7am | Physical drill | |
| | | 9.15 | 2Lt HENDERSON & 20 O.R. paraded under Divisional Bombing Officer for instruction. | |

Instructions regarding War Diaries and Intelligence Summaries are contained in F. S. Regs., Part II. and the Staff Manual respectively. Title pages will be prepared in manuscript.

# WAR DIARY
*or*
# INTELLIGENCE SUMMARY.
*(Erase heading not required.)*

Army Form C. 2118. 8

| Place | Date | Hour | Summary of Events and Information | Remarks and references to Appendices |
|---|---|---|---|---|
| NOYELLETTE | 29.3.17 | 9.15a | Nos 1 & 2 paraded under C.O. on range for revolver shooting | |
| | | | Range takers paraded under C.S.M. | |
| | | | Remainder of Company Immediate Action & Mechanism | |
| | | 2p | Gun cleaning & rifle instruction. | |
| | | | Weather terribly wet and windy | |
| | | | Orders received that Company moves into line on 30th inst. | III |
| | | | Offrs & Company Relief orders issued accordingly | |
| | | | 12 O.R. reinforcements reported arrived at Railhead. | |
| " | 30.3.17 | 9.15 | 2 Lt W.C. DICKINSON & 20 O.R paraded under Divisional Bombing Officer for instruction. | |
| | | | Rangetakers paraded under C.S.M. | |
| | | | Remainder of Company Immediate Action & Lecture on overhead fire | |
| | | 2p | Packing limbers | |
| | | 6 | Company paraded as per relief orders & marched to ARRAS. | |
| | | | weather fine Company arrived in billets about 11 p.m. | |
| | | | 12 O.R. joined Company from Base | |

2353 Wt. W2544/1454 700,000 5/15 D. D. & L. A.D.S.S./Forms/C. 2118.

Army Form C. 2118.

9

Instructions regarding War Diaries and Intelligence Summaries are contained in F. S. Regs., Part II. and the Staff Manual respectively. Title pages will be prepared in manuscript.

# WAR DIARY
*or*
# INTELLIGENCE SUMMARY.
*(Erase heading not required.)*

| Place | Date | Hour | Summary of Events and Information | Remarks and references to Appendices |
|---|---|---|---|---|
| ARRAS | 31.3.17 | 2 pm | 3 teams under Lt LIPSCOMB & 2Lt HENDERSON relieved 3 teams of 46 M.G.C at positions R8. R9 & B6. | |
| | | 5 pm | 2 teams under 2Lt DICKINSON relieved 2 teams of 46 MGC at positions B4 & B5 | |
| | | | ARRAS shelled heavily all day revived gas shells at 7 pm. weather showery. | |
| | | | Company Headquarters moved to 40 BOULEVARD. FAIDHERB. | |
| | | | R9 gun position blown in by shell during night. | |
| | | | amount of Company Cash in hand ~~76~~ 58 Frs 40 C. | |
| | | 12 noon | 8 Teams under 2nd Lts THOMSON & BRUNSDEN. for Barrage came under the orders of the D. M. G. O. | |

[signature]
Major.

O.C. No. 45 COY.
MACHINE GUN CORPS.

A5834 Wt. W4973/M687 750,000 8/16 D. D. & L. Ltd. Forms/C.2118/13.

OPERATION ORDERS by LIEUT: F.C. NAWTON
Commanding 45th Machine Gun Coy

NOYELLETTE
1st March 1917

1. The 45th Machine Gun Coy. will move to ARRAS to-morrow the 2nd inst and relieve 46th M.G. Coy.

2. Company parade in full marching order 4.45 p.m. and move off 5.0 p.m.

3. 2/Lt. H.H. HENDERSON and 4 Signallers will parade at 10.0 a.m and proceed to Hdqrs 46th Machine Gun Coy. ARRAS to take over billets and meet the Coy. at 8.0 p.m at the Archway ARRAS

4. All blankets to be tied in bundles of 10s and handed into Q.M. Stores at Reveille: Labels and string will be drawn from Q.M. Stores to-night

5 On the morning of 3rd Mch 2 teams of "A" Section under 2/Lt. R.J. THOMSON, 2 teams of "C" Section

under 2/Lt. H. H. HENDERSON, and remaining 2 teams of "A" under 2/Lt. F. R. KEITH and 1 team of "D" will relieve 7 teams of 46th M. G. Coy.

6. All ranks are reminded that the Town Orders ARRAS are strictly to be complied with.

J. Kenneth Lipscomb
Lieut.
2nd In Command
45th M. G. Coy

RELIEF ORDERS by MAJOR H.Y. WILKINSON
Commanding 45th Machine Gun Coy.

NOYELLETTE
29th March 1917

1. The 48th M.G. Coy, will relieve the 46th M.G Coy. in the left Sub-section I. 3. Sector on the 30th inst

2. 2/LT. F. MICHELMORE and 2 Signallers will proceed in advance and take over Billets, leaving here by 2.0 p.m.

3. The Company will parade at 6-0 p.m. (dress will be notified later) and will march to ARRAS via HABARCQ, and will follow the 45th T.M. Battery

4. Relief for the guns in the Trenches will commence at 2-0 p.M. on the 31st inst;

5. ~~LT. J.K. LIPSCOMB and teams 15 & 16 will take over positions at R. 6 & R. 7.~~

~~2/LT. H. H. HENDERSON~~

1.

SECRET

# Preliminary Instructions

1. The object of the forthcoming operations, as far as the 15th Division is concerned, is to capture the enemy's 3rd Line from the Road in H.28.C.8.2. Northwards to the River SCARPE in H.~~2~~22

2. The attack will be in 3 stages, and the 45th I.B's objectives will be as follows:- approximately

1st objective: The "Black" Line H.19.c.1.9. through FRED'S WOOD to point (98)

2nd objective The "Blue" Line H.20.A.2.3. to point (74)

3rd objective The "Brown" Line The Enemy's 3rd Line.

3. The 12th Division will be on the right of the 15th Division and the 9th on its left.

The 37th Division will be in Corps Reserve

The 44th I.B. will be on our right H.Qrs. G 23.C.4.0
The 26th I.B. — " — left H.Qrs. G.17.A.70.45

The 44th & 45th Brigades will capture the "Black" and "Blue" Lines, whilst the 46th Brigade will advance through them and capture the "Brown" Line

There will be 1 hour's pause after capture of the "Black" Line, and 4 hours after capture of "Blue" Line

Two Battalions will advance to the capture of the first objective each on a 2 Platoon frontage of 8 waves. four waves will capture the first objective The other 2 ~~Battalions~~ Companies will come up pass through them & capture the 2nd objective. One Battalion will be in reserve & one in support.

4. The opening bombardment will last for 48 hours and will be continuous. There will also be a M.G. Barrage from 22 Machine Guns under Divisional arrangements.

The rate of advance for the Creeping barrage proposed, is, from ZERO + 4 minutes, the barrage will lift 100 yards every 4 minutes, until 200X beyond the "Black" Line.

5. The Guns and teams for the Barrage will come under the D.M.G.O. at 6.0 a.m on the 31st inst. and a guide to take them to their positions, will be at Hd. Qts. RUE DE DOUAI at 12.0 noon, under 2nd LTS. THOMSON and BRUNSDEN and Sergts. ROONEY and STEVENS.

6 other teams will be in the Line and the 2 remaining ones will be in reserve.

Positions, officers and teams will be notified on the morning of the 31st inst.

6. <u>GAS</u>.

When "GAS ALERT" is <u>ON</u> Inspections of Small Box Respirators and P.H. Helmets will be held daily.

[signature]

Lieut.

2nd In Command

45th M.G. Coy.

2.

If the wind is suitable a smoke barrage will be placed along the left bank of the SCARPE from ZERO to ZERO + 60 minutes.

5. The attack on the "Brown" Line will be carried out in conjunction with Tanks Whatever happens, never mind the ruins in BLANGY, but push on, and impress on all ranks that whatever happens they must show a stout heart and get to the different objectives.

6. The dispositions of Guns will probably be as follows:-

| | | | | |
|---|---|---|---|---|
| (a). <u>Corps Barrage</u> | 6 Guns | under | 2 | Officers |
| (b) <u>To go forward.</u> | 4 " | " | 2 | " |
| (c). Indirect Fire R.E. position etc. | 3 " | " | 1 | " |
| (d). In Reserve | 3 " | " | 2 | " |

The 4 guns will go forward when the first Objective is taken and go on to the 2nd when that is taken. The advance on the 2nd objective will be ZERO plus 1.40

7. Head Quarters will be 113 RUE de DOUAI

Advance Dumps will be:-

"A" Dump G 23. D. 9½. 9½
"B" " (12)
"C" " (98)
"D" " (48)

and Ration Dump in FREDS WOOD.

A Company's Advance Dump will be in the same place as that to be occupied by the teams that go forward.

8. The teams will advance as follows:-

3/

No. 1. Tripod
2/3 } Gun & 2 Belt Boxes : 500 rounds
4 Spare Parts & Water
5 500 "
6 500 "
2 Carriers 1000

Total 2,500 rounds.

Dress: Fighting order, and Section officers must see that each man has:-

Field Dressing
2 Identity Discs
Iron Rations
Water Bottle full
Correct amount of Ammunition
Rations for the day
A. B. 64.
Box Respirator & Gas Helmet

Section officers must also think about the 48 hours bombardment,
Where supply of fresh water can be stored and obtained also rations.
Where the latrine should be and the nearest 1st Aid Post

9. It is to be remembered that these are only preliminary instructions, liable to alterations: but the time has come when the smallest detail must be thought about & thought out.

H M Wilkinson

Major
Commanding 45th Machine Gun Coy.

14. 3. 1917.

Instructions regarding War Diaries and Intelligence Summaries are contained in F. S. Regs., Part II. and the Staff Manual respectively. Title pages will be prepared in manuscript.

# WAR DIARY

*or*

~~INTELLIGENCE SUMMARY.~~

*(Erase heading not required.)*

Army Form C. 2118.

Vol XI

| Place | Date | Hour | Summary of Events and Information | Remarks and references to Appendices |
|---|---|---|---|---|
| | | | CONFIDENTIAL. | |
| | | | WAR DIARY | |
| | | | OF | |
| | | | 45TH MACHINE GUN COY. | |
| | | | 1st to 30th APRIL, 1917. | |
| | | | VOLUME XI. | A.W. Williams Major |

A5834 Wt. W4973/M687 750,000 8/16 D. D. & L. Ltd. Forms/C.2118/13.

Instructions regarding War Diaries and Intelligence Summaries are contained in F. S. Regs., Part II. and the Staff Manual respectively. Title pages will be prepared in manuscript.

# WAR DIARY
*or*
# INTELLIGENCE SUMMARY.
(*Erase heading not required.*)

Army Form C. 2118.

| Place | Date | Hour | Summary of Events and Information | Remarks and references to Appendices |
|---|---|---|---|---|
| ARRAS | 1.4.17 | | CO & 2/i/command round all guns. Very quiet day. Weather cold and dry. | |
| " | 2.4.17 | | CO & 2/i/C round all guns. Orders received for all troops to be in Battle positions by the night of the 3rd inst. Hostile artillery very quiet. Heavy fall of snow in evening. | |
| " | 3.4.17 | | Lt BARNS joined Company from Base. | |
| | | 5pm | All teams moved off to their Bombardment positions. Two teams of C & two of D to go forward & two of A in reserve to cellar 28 BLANGY. Two teams of B to dugout near R8 position. The 8 Divisional Barrage already in position, A & B near R9 & C & D at mouth of sewer. All in position by 7 pm. Officers as follows. Lt LIPSCOMB & 2Lt HENDERSON to cellar 33 BLANGY. 2Lts MICHELMORE & DICKINSON to Battle Headquarters. 2Lts THOMSON & BRUNSDEN to R9 cellar. Lts NAWTON & BARNS returned to DUISANS. CO & CSM remained at Company Headquarters 40 BOULEVARD FAIDHERBE. CO visited all teams at 10.30 pm. Weather wet. | |
| | 4.4.17 | | Bombardment commenced at 6.30 am. Hardly any retaliation. CO round all teams at 11 am. Gas discharged at 4.30 pm. Weather wet. | |

A5834 Wt. W4973/M687 750,000 8/16 D. D. & L. Ltd. Forms/C.2118/13.

Instructions regarding War Diaries and Intelligence Summaries are contained in F. S. Regs., Part II. and the Staff Manual respectively. Title pages will be prepared in manuscript.

# WAR DIARY
*or*
# INTELLIGENCE SUMMARY.
*(Erase heading not required.)*

Army Form C. 2118. 2

| Place | Date | Hour | Summary of Events and Information | Remarks and references to Appendices |
|---|---|---|---|---|
| ARRAS. | 4.4.17 | | Hostile artillery more active at night our guns did indirect fire 8.000 rounds on gaps in enemy wire | |
| " | 5.4.17 | | C.O. round all positions & teams. | |
| | | 12 mn | Our guns fired 1500 rounds during raid by ROYAL SCOTS. R8 position blown in by a shell | |
| | | | weather fine. Hostile artillery quiet. | |
| | | | our guns fired 5000 rounds at night on gaps in wire | |
| | 6.4.17 | | Bombardment continued | |
| | | | C.O. visited all officers and teams during the day | |
| | | | Hostile artillery very quiet. Rain in afternoon & evening. | |
| | | | our guns carried out usual indirect fire. DUISANS shelled in evening | |
| | 7.4.17 | 10 am | C.O. round all guns | |
| | | | Bombardment continued but little reply from Bosch | |
| | | | Headquarters BOULEVARD FAIDHERBE heavily shelled about midnight. DUISANS also shelled by high velocity gun & several casualties inflicted | |
| " | 8.4.17 | | Bombardment continued & much heavier. C.O. saw all officers & moved his Headquarters from BOULEVARD FAIDHERBE to Battle Headquarters RUE DE DOUAI. | |
| | | | C.O.s conference at Brigade 3 pm. | |
| | | | C.O. round all officers and teams at 5.30. Hostile artillery very lively | |

Instructions regarding War Diaries and Intelligence Summaries are contained in F. S. Regs., Part II. and the Staff Manual respectively. Title pages will be prepared in manuscript.

Army Form C. 2118. 3

# WAR DIARY
*or*
# INTELLIGENCE SUMMARY.
*(Erase heading not required.)*

| Place | Date | Hour | Summary of Events and Information | Remarks and references to Appendices |
|---|---|---|---|---|
| ARRAS | 9.4.17 | | Lt LIPSCOMB moved into No 12 cellar at 12.30 midnight & 2Lt HENDERSON to No 28 at same time. CO went to Brigade at 2.20 am to check watches. | |
| | | 5.30 | ZERO. | |
| | | | ROYAL SCOTS were held up slightly in BLANGY, but 1st objective easily taken. Hostile barrage feeble. | |
| | | 6.30 | Brigadier ordered our 4 guns to go forward & Lts LIPSCOMB & HENDERSON reported at 8 and 8.30 am respectively that they were in position at 1st objective & moved forward later to 2nd objective. 2Lt HENDERSON got across without a casualty, but Lt LIPSCOMB had L/c WOODBRIDGE & Pte KERR killed Sgt BROWN severely wounded L/c COLE wounded, and was also himself wounded in the back but carried on with his teams. | |
| | | 11 pm. | Received news that 2Lt HENDERSON had dug in about 200 yards from RAILWAY TRIANGLE as the battalions had been held up there & same news received from Lt LIPSCOMB about 20 minutes later. | |
| | | 11.40 am | Our troops withdrawn & an intense bombardment put on Railway Embankment, when our troops again went forward & carried the second objective. | |
| | | | 2Lt DICKINSON & 3 O.R. sent up to relieve Lt LIPSCOMB & replace his casualties. | |
| | | | 2Lt MICHELMORE & 2 teams sent up to Strong point near RAILWAY TRIANGLE. | |
| | | 6.30 pm | Orders received to move forward & close up. | |

A5834 Wt. W4973/M687 750,000 8/16 D. D. & L. Ltd. Forms/C.2118/13.

Army Form C. 2118. 4

# WAR DIARY
*or*
# INTELLIGENCE SUMMARY.
*(Erase heading not required.)*

Instructions regarding War Diaries and Intelligence Summaries are contained in F. S. Regs., Part II. and the Staff Manual respectively. Title pages will be prepared in manuscript.

| Place | Date | Hour | Summary of Events and Information | Remarks and references to Appendices |
|---|---|---|---|---|
| | 9.4.17 | | Headquarters moved to RAILWAY TRIANGLE | |
| | | | CO got in touch with 2LT THOMSON found he had 1 man killed & 3 wounded | |
| | | | Disposition of teams at this time as follows. | |
| | | | 2LT BRUNSDEN & 2 teams with Camerons to E of FEUCHY. | |
| | | | " DICKINSON " " with RSF about FEUCHY. WORKS. | |
| | | | " MICHELMORE " " in Strong point W of TRIANGLE. | |
| | | | " HENDERSON 4 " in dugout in N end of RAILWAY EMBANKMENT. | |
| | | | Two teams in dugout near Headquarters | |
| | | | 2LT THOMSON & 4 teams reported about H 20C.8.0 | |
| | | | Night very dark but quiet Early morning was wet but weather improved later in day. | |
| | | | Our Casualties to date. LT. J.K. LIPSCOMB wounded. | |
| | | | Killed Pte NORTH. Pte KERR L/C WOODBRIDGE | |
| | | | Wounded. Sgt BROWN. L/C COLE Pte NOON. Pte WYLIE. Pte VAUGHAN | |
| | | | Pte RICHARDSON Pte CAGLAIRI. | |
| RAILWAY TRIANGLE | 10.4.17 | | Heavy snow in morning | |
| | | 8 am | 2LT THOMSON reported, had missed HQ in dark & took his teams to ARRAS. | |
| | | 9.30 | CO went up to FEUCHY with Brigadier | |
| | | 12. | 37th Division attacked MONCHY | |
| | | 2.30 pm | Received orders to move forward & support 37th Division. | |

A5834 Wt. W4973/M687 750,000 8/16 D. D. & L. Ltd. Forms/C.2118/13.

Instructions regarding War Diaries and Intelligence Summaries are contained in F. S. Regs., Part II. and the Staff Manual respectively. Title pages will be prepared in manuscript.

# WAR DIARY
*or*
# INTELLIGENCE SUMMARY.
*(Erase heading not required.)*

Army Form C. 2118. 5

| Place | Date | Hour | Summary of Events and Information | Remarks and references to Appendices |
|---|---|---|---|---|
| FEUCHY | 10.4.17 | | 2Lt MICHELMORE & 2 teams to RSFs | |
| | | | " THOMSON " " to A & S.H | |
| | | | Sgt ROONEY " " to Royal Scots. | |
| | | 3 pm | Headquarters moved to FEUCHY & remainder of Company moved up at 5.30 pm weather cold & snowing hard. | |
| | | | Brigade ordered to move up & came under shell & machine gun fire, but dug in about H 23 d to H 29 central | |
| | 11.4.17 | 2.30 am | Received orders that Brigade was to attack all along the line at 5. am 4 guns ordered up to play into MOUNT PLEASANT WOOD and the wood W of ROEUX | |
| | | 3.15 am | Co. guided up 4 teams under 2Lts. MICHELMORE & BRUNSDEN & dug in about H 23 a 7½.6½ | |
| | | | Brigade went through MONCHY twice, also the Cavalry, but were driven out by shell fire | |
| | | 9 am | 2Lt THOMSON & 2 guns went up to H29. b 8.2 Rest of Company carrying S.A.A. from RAILWAY TRIANGLE to sunken cross road in H23.b. | |
| | | | Heavy fall of snow commenced about 4 pm. & continued for some time | |
| | | | Much aeroplane activity | |
| | | 5 pm | Heard 15th Division was to be relieved by 17th Division during the night | |
| | | 9 pm | Heard 50th Brigade were to relieve & guides sent out | |
| | | | Very cold night much snow. | |

A5834 Wt. W4973/M687 750,000 8/16 D. D. & L. Ltd. Forms/C.2118/13.

Army Form C. 2118. 16

Instructions regarding War Diaries and Intelligence Summaries are contained in F. S. Regs., Part II. and the Staff Manual respectively. Title pages will be prepared in manuscript.

# WAR DIARY
*or*
# INTELLIGENCE SUMMARY.
*(Erase heading not required.)*

| Place | Date | Hour | Summary of Events and Information | Remarks and references to Appendices |
|---|---|---|---|---|
| FEUCHY | 12.4.17 | 4 am | No relief arrived, heard from 50th Brigade that relief was complete & that they knew nothing about 45th MGC. | |
| | | | All teams instructed to return to FEUCHY & there by 7 am except Sgt ROONEY. | |
| | | | Teams returned to dugouts in old German support line. Snowing hard & ground very heavy. All officers returned to billet in ARRAS. | |
| | | 1 pm | Lts NAWTON & BARNS arrived from DUISANS | |
| | | 3 | Company brought out of O G line into billets in ARRAS & all guns &c brought by Transport to Battle Headquarters. | |
| ARRAS | 13.4.17 | | Men spent all morning getting themselves & clothes clean. | |
| | | | Huge accumulation of Orderly Room papers attended to. | |
| | | 2 pm | Gun cleaning &c | |
| | | 6 | Medals distributed to D Section winners of Company Football Competition | |
| | | | 2Lt KEITH & 2 OR returned from Machine Gun School CAMIERS. | |
| | | | Weather much warmer & more settled. | |
| | 14.4.17 | 9-12 am | Sections paraded under Section officers for gun & ammunition cleaning | |
| | | 2 pm | Sections paraded for inspection of gas apparatus, iron rations & ammunition | |
| | | 830 pm | A & D Sections paraded under Orderly Officer for Baths | |
| | | | Weather fine until evening then wet. | |

Instructions regarding War Diaries and Intelligence Summaries are contained in F. S. Regs., Part II. and the Staff Manual respectively. Title pages will be prepared in manuscript.

# WAR DIARY
*or*
# INTELLIGENCE SUMMARY.
*(Erase heading not required.)*

Army Form C. 2118. 7

| Place | Date | Hour | Summary of Events and Information | Remarks and references to Appendices |
|---|---|---|---|---|
| ARRAS. | 15.4.17 | 10.40 am | Church of England Parade | |
| | | 10. | R. C.'s Parade | |
| | | 11 am | Presbyterian Church Parade. | |
| | | 230 | Company pay. Party of 1 NCO & 15 men burying horses in ARRAS. | |
| | | 7.30 pm | B & C Sections paraded for baths. | |
| | | | Weather very wet & miserable | |
| | 16.4.17 | 9-12. | Cleaning guns, ammunition &c. | |
| | | 2 pm | Company moved into new Billets in new area allocated to Brigade. | |
| | | | Weather wet & stormy. | |
| | 17.4.17. | 9-12 am | Cleaning billets, guns & ammunition | |
| | | 2 pm. | Inspection of Sections in Battle order | |
| | | | 20 O R joined Company from Base & were posted to Sections. | |
| | | | Weather wet & windy. | |
| | | | CO's conference at Brigade in morning. CO. went up line to see 87 Company re relief. | |
| | | 7 pm. | Further CO's conference. Company to go into line on night of 19/20 & attack on morning of 22nd. Preliminary Instructions issued to all Officers. | I |

A5834 Wt. W4973/M687 750,000 8/16 D. D. & L. Ltd. Forms/C.2118/13.

Instructions regarding War Diaries and Intelligence Summaries are contained in F. S. Regs., Part II. and the Staff Manual respectively. Title pages will be prepared in manuscript.

# WAR DIARY
*or*
# INTELLIGENCE SUMMARY.
*(Erase heading not required.)*

Army Form C. 2118. 8/1

| Place | Date | Hour | Summary of Events and Information | Remarks and references to Appendices |
|---|---|---|---|---|
| ARRAS. | 18.4.17 | 9 am | Route march. | |
| | | 2 pm | Inspection of Company by C.O. | |
| | | | weather wet & miserable all day. | |
| " | 19.4.17 | 9 am | Gun cleaning & points before firing | |
| | | 12 " / 12 a | Box respirator inspection & drill | |
| " | | | 2/i/c went up to line to see O.C. 87th Coy re relief. | |
| | | 4 30 | C.O. & 10 teams left ARRAS to relieve 87th Company in the line. 2/i/c & remaining 6 teams stopped in ARRAS. | |
| | | | Weather dull but dry. | |
| " | ~~20.4.17~~ | | C.O. turned out of Headquarters dugout by 44 Brigade & after much difficulty found a fresh dugout | |
| | | | Relief complete by midnight. | |
| | | 11 50 pm | C.O. started out to find gun teams & after some time managed to locate them all. | |
| | 20.4.17. | | C.O. went to Brigade about noon. Bosch artillery very active all the morning | |
| | | 7 30 | C.O. round all 2Lt DICKINSON'S gun positions. Rations arrived at 9 pm. after much difficulty on road & were all away to teams by midnight. | |

A5834 Wt. W4973/M687 750,000 8/16 D. D. & L. Ltd. Forms/C.2118/13.

Instructions regarding War Diaries and Intelligence Summaries are contained in F. S. Regs., Part II. and the Staff Manual respectively. Title pages will be prepared in manuscript.

# WAR DIARY
*or*
# INTELLIGENCE SUMMARY.
*(Erase heading not required.)*

Army Form C. 2118.

9

| Place | Date | Hour | Summary of Events and Information | Remarks and references to Appendices |
|---|---|---|---|---|
| In the Line | 21.4.17 | 3.30 am | CO. went round Lt BARNS guns. Shelling very heavy. Called on 2Lt DICKINSON on way back. | |
| | | | S.A.A. had been unable to get through on previous night owing to road being blocked by shelling. | |
| | | | Lt NAWTON & 2Lt MICHELMORE went from ARRAS to see the Co. in morning | |
| | | 7pm. | 2Lt F.R. KEITH & 2 teams of 'B' Section left with R.S.F's to take up Battle position | |
| | | 7.45 | 2Lt R.J. THOMSON & 2 teams of 'A' Section left with A&SHYs to take up Battle position | |
| | | 6.30 | Sgt SHERWOOD & 2 teams of A Section left for forward Headquarters. | |
| | | 7pm | 2Lt H.H. HENDERSON guided 48.000 rounds of S.A.A. up to CO's dugout. | |
| | | 9. | Capt MORROGH 46 M.G.C. arrived to share Headquarters. Cpl WARD who had been sent to guide him, being killed on the way back. | |
| | 22 | 330 am | 2 Lt BRUNSDEN went round to see all officers & saw to supply of ammunition. He was slightly wounded in the arm but remained at duty. Sgt BUCHAN also wounded | |
| | | 11am | CO went to see Lt BARNS & 2Lt DICKINSON to talk over final arrangements. | |
| | | 2pm | CO had conference with CO's of 44 & 46 Coy re barrage | |
| | | 7pm | Brigadier & Brigade Major called to see CO. with reference to our barrage after 1st & 2nd objectives have been taken. Changed one of our gun positions in front line with 88 Coy on our left, for one of theirs in support line | |

A5834 Wt. W4973/M687 750,000 8/16 D. D. & L. Ltd. Forms/C.2118/13.

Instructions regarding War Diaries and Intelligence Summaries are contained in F. S. Regs., Part II. and the Staff Manual respectively. Title pages will be prepared in manuscript.

# WAR DIARY
*or*
# INTELLIGENCE SUMMARY.
*(Erase heading not required.)*

Army Form C. 2118. 10

| Place | Date | Hour | Summary of Events and Information | Remarks and references to Appendices |
|---|---|---|---|---|
| In the line | 23.4.17 | 4.45 am | Attack launched. | |
| | | | Enemy put over a heavy barrage & also much machine gun fire & attack held up for a time. A second attempt made at 8 am 2Lt THOMSON wounded. Counter attack reported from S.E. & all available guns turned in that direction | |
| | | 2pm | CO. went to Brigade to find out situation. 29th Division on left had their objective & on the left our Brigade advanced about 800x, thence line runs S.S.W. to centre of GUÉMAPPE | |
| | | 4pm | 46th Brigade to go through & take ~~Second~~ First Ger. objective at 6pm. Four guns to give covering fire. 2Lt DICKINSON with 4 guns Lt BARNS with 2 guns on N side of CAMBRAI. Rd & 2Lt BRUNSDEN with 2 guns & 2 guns with Sgt ROONEY. | |
| | | 5pm | 2Lt KEITH reported only himself Sgt STEVENS & 2 men left of his 2 teams | |
| | | 11.30 pm | Brigade ordered all guns to be withdrawn except 4. 2 with Camerons & 2 with R.S.F. 2Lt BRUNSDEN to be in charge of these guns. Remaining officers & men to return to BROWN LINE. | |
| | 24.4.17 | 4.30 am | All teams back in old German line | |
| | | 4pm | 46 Brigade made another attack on 1st objective with 8 of our guns in support. Bosch put over a heavy barrage on to our front line. 2Lt BRUNSDEN badly wounded his runner & two of his teams also being hit. | |

A5834 Wt. W4973/M687 750,000 8/16 D. D. & L. Ltd. Forms/C.2118/13.

Instructions regarding War Diaries and Intelligence Summaries are contained in F. S. Regs., Part II. and the Staff Manual respectively. Title pages will be prepared in manuscript.

# WAR DIARY
*or*
# INTELLIGENCE SUMMARY.
*(Erase heading not required.)*

Army Form C. 2118. 11

| Place | Date | Hour | Summary of Events and Information | Remarks and references to Appendices |
|---|---|---|---|---|
| In the line | 25.4.17 | 4.40 am | CO sent water & rations to forward teams & then visited all teams. Everything alright but had had a rough time during the night. | |
| | | 2.15 pm | Conference of CO's at Brigade. 44 & 45 Brigades to relieve 46 Brigade in front line, one of our guns to be attached to each Battalion | |
| | | 9 pm | Sgt SHERWOODS teams withdrawn & return to H.Q | |
| | 26.4.17 | | Lt BARNS went up to relieve 2Lt DICKINSON. 5 Casualties during night. | |
| | | 2.30 pm | Instructions received that Brigade is to attack CAVALRY FARM at 10.35 pm | |
| | | 7 pm | Reliefs sent up to teams in the line. Bosch artillery very active all day. | |
| | 27.4.17 | 5.45 am | CO. round all guns & teams<br>Barrage guns fired 8.500 rounds during night.<br>No 8 team completely knocked out during the night 3 killed & 2 wounded.<br>attack on Cavalry Farm not a success. Camerons & 44 Brigade advanced rdy in, but Bosch counter attacked & forced them back.<br>Barrage guns ordered to fire bursts during the day. | |
| | | 12.30 pm | CO. 167 Company arrived, they were to relieve 46 Company that night & 44th & 45th Companys tomorrow.<br>CO. went to GUEMAPPE in afternoon to see CO. 44 Company. | |
| | | 9 pm | 2Lt F KEITH took up another team to replace the one knocked out & to make a fresh emplacement. | |

A5834 Wt. W4973/M687 750,000 8/16 D. D. & L. Ltd. Forms/C.2118/13.

Army Form C. 2118. 12

Instructions regarding War Diaries and Intelligence Summaries are contained in F. S. Regs., Part II. and the Staff Manual respectively. Title pages will be prepared in manuscript.

# WAR DIARY
*or*
# INTELLIGENCE SUMMARY.
*(Erase heading not required.)*

| Place | Date | Hour | Summary of Events and Information | Remarks and references to Appendices |
|---|---|---|---|---|
| In the Line | 28.4.17 | 10.30 am | C.O. 167 Company arrived & C.O. 44 Coy, went to Brigade to meet Divisional M.G. Officer of No 193 & relief fixed up. 193 Company to take over our 4 Barrage guns only | |
| | | | Relieving Company arrived at 7.30 pm. & sent off with guides & 4 relieved teams back by 9.15 pm. & went straight to limbers on WANCOURT-TILLOY ROAD. | |
| | | | Teams with Battalions came out with the Battalions & 3 were back by 10 pm but the last one not back until 2 am. These 4 teams & the C.O. arrived back at ARRAS at 5. am. | |
| | 29.4.17 | | Company cleaned themselves & packed limbers | |
| | | 1.30 pm | Company paraded & marched with Brigade to BERNEVILLE & arrived about 3.30 pm. Passed Divisional Commander & the Brigadier on the road. | |
| | | | Men very good billets. Weather a perfect spring day. | |
| BERNEVILLE | 30.4.17 | 9-12 am | Sections sorting out their gun kit & cleaning same. | |
| | | 2-3 pm | Cleaning equipment. | |
| | | 6-7.30 pm | Baths. Weather fine & warm. | |
| | | | Total Casualties for the Month. Officers: killed NIL, wounded 3. O Rank: killed 11, wounded 34, missing 3 | |

A H Wilkinson Major.

CONFIDENTIAL.

Instructions regarding War Diaries and Intelligence Summaries are contained in F. S. Regs., Part II. and the Staff Manual respectively. Title pages will be prepared in manuscript.

# WAR DIARY
*or*
# INTELLIGENCE SUMMARY.
*(Erase heading not required.)*

Army Form C. 2118.

Vol 12

| Place | Date | Hour | Summary of Events and Information | Remarks and references to Appendices |
|---|---|---|---|---|
| | | | 45th Company Machine Gun Corps | |
| | | | WAR DIARY | |
| | | | for month of | |
| | | | MAY 1917. | |
| | | | —— O —— | |
| | | | VOLUME X.I.I. | |
| | | | [illegible signature] | |
| | | | Major. | |

A5834 Wt. W4973/M687 750,000 8/16 D. D. & L. Ltd. Forms/C.2118/13.

Instructions regarding War Diaries and Intelligence Summaries are contained in F. S. Regs., Part II. and the Staff Manual respectively. Title pages will be prepared in manuscript.

# WAR DIARY
*or*
# INTELLIGENCE SUMMARY.
*(Erase heading not required.)*

Army Form C. 2118.

1

| Place | Date | Hour | Summary of Events and Information | Remarks and references to Appendices |
|---|---|---|---|---|
| BERNEVILLE | 2.5.17 | 8.30 10am | Parade for Baths | |
| | | 9-10 | Cleaning billets & streets in neighbourhood of billets | |
| | | 10.30 to 12.30 | Gun cleaning and instruction under Section Officers | |
| | | 2.3 pm | Inspection of kit | |
| | | 3.15 | Company pay | |
| | | | Brigadier inspected billets during morning | |
| | | | 2Lt A. McLEOD joined Company from Reinforcement Camp & 1 3 O R | |
| | | | Weather gloriously fine & warm | |
| | | | 22632 L/C LEES awarded Military Medal. | |
| | 2.5.17 | 8.9 am | Baths | |
| | | 9.12 | Cleaning ammunition & gun instruction | |
| | | 2-3 pm | Inspection of gas helmets, box respirators, Iron rations & ammunition | |
| | | | Weather fine. | |
| | 3.5.17 | 7 730 am | Physical drill | |
| | | 9.12 am | advanced gun drill | |
| | | 2 3 pm | Company & rifle drill | |
| | | | Weather fine & warm. | |

A5834 Wt. W4973/M687 750,000 8/16 D. D. & L. Ltd. Forms/C.2118/13.

2

Army Form C. 2118.

Instructions regarding War Diaries and Intelligence Summaries are contained in F. S. Regs., Part II. and the Staff Manual respectively. Title pages will be prepared in manuscript.

# WAR DIARY
*or*
# INTELLIGENCE SUMMARY.
*(Erase heading not required.)*

| Place | Date | Hour | Summary of Events and Information | Remarks and references to Appendices |
|---|---|---|---|---|
| BERNEVILLE | 4.5.17 | 7-7.30 am | Physical drill A B & D Sections C Section points before firing | |
| | | 9-12 | Advanced gun drill A B & D. 'C' on range. | |
| | | 2-3 pm | A B D Cleaning limber 'C' Cleaning guns & belt filling. | |
| | | 3 pm | Brigade boxing competition commenced | |
| | | 6 | 44 45 46 Machine Gun Coys v Royal Scots at football Royal Scots won 3-0. | |
| | | | Company promotions appeared in Company orders | |
| | | | Commanding Officer proceeded on special leave to England | |
| | | | weather fine. | |
| " | 5.5.17 | 7-7.30 am | Physical Drill B C & D Sections. A Section Points before firing | |
| | | 9-12 am | 'A' on Range. B C D advanced Drill | |
| | | 2-3 | B C D Company & Rifle Drill under Company S M | |
| | | | A Cleaning guns. | |
| " | 6.5.17 | 9 am | C of E. Parade | |
| | | 9.30 | Presbyterians Parade. | |
| | | 2-3 | Belt filling | |
| | | | weather fine & warm. | |
| | | 3.45 pm | Parade for baths. | |

A5834 Wt. W4973/M687 750,000 8/16 D. D. & L. Ltd. Forms/C.2118/13.

Instructions regarding War Diaries and Intelligence Summaries are contained in F. S. Regs., Part II. and the Staff Manual respectively. Title pages will be prepared in manuscript.

# WAR DIARY
*or*
# INTELLIGENCE SUMMARY.
*(Erase heading not required.)*

Army Form C. 2118. 3.

| Place | Date | Hour | Summary of Events and Information | Remarks and references to Appendices |
|---|---|---|---|---|
| BERNEVILLE | 7.5.17 | 9.45 am | Company paraded & marched to WANQUENTIN & arrived in Billets about 12.15 | |
| | | 12.45 | Foot and Rifle Inspection of Company. | |
| WANQUENTIN | 8.5.17 | 9.30 | Company paraded & marched to BEAUDRICOURT VIA HAUTEVILLE, AVESNES & GRAND RULLECOURT & arrived in Billets at 2.15. | |
| | | | No one fell out on the march. | |
| | | | Brigade marched past Divisional General en route | |
| | | | Weather very wet in early part of the day but improved later | |
| | | | Billets good | |
| BEAUDRICOURT | 9.5.17 | 7-7.30 am | Physical drill | |
| | | 9-12 | Cleaning guns & advanced gun drill | |
| | | 2-3 | Rifle & Company Drill | |
| | | | Instructional classes for attached men commenced. | |
| | | 4.45 | Conference of CO's at Brigade H.Q. to discuss Brigade Scheme for next day. | |
| | 10.5.17 | 8 am | 8 Gun Teams parade to take part in Brigade Scheme 2 guns being with each Battalion. Weather delightfully fine. Teams back in Billets about 3.15 pm. | |
| | | | Rest of Company. Gun drill & cleaning. | |
| | | | 2 O.R. proceeded to Army Rest Camp. | |
| | | 5.30 pm | Conference of CO's at Brigade to discuss Scheme. | |

A5834 Wt. W4973/M687 750,000 8/16 D. D. & L. Ltd. Forms/C.2118/13.

4

Instructions regarding War Diaries and Intelligence Summaries are contained in F. S. Regs., Part II. and the Staff Manual respectively. Title pages will be prepared in manuscript.

# WAR DIARY
*or*
# INTELLIGENCE SUMMARY.
*(Erase heading not required.)*

Army Form C. 2118.

| Place | Date | Hour | Summary of Events and Information | Remarks and references to Appendices |
|---|---|---|---|---|
| BEAUDRICOURT | 11/5/17 | 7-7.30 am. | Physical Drill | |
| | | 9-4 | B & C Section on Field Firing Range | |
| | | 9-12 | A & D Advanced gun drill | |
| | | 2-3 pm | Company & rifle drill | |
| | | | Weather very hot | |
| | 12/5/17 | 7.30 am | Parade for baths | |
| | | 9-11 am | Gun cleaning & advanced gun instruction | |
| | | 11-12 | Cleaning equipment | |
| | | 2-3 | Inspection of Sections in Fighting Kit by Section Officers | |
| | | | Instructional classes continued. | |
| | 13/5/17 | | Divisional Horse Show Splendid turnout & weather perfect. | |
| | | | Company secured Second place in Officers Horse Race | |
| | 14/5/17 | 8 am. | Company paraded for Brigade Scheme. 2 guns attached to each Battalion | |
| | | 5.30 pm | Conference of COs to discuss the days scheme | |
| | | | Weather fine & dry | |
| | 15/5/17 | 7-7.30 am. | Physical drill | |
| | | 9-10 | Rifle and Company drill | |
| | | 10-12 | Gun drill & instruction | |
| | | 2 pm | Inspection of Company by the Brigadier Weather fine but much cooler | |

A5834 Wt. W4973/M687 750,000 8/16 D. D. & L. Ltd. Forms/C.2118/13.

5.

Army Form C. 2118.

Instructions regarding War Diaries and Intelligence Summaries are contained in F. S. Regs., Part II. and the Staff Manual respectively. Title pages will be prepared in manuscript.

# WAR DIARY
*or*
# INTELLIGENCE SUMMARY.
*(Erase heading not required.)*

| Place | Date | Hour | Summary of Events and Information | Remarks and references to Appendices |
|---|---|---|---|---|
| BEAUDRICOURT | 15/5/17 | 4.30 | Company pay. | |
| | | 7-7.30 am | Physical drill. | |
| | 16/5/17 | 9-12 | Gun cleaning & instruction. | |
| | | 2 pm | Brigade Sports Weather unfortunately changed & the meeting was unfinished owing to rain. | |
| " | 17/5/17 | 7-7.30 am | Physical drill | |
| | | 9-12 | Cleaning guns & ammunition | |
| | | 2-3 pm | Company & Rifle drill | |
| | | | C.O returned from Leave | |
| | | | Instructional Classes continued | |
| | | | Weather wet & stormy in early part of day, improved later. | |
| " | 18/5/17 | 7-7.30 | Physical drill. | |
| | | | Attached men Points before firing | |
| | | 9 am | Company paraded for route march | |
| | | | Attached men on range | |
| | | 2 pm | Attached men gun cleaning. Company Company & rifle drill | |

2353 Wt W2544/1454 700,000 5/15 D. D. & L. A.D.S.S./Forms/C. 2118.

6.

Army Form C. 2118.

Instructions regarding War Diaries and Intelligence Summaries are contained in F. S. Regs., Part II. and the Staff Manual respectively. Title pages will be prepared in manuscript.

# WAR DIARY
*or*
# INTELLIGENCE SUMMARY.
*(Erase heading not required.)*

| Place | Date | Hour | Summary of Events and Information | Remarks and references to Appendices |
|---|---|---|---|---|
| BEAUDRICOURT | 18/5/17 | 5.30 pm | Parade for Baths. | |
| | 19/5/17 | 8 am | Company on Range | |
| | | 11 am | Inspection of Transport by G.O.C. | |
| | | | Corporal W. HORNBY & 16894 Pte M. DOYLE awarded the Military Medal | |
| | | | Court Martial on 72213 Pte WEIR J. at 6th Camerons Headquarters | |
| | | | Two other Ranks proceeded on leave | |
| | 20/5/17 | 9 am | Church of England Parade. | |
| | | 10.30 | Presbyterian Parade. | |
| | | 10.45 am | Roman Catholic | |
| | | | Weather fine & very hot. | |
| | | | Orders received that 15th Division will join 19th Corps & move to a new area. | |
| | 21/5/17 | 8.45 am | Company paraded & marched to BONNIERES, weather very wet in early part of day but improved later. Arrived in billets about 1 pm. | |
| | | | 2Lt G.H.S. HOPKINS joined from Base | |
| BONNIERES | 22/5/17 | 7.45 am | Company paraded & marched off 8.30 to QUOEUX | |

2353 Wt. W2544/1454 700,000 5/15 D. D. & L. A.D.S.S./Forms/C. 2118.

7.

Army Form C. 2118.

Instructions regarding War Diaries and Intelligence Summaries are contained in F. S. Regs., Part II. and the Staff Manual respectively. Title pages will be prepared in manuscript.

# WAR DIARY
*or*
# INTELLIGENCE SUMMARY.
*(Erase heading not required.)*

| Place | Date | Hour | Summary of Events and Information | Remarks and references to Appendices |
|---|---|---|---|---|
| BONNIERS | 22/5/17 | | Arrived in billets about 1 30 Weather wet at starting but improved later. Billets good & showed be very comfortable | |
| | | 5 pm | Company parades for gun cleaning | |
| OUDEUX | 23/5/17 | 7-730 am | Running | |
| | | 9-11.15 | Gun cleaning & drill | |
| | | 1150 1230 | Physical drill | |
| | | 2-3 pm | Rifle and Company drill | |
| | | | Weather fine & very hot 2/Lt J.R. STRANGE proceeded on leave to U Kingdom | |
| | 24/5/17 | | Six teams detailed to go with Camerons RSF & Royal Scots on their scheme. | |
| | | | Attached men continued instructional classes & remainder of Company on Town Majors fatigue. | |
| | | | 26 other ranks joined from Base. | |
| | 25/5/17 | 7-730 am | Running. | |
| | | 9.45 am | D Section paraded & proceeded to Range | |
| | | 9-1230 | A B & C Sections Gun drill & instruction | |

2353 Wt. W2544/1454 700,000 5/15 D. D. & L. A.D.S.S./Forms/C. 2118.

8

Army Form C. 2118.

Instructions regarding War Diaries and Intelligence Summaries are contained in F. S. Regs., Part II. and the Staff Manual respectively. Title pages will be prepared in manuscript.

# WAR DIARY
*or*
# INTELLIGENCE SUMMARY.
*(Erase heading not required.)*

| Place | Date | Hour | Summary of Events and Information | Remarks and references to Appendices |
|---|---|---|---|---|
| QUEUX | 25/5/17 | 2-3 pm | Kit inspection by Section Officers | |
| | | | Instructional Classes for attached men continued. | |
| | | | Weather perfect. | |
| | 26/5/17 | 7am | Running | |
| | | 8.45 am | B Section on Range | |
| | | 9-11.30 | A C D Sections Advanced gun drill | |
| | | 11 a.m | XIX Corps M G Officer visited Company. | |
| | | 2-3 pm | Inspection of Box Respirators by Gas N C O | |
| | | 5 pm | Baths | |
| | | | Instructional Classes continued | |
| " | 27/5/17 | 9 am | C of E Parade | |
| | | 8.50 | Presbyterian Parade | |
| | | | Weather fine | |
| | 28/5/17 | | Brigade Tactical Scheme 10 Teams attached to Battalions | I |
| | | | Remainder of Coy Town Majors fatigue & cleaning limbers. | |
| | 29/5/17 | 6.30-7.30 | Company & Rifle drill | |
| | | 9- | C. D Sections Route march & tactical scheme | |
| | | 3 P.M | General Hill. G.O.C Grantham visited Company. | |

Instructions regarding War Diaries and Intelligence Summaries are contained in F. S. Regs., Part II. and the Staff Manual respectively. Title pages will be prepared in manuscript.

# WAR DIARY
*or*
# INTELLIGENCE SUMMARY.
*(Erase heading not required.)*

Army Form C. 2118. 9

| Place | Date | Hour | Summary of Events and Information | Remarks and references to Appendices |
|---|---|---|---|---|
| QUŒUX | 29/5/17 | 8.45 am | A Section on Range B Section Advanced gun drill | |
| | | | 2Lt G. H. S. HOPKINS detailed for Court Martial at CHERIENNE | |
| | | | weather cloudy & much cooler | |
| | | 4.45 pm | Baths parade | |
| | 30/5/17 | 7 7.45 am | Running | |
| | | 9.30 | Company parade to rehearse inspection by French Commander in Chief | |
| | | 2 pm | Gun drill under Section officers | |
| | 31/5/17 | | Inspection by French C in C Cancelled | |
| | | 6.30-7.30 am | Company and Physical drill | |
| | | | C Section on Range | |
| | | 8.45 am | A & B Sections, Scheme on Brigade Training Ground | |
| | | | Company played 45 TMB in Brigade Competition Result | |
| | | | TMB 4 goals MGC 2 | |
| | | | Weather greatly improved much warmer again | |
| | | | 3226 Cpl HORNBY W. promoted Acting Sgt vice 3161 Sgt SMITH. W to hospital | |
| | | | 72194 L/C McKINNON K " A/Cpl vice 3226 Cpl HORNBY W promoted. | |

A. W. Wilkinson Major

2353 Wt. W2544/1454 700,000 5/15 D. D. & L. A.D.S.S./Forms/C. 2118.

# Tactical Scheme 28.5.17

REF. 15th Div: Map No. 1
WAIL Manoeuvre area 1/20,000

## General Idea

The British Front Line is on the ERQUIERES – WAIL ROAD. The German Line facing it runs N.E. and S.W. through QUATREVAUX

## Special Idea

1. On the night of 27th inst: our Patrols report that there are indications that the enemy is withdrawing and orders are received to push forward with vigour to-morrow and consolidate on the GALAMETZ – ERQUIERES ROAD from Cross Roads in A. 17. B. to A. 17. C. 5. 6

Our Brigade Front is held by 6/7th R. SCOTS FUSRS: from A. 4. D. 1. 8. to A. 4. C. 6. 4. left and 6th CAMERON HIGHRS. from A. 4. C. 6. 4. to A. 4. C. 0. 0. right. The Dividing Line on the objective is A. 17. central.

The 11th A. & S. HIGHRS. will be in reserve on the road running through A. 3.

The 13th ROYAL SCOTS will act as enemy.

2. Two Vickers Guns are attached to each Battalion as follows:-

6/7th R. SCOTS FUSRS: 2/LT: G. H. S. HOPKINS & 2 Guns & Teams of "B" Section
6th CAMERON HIGHRS. 2/LT: A MacLEOD & 2 — " — "D" "
11th A. & S. HIGHRS LT: H. M. BARNES & 2 — " — "D" "
13th ROYAL SCOTS 2/LTS: KEITH & HENDERSON & 2 — " — "A & C" Sections

and will report to O.C. Battalions & receive Orders from them direct

3. All Transport required for carrying Lewis Guns, Machine Guns, & Trench Mortars, will go to rendezvous with Battalions but will move forward when unloaded to WAIL and along the Road as far as GALAMETZ, where it will turn into the Road leading to ERQUIERES and await the arrival of Battalions etc. on completion of Field Day.

2/LT. F. MICHELMORE will supervise the Move and make arrangements to collect all Transport of the Brigade.

4. Brigade Headquarters will be at Road Junction A. 3. B. 5. 0.

5. All ~~Battalions~~ will be in position ready to move at 9-15 a.m

H. M. Wilkinson
Major

26/5/17

Instructions regarding War Diaries and Intelligence Summaries are contained in F. S. Regs., Part II. and the Staff Manual respectively. Title pages will be prepared in manuscript.

# WAR DIARY
*or*
# INTELLIGENCE SUMMARY.
*(Erase heading not required.)*

Army Form C. 2118.

Vol 13

| Place | Date | Hour | Summary of Events and Information | Remarks and references to Appendices |
|---|---|---|---|---|
| | | | CONFIDENTIAL<br>War Diary<br>of<br>45th Machine Gun Company<br>1st to 30th June 1917<br>VOLUME XIII<br>H. Mawston<br>Lieut<br>Commanding 45th Machine Gun Coy. | |

2353 Wt. W2544/1454 700,000 5/15 D. D. & L. A.D.S.S./Forms/C. 2118.

Instructions regarding War Diaries and Intelligence Summaries are contained in F. S. Regs., Part II. and the Staff Manual respectively. Title pages will be prepared in manuscript.

# WAR DIARY
*or*
# INTELLIGENCE SUMMARY.
*(Erase heading not required.)*

Army Form C. 2118.

| Place | Date | Hour | Summary of Events and Information | Remarks and references to Appendices |
|---|---|---|---|---|
| QUOEUX | 1.6.17. | 6.30 | Company Physical Drill | |
| | | 7.30 am | D Section on Range. | |
| | | 8.45 am | 2 Teams of 'C' Section attached to A & S Hrs for scheme. | |
| | | | Remainder of Company gun drill | |
| | | | Instructional classes for attached men continued. | |
| | | | Football Result Brigade Hdqrs 3 MGC 1 | |
| | 2.6.17 | 6.30 | Company Physical Drill | |
| | | 7.30 a | Instructional Classes on Range | |
| | | 8.45 | Remainder of Company advanced gun drill | |
| | | | 2 Lts A. McLEOD & B.C. SIMMONS attended Army attack scheme at AUXI-LE CHATEAU | |
| | | | Weather fine | |
| | | | Football Result 45 F.A. 8. MGC 1. | |
| | 3.6.17 | 8.30 | Church of England and Presbyterian Church Parades | |
| | | 2 pm | Company Pay. | |
| | | | Football Result 45 TMB 3 MGC 0 | |
| | | | Weather fine & very hot. | |
| " | 4.6.17 | 6.30–7.30 am | Physical and Company Drill | |
| | | 9 am | Route March | |
| | | 5 pm | Brigade Concert Party gave a performance in Company Transport Lines | |
| | | | Football Result 6th Camerons 5 MGC 0. | |
| | | | Weather still fine & very hot. | |

A5834 Wt. W4973/M687 750,000 8/16 D. D. & L. Ltd. Forms/C.2118/13.

Army Form C. 2118.

Instructions regarding War Diaries and Intelligence Summaries are contained in F. S. Regs., Part II. and the Staff Manual respectively. Title pages will be prepared in manuscript.

# WAR DIARY
*or*
# INTELLIGENCE SUMMARY.
*(Erase heading not required.)*

| Place | Date | Hour | Summary of Events and Information | Remarks and references to Appendices |
|---|---|---|---|---|
| QUOEUX | 5.6.17 | 6.30 am | Company & Rifle Drill | |
| | | 9am–11.15 | Gun drill & Instruction | |
| | | 11.30 | Physical Drill | |
| | | 2 pm | Inspection of Sections in Fighting order by Section officers | |
| | | | Football Result 11th A&SH 6 45 MGC 0 | |
| | 6.6.17 | 6.30 am | Company & Physical Drill | |
| | | 8.45 am | B Section on Range | |
| | | 9am | Remainder of Company advanced Drill on Training Ground | |
| | | 2 pm | Inspection of Company by CO | |
| | | 3.45 pm | Bath Parade | |
| | | | Weather fine but heavy thunderstorm at night | |
| | | | Football Result 45 MGC 5 45 FA. 3 | |
| " | 7.6.17 | 6.30 am | Company & Physical Drill | |
| | | 8.45 am | A Section on Range | |
| | | 9 am | Remainder of Company advanced gun drill | |
| | | | Lt H.M.BARNS attended Court Martial at Headquarters 11th A&SH | |
| | 8.6.17 | 6.30 am | Company & Physical Drill | |
| | | 8.45 am | C Section on Range | |
| | | 9am | Remainder of Company Gun Drill | |
| | | 2 pm | Cleaning equipment | |
| | | | Football Result 13 Royal Scots 3 MGC 0 | |
| | | | 2 OR returned from MG School CAMIERS | |

Instructions regarding War Diaries and Intelligence Summaries are contained in F. S. Regs., Part II. and the Staff Manual respectively. Title pages will be prepared in manuscript.

# WAR DIARY
*or*
# INTELLIGENCE SUMMARY.
*(Erase heading not required.)*

Army Form C. 2118.

| Place | Date | Hour | Summary of Events and Information | Remarks and references to Appendices |
|---|---|---|---|---|
| QUOEUX | 9.6.17 | 6.30 | Company parade to pack limbers. | |
| | | 8 am | Company parade for Brigade Tactical Scheme | |
| | | | 2 guns attached to each of R.S.F. R.S. & A.&S.Hrs & 4 to 6th Camerons who acted as enemy. | |
| | | | Football Result 11th A.S.Hrs 5 M.G.O. | |
| | | | Weather fine & warm. | |
| | | | 2Lt W C DICKINSON & 2 O.R. returned from 6th Corps School | |
| | 10.6.17 | 8.30 am | Presbyterian Parade | |
| | | 9.15 am | Church of England Parade | |
| | | 10.15 | Roman Catholic Parade | |
| | | 2 pm | Company Pay. | |
| | | | Football Result 6th Camerons 5 M.G.C. 1. | |
| | 11.6.17 | | Inspection of Company by Divisional Commander postponed owing to wet Company carried on with work in billets | |
| | | | Weather improved later in day | |
| | | | Football Result 45 M.G.C. 2 3rd Train A.S.C. 0 | |
| | | | Brigade Concert Party performed for Company. | |
| | 12.6.17 | 6.30 am | Packing limbers | |
| | | 9 am | Parade under Section Officers | |
| | | 10.30 | Company parade in full marching order | |

A5834 Wt. W4973/M687 750,000 8/16 D. D. & L. Ltd. Forms/C.2118/13.

Instructions regarding War Diaries and Intelligence Summaries are contained in F. S. Regs., Part II. and the Staff Manual respectively. Title pages will be prepared in manuscript.

# WAR DIARY
*or*
# INTELLIGENCE SUMMARY.
(*Erase heading not required.*)

Army Form C. 2118.

| Place | Date | Hour | Summary of Events and Information | Remarks and references to Appendices |
|---|---|---|---|---|
| QUOEUX | 12.6.17 | 12.30 pm | Company parade for inspection by Divisional Commander. | |
| | | | Weather very hot. | |
| | | | 2Lt F MICHELMORE rejoined from Paris Leave. 2Lt F KEITH rejoined from United Kingdom leave. | |
| " | 13.6.17 | | Brigade Field Firing Scheme | |
| | | | A & C Sections with A & S Hrs | |
| | | | B & D " Camerons. | |
| | | | Weather dull & visibility very poor which made it very difficult for guns to get on to targets | |
| " | 14.6.17 | 6.30 | Company Physical Drill | |
| | | 8.30 am | A & B Sections & half Transport parade for route march to Baths | |
| | | 9.30 am | C & D " " " " " " " | |
| | | | 19 other ranks joined Company from Base. | |
| " | 15.6.17 | 6.30 am | Nos 1 & 2 of all gun teams Points before firing remainder Company & Physical Drill. | |
| | | 8.45 am | All Nos 1 & 2 on range. | |
| | | 9-11 am | Remainder of Company Gun Instruction | |
| | | 11.15-12.30 | Musketry Instruction | |
| | | 2 pm | Belt Filling & Cleaning equipment | |
| | | 3.45 pm | Parade for Baths. | |

A5834 Wt. W4973/M687 750,000 8/16 D. D. & L. Ltd. Forms/C.2118/13.

Army Form C. 2118.

Instructions regarding War Diaries and Intelligence Summaries are contained in F. S. Regs., Part II. and the Staff Manual respectively. Title pages will be prepared in manuscript.

# WAR DIARY
*or*
# INTELLIGENCE SUMMARY.
*(Erase heading not required.)*

| Place | Date | Hour | Summary of Events and Information | Remarks and references to Appendices |
|---|---|---|---|---|
| QUOEUX | 16.6.17 | 6.30 am | Company Physical Drill | |
| | | 8.30 am | Half Company on Rifle Range | |
| | | | Remainder of Company Gun drill & instruction | |
| | | 2.3 pm | Cleaning Kit & Equipment | |
| | | | Weather very hot. Sent to draw money to pay the Company, but after waiting from 3.45 to 6 p.m. told no more money left. | |
| — | 17.6.17. | | Church Parades. R Cs 8 a.m. Presbyterian 8.30 and C of E 11.15 a.m | |
| — | 18.6.17. | 7. am | 2 Teams attached to Battalions for schemes. | |
| | | 6.30 | Remainder of Coy. Coy. & Physical Drill. | |
| | | 9 am | Gun drill & instruction | |
| | | 10 am | No. 72207. Pte Elder R. tried by F.G.C.M. Case dismissed. | |
| | | 8 pm | Brigadier & Brigade major to dinner. | |
| | 19.6.17 | 4 am | Reveille. | |
| | | 5.30 | Company Parade. Teams 3. 4. 7. 8 9. 10. 15. 16. on Range then on to Baths at 9. a.m | |
| | | | Teams 1.2. 5 6. 11 12 13 & 14. Field Firing near VAUX with 2 Battalions. | |
| | | | Weather cooler. | |
| | | 10. am | Lt Newton & 2/Lt Henderson to Paris for 3 days leave | |
| | 20.6.17. | 6.30 am | Company & Physical Drill. | |
| | | 9 am | Gun Instruction | |
| | | 11 am | Packing Limbers. | |

A5834 Wt. W4973/M687 750,000 8/16 D. D. & L. Ltd. Forms/C.2118/13.

Instructions regarding War Diaries and Intelligence Summaries are contained in F. S. Regs., Part II. and the Staff Manual respectively. Title pages will be prepared in manuscript.

# WAR DIARY
*or*
# INTELLIGENCE SUMMARY.
*(Erase heading not required.)*

Army Form C. 2118.

| Place | Date | Hour | Summary of Events and Information | Remarks and references to Appendices |
|---|---|---|---|---|
| QUOEUX | 20.6.17 | 2 p.m. | Sections inspected in marching order by C.O. Orders for the move tomorrow received, & Company movement Orders issued | I |
| | | 3.30 p.m. | One 1 per section under 2/Lts Hopkins & MacLeod. Paraded for Tactical Scheme with Battalions. | |
| | | 7.30 | Corporal Parkin. Ptes Priestly + [illegible] interviewed by Brigadier for Commissions. | |
| | | 6 p.m | Brigade Concert Party here. stopped by Rain after ½ hour. | |
| | 21.6.17. | 9 a.m | Corporal Pritchard to III Army School. Packing Limbers & cleaning Billets etc. | |
| | | 5 p.m | Company Parade to march to PETIT HOUVIN, as per movement orders. Very heavy thunderstorm just after starting. then cleared up | I |
| PETIT HOUVIN. | | 10.5 | arrived. Tea all ready for the Company. Foot inspection. | |
| — | 22.6.17 | | Rain on + off all day. | |
| | | 10. a.m | Rifle inspection. | |
| | | 2 p.m | Parade for march to CONTEVILLE via St POL | |
| CONTEVILLE | 23-6-17 | 2 pm | Company Parade for march to LA COUTURE. Arrived about 6 pm billets very scarce as village very small. | |
| | | 10.30 am | Rifle Inspection and Foot Inspection. | |
| | | 11.30 am | Major H.W. Wilkinson left to join Div'l H'qrs. as Div'l M.G. Officer. Lieut H.M. Burns took over command of Company owing to Lieut Newton being on leave 2/Lieut Mickelmore acting as second in Command | |

A5834 Wt. W4973/M687 750,000 8/16 D. D. & L. Ltd. Forms/C.2118/13.

Army Form C. 2118.

# WAR DIARY
*or*
# INTELLIGENCE SUMMARY.
(*Erase heading not required.*)

Instructions regarding War Diaries and Intelligence Summaries are contained in F. S. Regs., Part II. and the Staff Manual respectively. Title pages will be prepared in manuscript.

| Place | Date | Hour | Summary of Events and Information | Remarks and references to Appendices |
|---|---|---|---|---|
| LA COUTURE | 24-6-17 | 10 am | Company employed by cleaning guns and limbers<br>~~Lieut~~ Lieut Nawton and 2/Lieut Henderson expected back from leave but did not arrive having apparently proceeded further in advance to await arrival of the Brigade | |
| LA COUTURE | 25/6/17 | 8.30 am | Inspection of Billets by O.C | |
| | | 9 am | Coy parade for March to AIRE area. Coy billeted at Neuffré | |
| NEUFPRE | 26/6/17 | 2.30 | Reveille. Breakfasts at 3 am. | |
| | | 4.30 | Coy parade for March to PRADELLES via STEENBECKE and HAZEBROUCK. Arrived 10.15 am. Great difficulty in obtaining billets as our area seems to have overlapped the 13th Royal Scots. Coy finally settled down at 2 pm. | |
| PRADELLES | 27/6/17 | 2.30 am | Reveille. Breakfasts 3 am. | |
| | | 4.30 am | Coy paraded to March to WATOU area. Arrived 11 am. Billets very scarce and very little accomodation for Officers. Two Officers forced to bivouac in a field close by the Mess. Lieut Nawton and 2/Lieut Henderson rejoined from Paris leave at 6 pm. Lieut Nawton took over command of the Coy. C.Q.M.S. Lewis left to join 122nd Coy to take over duties of CSM to this Coy | |

Instructions regarding War Diaries and Intelligence Summaries are contained in F. S. Regs., Part II. and the Staff Manual respectively. Title pages will be prepared in manuscript.

# WAR DIARY
*or*
# INTELLIGENCE SUMMARY.
(*Erase heading not required.*)

Army Form C. 2118.

| Place | Date | Hour | Summary of Events and Information | Remarks and references to Appendices |
|---|---|---|---|---|
| WATOU area | 28/6/17 | 7 am | Reveille | |
| | | 8 am | Breakfasts | |
| | | 9 – 12.30 am | Cleaning Guns and Equipment. Section Officers held various inspections Gas Helmet Iron Rations etc. | |
| | | 2–5 pm | Continuation of above inspections by Section Officers and a return showing all deficiencies was rendered to Orderly Room by 5 pm | |
| " | 29/6/17 | 6.30 – 7.30 am | Physical Drill | |
| | | 9 – 12.30 pm | Gun Cleaning & Instruction | |
| | | 10 am | The following Officers attended a Field General Court Martial at Hqrs 11th A & S Highrs for various duties – Lieut H. M. Boons. Privates F. Micklemore B.C. Simmonds G.H.S. Hopkins. CSM. Lukes P. Sergt. Rooney Cpl Miller | |
| | | 2–5 pm | Packing limbers 6 pm. Private Keith left for Anti Aircraft Course at Hqrs 21 Squad. R.F.C. Coy pay at 2 pm while packing limbers | |
| " | 30/6/17 | 1.30 am | Reveille. Breakfast on line of March at 8 am | |
| | | 2.45 am | Coy Paraded to March to BROXEELE area. arrived 1.20 pm Rain fell during practically the whole of the march. Billets much better plenty of room for men. | |

H. Mawston Lieut
Commanding 45th Machine Gun Coy

A5834 Wt. W4973/M687 750,000 8/16 D. D. & L. Ltd. Forms/C.2118/13.

45/15

Army Form C. 2118.

Instructions regarding War Diaries and Intelligence Summaries are contained in F. S. Regs., Part II. and the Staff Manual respectively. Title pages will be prepared in manuscript.

# WAR DIARY

*or*

~~INTELLIGENCE SUMMARY.~~

*(Erase heading not required.)*

Vol 14

| Place | Date | Hour | Summary of Events and Information | Remarks and references to Appendices |
|---|---|---|---|---|
| | | | CONFIDENTIAL<br>WAR DIARY<br>of<br>45th MACHINE GUN COMPANY<br>1st to 31st July 1917<br>VOLUMN XIV<br><br>[signature]<br>Capt<br>O.C. 45th Machine Gun Company | |

A5834 Wt. W4973/M687 750,000 8/16 D. D. & L. Ltd. Forms/C.2118/13.

Instructions regarding War Diaries and Intelligence Summaries are contained in F. S. Regs., Part II. and the Staff Manual respectively. Title pages will be prepared in manuscript.

# WAR DIARY
*or*
# INTELLIGENCE SUMMARY.
*(Erase heading not required.)*

Army Form C. 2118.

| Place | Date | Hour | Summary of Events and Information | Remarks and references to Appendices |
|---|---|---|---|---|
| | 1/7/17 | 10am | Presbyterian Church Parade at 10.30 with 11th Argyll + Suth. Highrs | |
| Brocourt Area | | 2pm | Coy paraded at Transport Lines to practise Pack Mule Drill | |
| | 2/7/17 | 8.45am | Coy paraded at Transport Lines for Pack Animal Drill | |
| | | 10am | Inspection of Coy at Pack Animal Drill by G.O.C. 45th Inf. Bde. Two teams from each Section at work | |
| | | 8.45 –12.30 | Remainder of Coy Gun Drill Cleaning and Instruction 2-3pm Inspection of Sections by Section Officers. | |
| | 3/7/17 | 8.45am –12.30pm | Coy paraded for Coy Scheme on Training Area, visited by Corps Commander and G.O.C. 45th Inf. Bde | |
| | | 2-3pm | Inspection of Coy in Fighting Order by C.O. New fighting order instituted, Haversack changed for the valise | |
| | 4/7/17 | 7.30am | Two teams from A and C Sections and four teams from D Section paraded for Brigade Scheme. | |
| | | 2-3pm | Brigade Gas N.C.O. Inspected helmets of Company. | |
| | | 10am | 2/Lieut MACLEOD detailed as a member of a Field General Court Martial which assembled at HQrs of 13th Royal Scots. 6pm 2/Lieut Keith rejoined from Anti-Aircraft Course | |
| | 5/7/17 | 7.45 –9am | Gun Drill Repacking and overhauling Contents of Limbers to Check S.A.A. etc. | |
| | | 2-3pm | Coy and Rifle Drill | |

2353 Wt. W2544/1454 700,000 5/15 D. D. & L. A.D.S.S./Forms/C. 2118.

Army Form C. 2118.

Instructions regarding War Diaries and Intelligence Summaries are contained in F. S. Regs., Part II. and the Staff Manual respectively. Title pages will be prepared in manuscript.

# WAR DIARY
*or*
# INTELLIGENCE SUMMARY.
*(Erase heading not required.)*

| Place | Date | Hour | Summary of Events and Information | Remarks and references to Appendices |
|---|---|---|---|---|
| | 6-7-17 | 8am | Four teams of D. Section, and two of A and C Sections paraded for Brigade Scheme | |
| | | 9-12.30pm | Remainder of Coy under Brigade Physical Training Instructor for Physical Drill and Bayonet Fighting. | |
| | | 2-3pm | Instructional Class for N.C.O.s under Brigade Instructor. | |
| | 7-7-17 | 9am | Physical Training | |
| | | 10-11am | Bayonet Fighting | |
| | | 11-12pm | Rifle and Coy. Drill. 2-3pm Sections paraded under Section Officers. | |
| | 8-7-17 | 9am | Coy paraded to march to ARNEKE to entrain for Toronto Camp | |
| | | 11.30am | Coy Entrained arriving at Camp about 2.30pm | |
| | | 8pm | Coy paraded to move up to the line to relieve 44th. M.G. Coy. Nine teams with ten Guns in the line remainder at Company HQrs at Ecole. Relief Completed at 2.30am 9/7/17. Enemy very quiet all night. | |
| | 9-7-17 | 9.30am | C.O. visited Lieuts. Hopkins Dickinson and Keith. and went round their Guns returning to HQrs about 1.15pm. | |
| | | 5pm | Corps Machine Gun Officer visited HQrs | |
| | | 12 mdt | Transport Arrived with rations. Enemy Artillery and our own became very active about | |

2353 Wt. W2544/1454 700,000 5/15 D. D. & L. A.D.S.S./Forms/C. 2118.

Instructions regarding War Diaries and Intelligence Summaries are contained in F. S. Regs., Part II. and the Staff Manual respectively. Title pages will be prepared in manuscript.

# WAR DIARY
*or*
# INTELLIGENCE SUMMARY.
*(Erase heading not required.)*

Army Form C. 2118.

| Place | Date | Hour | Summary of Events and Information | Remarks and references to Appendices |
|---|---|---|---|---|
| | 9.7.17 (cont) | | this time, but became quieter towards the early morning. | |
| In the Line | 10-7-17 | 2.30 am | CO. round guns Bosch attempted to raid our Front Line about 12.30a.m. | |
| | | | Major Wilkinson arrived at Coy HQ at 3.30am & went round line with CO. | |
| | | | Carrying party took 20000 rounds SAA up to EAST LANE. | |
| | | | Ptes JEPPS & MCDONALD both Officers Servants wounded by Shrapnel while coming to HQ. for rations. | |
| | 11.7.17 | | Fairly quiet day. | |
| | | | Carrying party took 50 Boxes SAA to EAST LANE & at night Gas Bombs to front line | |
| | | 3 pm | Conference at Brigade Headquarters | |
| | | | Rations arrived about 1.30 pm & were duly issued. | |
| | 12.7.17 | | Major WILKINSON came to Company Headquarters ~~with proposed alterations~~ | |
| | | | SAA taken up to positions in HAYMARKET. Rations arrived very late having been heavily shelled while coming up. one limber was knocked out on the way back & two mules hit. | |

Instructions regarding War Diaries and Intelligence Summaries are contained in F. S. Regs., Part II. and the Staff Manual respectively. Title pages will be prepared in manuscript.

# WAR DIARY
*or*
# INTELLIGENCE SUMMARY.
*(Erase heading not required.)*

Army Form C. 2118.

| Place | Date | Hour | Summary of Events and Information | Remarks and references to Appendices |
|---|---|---|---|---|
| In the Line | 13.7.17 | | Divisional MGO & DMGO 25th Division came to Coy HQ re proposed alteration of M.G defence scheme 5 additional barrage guns put in line at I 9 c & gun at DILLY FARM & one on RAILWAY withdrawn. Working party under 2LT H. HENDERSON out from 9 pm until 2 am making fresh emplacements & shelters & then forced to stop by gas shells. All returned to HQ safely. Rations arrived safely shortly before midnight. | |
| " | 14.7.17 | | CO & 2LT HOPKINS finished direction & aiming posts for Barrage guns. SAA taken up to ST JAMES ST | |
| | | 8 pm | 2LT B SIMMONDS arrived at HQ to relieve 2LT FR KEITH & No 16 team left to relieve 15 Team in DILLY TRENCH. 5 Barrage teams of 1 NCO & 4 men of C under 2LT H HENDERSON occupied new | |
| " | 14.7.17 | | positions made on previous night. HQ heavily shelled just as they were about to leave. SAA taken up to these positions & NCO & 8 men sent to finish off shelters. | |
| | | 10 pm | Boche commenced a terrific bombardment with gas shells & 5'9's | |

2353 Wt. W2544/1454 700,000 5/15 D. D. & L. A.D.S.S./Forms/C. 2118.

Instructions regarding War Diaries and Intelligence Summaries are contained in F. S. Regs., Part II. and the Staff Manual respectively. Title pages will be prepared in manuscript.

# WAR DIARY
*or*
# INTELLIGENCE SUMMARY.
*(Erase heading not required.)*

Army Form C. 2118.

| Place | Date | Hour | Summary of Events and Information | Remarks and references to Appendices |
|---|---|---|---|---|
| In the Line | 14.7.17 | | which lasted until 3.30am, much damage done to the School House and its environs. Several men gassed | |
| | | 3.45 am | 2Lt STRANGE arrived but had been unable to get the rations & water cart through & had dumped the contents of limbers W of YPRES. Very heavy fall of rain about this time. | |
| .. | 15.7.17 | 10 am | Major WILKINSON arrived with a party of officers of 47 MGC & arrangements made for relief of 3 gun positions B. D. & E to take place that night. | |
| | | | CO round line in afternoon. Weather much improved & Bosch inclined to be a little more friendly | |
| | | 9.30 pm | Carrying party took S.A.A to Barrage guns. | |
| | | | Carrying party of 47 MGC took S.A.A to Haymarket dump. | |
| | | 10.30 pm | 3 Teams of 47 MGC left HQ to relieve 3 teams of 45 MGC in the line. Relief complete & teams back by 1.30 am. | |
| | | | Rations arrived safely about 11.45 pm. | |
| | | | Fairly quiet night except for a few gas shells | |

2353 Wt. W2544/1454 700,000 5/15 D. D. & L. A.D.S.S./Forms/C. 2118.

Instructions regarding War Diaries and Intelligence Summaries are contained in F. S. Regs., Part II. and the Staff Manual respectively. Title pages will be prepared in manuscript.

# WAR DIARY
*or*
# INTELLIGENCE SUMMARY.
*(Erase heading not required.)*

Army Form C. 2118.

| Place | Date | Hour | Summary of Events and Information | Remarks and references to Appendices |
|---|---|---|---|---|
| In the Line | 16.7.17 | | Bombardment commenced<br>Bosch artillery fairly quiet until about 11 p.m. when the SCHOOL HOUSE & vicinity was heavily shelled just as rations were being unloaded. Water Cart & 4 mules knocked out & Mr Strange's horse had to be let loose owing to the shelling & gas. Barrage guns which were firing on enemy wire also heavily shelled & Sgt BUCHAN killed Pte STIRLING & Pte BRUNTON wounded & several men slightly gassed. Two emplacements knocked in by a tree falling on them. | |
| | 17.7.17 | | Fairly quiet day<br>CO round guns in morning & arrangements made to make fresh emplacements for Barrage guns damaged on previous night.<br>Sgt BUCHAN buried by the gun position where he was killed.<br>Major WILKINSON & Lt BARNS also went round line.<br>Rations up by 11 p.m. after a quiet journey.<br>2Lt H. HENDERSON teams at I 9 6 finished the two new emplacements one NCO & 12 men went as carrying party to 45 T.M.B | |

2353 Wt. W2544/1454 700,000 5/15 D. D. & L. A.D.S.S./Forms/C. 2118.

Instructions regarding War Diaries and Intelligence Summaries are contained in F. S. Regs., Part II. and the Staff Manual respectively. Title pages will be prepared in manuscript.

# WAR DIARY
*or*
# INTELLIGENCE SUMMARY.
*(Erase heading not required.)*

Army Form C. 2118.

| Place | Date | Hour | Summary of Events and Information | Remarks and references to Appendices |
|---|---|---|---|---|
| In the Line | 18.7.17 | 10 am | CO round all guns. | |
| | | | Things very quiet. | |
| | | 6.30 pm | Co's 44 & 46 M.G.C. arrived at HQ re relief on following night. | |
| | | | 8 guns got in position to assist Company of RSF in raid | |
| | | | Guns fired 12,000 rounds & all teams returned safely. Very wet night | |
| | 19.7.17 | | Relief orders sent to officers in line | |
| | | | Very quiet day weather much improved | |
| | | 10.45 pm | Teams of 44 & 46 M.G.Cs arrived at Company HQrs | |
| | | | Relief carried out quietly last two teams back at HQ by 2.30 am | |
| | | | CO last party left ECOLE at 3 am & arrived at TORONTO CAMP | |
| | | | at 5.15 am. Very quiet coming out. | |
| Toronto Camp | 20-7-17 | | Morning spent at rest. | |
| | | 3 pm. | Guns Cleaned and overhauled, contents of limbers checked | |
| " | 21-7-17 | 9-12 noon | Gun Cleaning and Packing Limbers | |
| | | 3.30 pm. | Coy Paraded in full marching order and marched to Camp in WATOU area arriving 6.30 pm | |
| " | 22-7-17 | 9-11.45 am | Gun and Ammunition Cleaning | |

2353 Wt. W2544/1454 700,000 5/15 D. D. & L. A.D.S.S./Forms/C. 2118.

Instructions regarding War Diaries and Intelligence Summaries are contained in F. S. Regs., Part II. and the Staff Manual respectively. Title pages will be prepared in manuscript.

# WAR DIARY
*or*
# INTELLIGENCE SUMMARY.
(*Erase heading not required.*)

Army Form C. 2118.

| Place | Date | Hour | Summary of Events and Information | Remarks and references to Appendices |
|---|---|---|---|---|
| ~~[illegible]~~ Fins Waton Area | 22-7-17 Contd. | 11.45am -12.30pm | Sections Paraded for Clothing Inspection by C.O. | |
| | | 2-3pm | Cleaning Equipment. | |
| " | 23-7-17 | 8.30am | 2/Lieuts Mickelmore and Dickinson proceeded to XIX Corps HQrs to view model of ground in the line | |
| | | 9am | Coy Paraded for route march under Lieut. H.M. Boons returning at 12 noon. | |
| | | 2pm | Coy Pay. | |
| " | 24-7-17 | 9-11.30 am | Coy Paraded under Brigade Gas N.C.O for inspection of respirators and helmets | |
| | | 10am | 2/Lieut. Mickelmore detailed as a member of a F.G.C.M. assembling at HQrs 11th Argyll and Sutherland Highrs. | |
| " | | 11.45-12.30pm | Inspection of Iron Rations and Ammunition by Section Officer | |
| | | 2-3pm | Cleaning Limbers | |
| " | 25-7-17 | 9-11.30 am | Repacking Limbers and Parades under Section Officers | |
| | | 11.45 am | Inspection of Sections in 'Battle Order' by Section Officers | |
| | | 2-3pm | Inspection of Company in 'Battle Order' by C.O | |
| | | 8.20am | Following Officers and NCOs, [illegible] to proceed to Corps HQrs to view Model of Ground. 2/Lieuts. Keith, Simonds, Macleod and Davies, Sergts. Rooney and Ward, Cpl. Combes and L/Cpl. Chilcott. | |

Instructions regarding War Diaries and Intelligence Summaries are contained in F. S. Regs., Part II. and the Staff Manual respectively. Title pages will be prepared in manuscript.

# WAR DIARY
*or*
# INTELLIGENCE SUMMARY.
*(Erase heading not required.)*

Army Form C. 2118.

| Place | Date | Hour | Summary of Events and Information | Remarks and references to Appendices |
|---|---|---|---|---|
| In the Line | 30-7-17 | 1.30 pm | School shelled, otherwise very quiet day. Men got guns and ammunition cleaned and spent best part of days resting | |
| | 31-7-17 | 3.50 am | ZERO Retaliation on back area very feeble. | |
| | | | C.O left HQrs. with 2 reserve teams at 6.10am and proceeded to CAMBRIDGE TRENCH, fairly quiet except for a few Gas Shells. C.O reported to Brigade HQrs and returned to Dugout to await orders to move forward. Heard BLACK LINE had been taken. Barrage Guns under 2/Lts KEITH and HOPKINS had meanwhile advanced to BLACK LINE. 45th Bde. moved forward from BLACK LINE to attack GREEN LINE at 10.18am | |
| | | 11.30 am | Instructions from Brigade as follows "Don't move forward as position very obscure". Heard later Division on right had failed to get GREEN LINE. Camerons on left had got to objective but not the Royal Scots Fus. so Camerons forced to drop back. | |
| | | 3 pm. | C.O. Went to Brigade. No news. | |
| | | 4.30 pm | Sent for by Brigadier, and later C.O. went up line to try and get in touch with teams but without success. Met Cpl. TAYLOR of C Section who informed him 2/LT DAVIES was wounded. Shelling very heavy on both sides. On C.O's arrival back at HQrs. warning orders received of relief by 44 & 46 Bdes. | |

Instructions regarding War Diaries and Intelligence Summaries are contained in F. S. Regs., Part II. and the Staff Manual respectively. Title pages will be prepared in manuscript.

# WAR DIARY
*or*
# INTELLIGENCE SUMMARY.
*(Erase heading not required.)*

Army Form C. 2118.

| Place | Date | Hour | Summary of Events and Information | Remarks and references to Appendices |
|---|---|---|---|---|
| | 25-7-17 cont. | 6.30pm | Voluntary Service and Celebration of Holy Communion for C of E | |
| | 26-7-17 | 8.45am | Coy Paraded to March to Toronto Camp Area arriving at 11.30 am | |
| | | | Day spent resting and settling down in Camp. Latrines dug etc. | |
| Toronto Camp Area | 27-7-17 | 9am -12noon | Gun Cleaning and Rifle Inspection. Parade under Section Officers Gas Helmet Drill etc. | |
| | | 10am | 2/Lieut. Dickinson detailed as member of F.G.C.M assembling at Hqrs. 13th The Royal Scots. | |
| | 28-7-17 | 9am | Rifle Inspection. | |
| | | 9.30am | Coy paraded in "Battle Order" for Inspection by Section Officers and C.O. | |
| | 29-7-17 | 9.45am | C.E. Church Parade at Y.M.C.A. Hut Erie Camp | |
| | | 10.45am | Presbyterian Parade at 6th Cam. Highrs Camp. | |
| | | 3.30pm | Teams 1 and 2 under 2/Lieut. Mickelmore reported to O.C. 6/7th R. Scots Fus. | |
| | | | Teams 13 and 15 under 2/Lieut. Dickinson reported to O.C. 6th Cam. Highrs. | |
| | | | Teams 14 and 16 under 2/Lieut. Macleod reported to O.C. 13th Bn. Royal Scots. | |
| | | | Teams 11 and 12 under 2/Lieut. Davies reported to O.C. 11th A. & Suth. Highrs. | |
| | | 9.35pm | Teams 5 6 7 8 under 2/Lt. Keith and Teams 9 and 10 under 2/Lt. Hopkins and Teams 3 and 4 under 2/Lt. Simmonds proceeded to Ecole with C.O. Arrived about midnight after a very quiet journey except for being held up by Artillery Limbers in HARRINGTON ROAD. Men's quarters quite good, Officers not so well off. | |

Instructions regarding War Diaries and Intelligence Summaries are contained in F. S. Regs., Part II. and the Staff Manual respectively. Title pages will be prepared in manuscript.

# WAR DIARY
*or*
# INTELLIGENCE SUMMARY.
*(Erase heading not required.)*

Army Form C. 2118.

| Place | Date | Hour | Summary of Events and Information | Remarks and references to Appendices |
|---|---|---|---|---|
| In the line | 31/7/17 | 11pm | Received relief orders and later instructions to vacate Coy. H.Qrs. dugout and move to a trench near Piccadilly, left dugout at 5am. Raining with rain and all ranks at H.Qrs. got wet through. C.O. sent 4 runners to get in touch with Officers. Several men returned wounded but no information received until runner from 2/LT DICKINSON arrived. Information received that 2/LT. HOPKINS had been killed. Messages also received from 2/LTS KEITH and MICHELMORE but no news of 2/LT MACLEOD. C.O. went to Brigade H.Qrs. and was told to withdraw all guns except those with Camerons & Royal Scots which would remain and come out that night with these battalions. C.O. sent these instructions to Officers concerned and received permission to return to old H.Qrs in dugout near railway. | |
| | | | Casualties for 31/7/17. Offrs. 1 Killed<br>1. Wounded.<br>O. Ranks. 3 Killed<br>22 wounded.<br>2. Missing (believed Killed)<br>7. Missing<br>Total. 2. Offrs. 34 Other Ranks. | |

H. Claw[illegible]
Capt.
O.C. 45th Machine Gun Coy

45
15

Army Form C. 2118.

Instructions regarding War Diaries and Intelligence Summaries are contained in F. S. Regs., Part II, and the Staff Manual respectively. Title pages will be prepared in manuscript.

# WAR DIARY
*or*
~~INTELLIGENCE SUMMARY.~~
*(Erase heading not required.)*

Vol 15

| Place | Date | Hour | Summary of Events and Information | Remarks and references to Appendices |
|---|---|---|---|---|
| | | | CONFIDENTIAL | |
| | | | WAR DIARY | |
| | | | OF | |
| | | | 45th Machine Gun Company | |
| | | | 1st to 31st August 1917 | |
| | | | VOLUMN XV | |
| | | | [signature] Capt | |
| | | | O. C. 45th Machine Gun Coy. | |

D. D. & L., London, E.C.
(A7883) Wt W8c9/M1672 350,000 4/17 Sch 52a Forms/C/2118/14

Instructions regarding War Diaries and Intelligence Summaries are contained in F. S. Regs., Part II. and the Staff Manual respectively. Title pages will be prepared in manuscript.

# WAR DIARY
*or*
# INTELLIGENCE SUMMARY.
(*Erase heading not required.*)

Army Form C. 2118.

| Place | Date | Hour | Summary of Events and Information | Remarks and references to Appendices |
|---|---|---|---|---|
| In the Line | 1/8/17 | 12 30pm | DM.G.O. visited Coy HQrs. Enemy counter-attacked in evening. 2/Lt DICKINSON returned with his two Guns | |
| | | | CO went to Brigade with 2/Lt DICKINSON and Brigadier ordered 4 Guns to C 30 central. Four Guns under 2/Lts DICKINSON and SIMMONDS who received orders that they were to report to HQrs of R. Scots Fusrs and A&S Hghrs respectively. 2/Lt DICKINSON had one Gun put out of action before reaching his destination. 2/Lt KEITH arrived back with the remainder of his teams about 5am and also heard from 2/Lt MICHELMORE with R. Scots Fusrs and from 2/Lt SIMMONDS with A&S Hghrs. | |
| | | 8 30pm | CO went to Brigade. Party under 2/Lt KEITH sent to Brigade Ration Dump to draw Coys rations. | |
| | | 10am | 2/Lt MICHELMORE arrived back at HQrs. Enemy shelling very heavy all morning. | |
| | | | C.O. sent out parties to find some lost Gun Kit, and they found one Gun and Tripod and several Belt Boxes | |
| | | 4pm | C.O. visited G.O.C. 47th Bde to inform him of position of MGs in line | |
| | | 6 30pm | Relief Orders arrived Company to withdraw at 8 40pm. | |
| | | | Many men returned during day, but no news of 2/Lt MACLEOD who must be either a prisoner | |

2353 Wt. W2544/1454 700,000 5/15 D. D. & L. A.D.S.S./Forms/C. 2118.

Army Form C. 2118.

Instructions regarding War Diaries and Intelligence Summaries are contained in F. S. Regs., Part II. and the Staff Manual respectively. Title pages will be prepared in manuscript.

# WAR DIARY
*or*
# INTELLIGENCE SUMMARY.
(*Erase heading not required.*)

| Place | Date | Hour | Summary of Events and Information | Remarks and references to Appendices |
|---|---|---|---|---|
| In the line | 1/8/17 contd | | or killed or wounded | |
| | | 7pm | A runner and three men sent to help Ptr DICKINSONS teams out. | |
| | | 8.30pm | All men except those in the line left CAMBRIDGE TRENCH for ECOLE to dump Guns etc and then march to H16. C.O. CSM and two signallers waited for return of teams in line. | |
| | | 10pm | All teams from line had arrived | |
| | | 10.30pm | Left Dugout and proceeded by Railway and MENIN ROAD to ECOLE and left all Guns etc. Then proceeded to point mentioned in Brigade Relief orders but found no Guide as mentioned, consequently Coy wandered about for some time | |
| | | | Finally found L/Cpl LARKIN who directed Coy to TORONTO CAMP | |
| | 3/8/17 | 3.30am | Coy arrived tired out and wet through at TORONTO CAMP. Very little accommodation but made the best of it. | |
| | | | Casualties 1/8/17 1 Off. missing (believed Killed) | |
| | | | 3 O.R. Killed | |
| | | | 3 O.R. Wounded | |
| | | | 3 O.R. Missing | |
| | | | Casualties 2/8/17 3 O.R. Wounded | |

Instructions regarding War Diaries and Intelligence Summaries are contained in F. S. Regs., Part II. and the Staff Manual respectively. Title pages will be prepared in manuscript.

# WAR DIARY
*or*
# INTELLIGENCE SUMMARY.
*(Erase heading not required.)*

Army Form C. 2118.

| Place | Date | Hour | Summary of Events and Information | Remarks and references to Appendices |
|---|---|---|---|---|
| TORONTO CAMP | 3/8/17 | | Coy spent morning resting | |
| | | 7.45 pm | Coy paraded and marched to entrain for WINNEZEELE arriving 7pm | |
| WINNEZEELE | 4/8/17 | 9.30 am | Foot & Rifle Inspections by Section Officers. | |
| | | 10-12.30 pm | Gun Cleaning and checking contents of limbers | |
| | | 2-3 pm | Cleaning Equipment. | |
| | 5/8/17 | 10.30 am | C.E. Church Parade. | |
| | | 11 am. | R.C. and Presbyterian Parades. | |
| | | 2-4 pm. | Gun and Ammn. Cleaning. | |
| | 6/8/17 | 9-11.30 pm | Cleaning Guns and Ammunition | |
| | | 11.30-12.30 pm | Inspection of Box Respirators and PH Helmets and Iron Rations. | |
| | | 2-3 pm | Coy Pay. | |
| | 7/8/17 | 9-11.30 | Cleaning Guns Ammunition and Equipment. | |
| | | 11.45-12.30 | Box Respirator Drill | |
| | | 2-3 pm | Coy Drill. | |
| | 8/8/17 | 9-10 | Cleaning Equipment for Inspection | |
| | | 10-11 | Inspection of Section in Drill order by Section Officers. | |

Instructions regarding War Diaries and Intelligence Summaries are contained in F. S. Regs., Part II. and the Staff Manual respectively. Title pages will be prepared in manuscript.

# WAR DIARY
*or*
# INTELLIGENCE SUMMARY.
*(Erase heading not required.)*

Army Form C. 2118.

| Place | Date | Hour | Summary of Events and Information | Remarks and references to Appendices |
|---|---|---|---|---|
| WINNEZEELE | 8/8/17 contd. | 11.15 - 12 p | Inspection of Coy in Drill order by C.O. | |
| | | 3.10 pm | Inspection of Coy by G.O.C. Divn. | |
| | 9/8/17 | 8.45 - 9.45 am | Physical Drill under 2/Lt MICHELMORE | |
| | | 10 - 12.30 pm | Coy Paraded for Inspection of Respirators by Divl Gas N.C.O. | |
| | | 2-3 pm | Advanced Gun Drill under Section Officer | |
| | 10/8/17. | 9 - 9.30 am | Section Drill under Section Officers. | |
| | | 9.30 - 10.15 am | Coy Drill under Lt H.M. BARNS | |
| | | 10.30 - 12.30 p | Gun Cleaning and Instruction. | |
| | | 2-3 | Gun Drill (Advanced). | |
| | | 5.30 pm | 20 men per Section and 20 Drivers to baths. | |
| | 11/8/17 | 9-10 am | Physical Drill | |
| | | 10.15 - 12.30 pm | Gun Drill and Instruction. | |
| | | 2-3 pm | Coy & Rifle Drill | |
| | 12/8/17 | 9.30 am | Presby. Church Parade. | |
| | | 10.30 | C.E. Church Parade | |
| | | 10.45 | Roman Catholic Parade. | |
| | 13/8/17 | 8.45 am | Coy paraded for Route March arriving back at Camp at 12 noon | |
| | | 2.45 p | Coy Paraded with Transport for inspection by Brigadier. | |

A5834 Wt. W4973/M687 750,000 8/16 D. D. & L. Ltd. Forms/C.2118/13.

Instructions regarding War Diaries and Intelligence Summaries are contained in F. S. Regs., Part II. and the Staff Manual respectively. Title pages will be prepared in manuscript.

# WAR DIARY
*or*
# INTELLIGENCE SUMMARY.

*(Erase heading not required.)*

Army Form C. 2118.

| Place | Date | Hour | Summary of Events and Information | Remarks and references to Appendices |
|---|---|---|---|---|
| Winnezeele | 13.8.17 | 9-11.15 | Lecture on ammunition by Section Officers. | |
| | | 11.30-12.30 | Physical Training. | |
| | | 2-3 | Company & Squad drill | |
| | 14.8.17 | 9-12.30 AM | Inspection of gas helmets by Div: Gas N.C.O. | |
| | | 2-3 PM. | Musketry & Immediate action. | |
| | 15.8.17 | 5 A.M. | Captain Hawker proceeded on leave to U.K.<br>Lt Barnes took over command of Company.<br>2Lt Strange 2nd in command. | |
| | | 9-11.30 AM | Guns Cleaning | |
| | | 2-30 PM | Packing Limbers | |
| | 16.8.17 | 9-12 AM | Cleaning up Camp. | |
| | | 1.30 PM. | Company paraded and marched to TORONTO Camp on WATOU-POPERINGHE Switchroad. arriving at that Camp at 8.30 P.M. | |
| | 17.8.17 | 9 A.M. | Foot inspection.<br>Company under orders to proceed to the trenches.<br>C.O. attended conference at Brigade. | |
| | 18.8.17 | 9.30 AM | Inspection of Company in new fighting order by C.O. | |
| | | 11 AM | Conference of all Officers & Section commanders. | |
| | | 2-30 PM | Gun cleaning and checking of ammunition. | |
| | 19.8.17 | 9 AM | Inspection of rifles & revolvers. | |
| | | 2-3 PM | Points before firing & precautions when going into the line. | |
| | | 3.30. | The C.O. & 16 gun teams proceeded to the [illegible]. | |

Instructions regarding War Diaries and Intelligence Summaries are contained in F. S. Regs., Part II. and the Staff Manual respectively. Title pages will be prepared in manuscript.

# WAR DIARY
*or*
# INTELLIGENCE SUMMARY.
(*Erase heading not required.*)

Army Form C. 2118.

| Place | Date | Hour | Summary of Events and Information | Remarks and references to Appendices |
|---|---|---|---|---|
| YPRES | 19.8.17 | 8.30pm | Coy arrived at ECOLE and found old Quarters occupied by a Battery of R.G.A. After much time and trouble everybody finally housed in adjacent building. Reported arrival through 46 Bde. | |
| | 20.8.17 | 9 am. | CO. and 2/Lt KEITH left to visit 46 Coy HQrs at HILL COT to arrange for relief. Found most of the Guns to be relieved belonged to 225 Coy. Then visited area given for forward HQrs at IBEX RESERVE and returned to ECOLE about 1.30pm. Found on return orders from Bde. correcting error in relief orders. CO arranged with 225 Coy to relieve 2 Guns and to relieve 46 Coy's 2 Guns with four of ours. | |
| | | 9pm. | 2/Lt HARD and four teams left with guides for FREZENBERG Cross Roads. | |
| | | 9.30pm. | Sergt. LAFFERTY and two teams left with guides for position in neighbourhood of BILL COT | |
| | | 9.45pm. | Received orders from Bde. that remaining Guns and HQrs to move to CAMBRIDGE TRENCH S of PICADILLY. As room very limited orders received later that HQrs and spare teams may remain at ECOLE. | |
| | | 1 am | 2/Lts KEITH and SIMMONDS with four and two teams respectively left for CAMBRIDGE TRENCH. | |
| | 21.8.17 | 9 am | CO visited 2/Lt KEITH at CAMBRIDGE TRENCH | |
| | | 12 noon. | Called at Bde and received orders that Guns at CAMBRIDGE TRENCH and spare gun teams and HQrs should move to IBEX RES after the R. Scots Fusrs. had moved about midnight. | |
| | | 11pm. | 2/Lt JACKSON and four spare teams left for IBEX RES. | |
| | | 11.30. | HQrs moved off and C.S.M. sprained his ankle just outside building and had to be left behind. | |
| | 22.8.17 | 1 am | HQrs arrived at IBEX RES and found 2/Lts KEITH and SIMMONDS had arrived with their teams but no sign of 2/Lt JACKSON who had apparently being wrongly directed | |

A5834 Wt. W4973/M687 750,000 8/16 D. D. & L. Ltd. Forms/C.2118/13.

Army Form C. 2118.

Instructions regarding War Diaries and Intelligence Summaries are contained in F. S. Regs., Part II. and the Staff Manual respectively. Title pages will be prepared in manuscript.

# WAR DIARY
*or*
# INTELLIGENCE SUMMARY.
*(Erase heading not required.)*

| Place | Date | Hour | Summary of Events and Information | Remarks and references to Appendices |
|---|---|---|---|---|
| | 22-8-17 cont. | | by Guide. Enemy shelling heavily with Gas shells and Respirators had to be worn. | |
| | | 2.30am | 2/Lt JACKSON and team arrived safely having discovered correct route. | |
| | ~~[illegible]~~ | 4.45am | Time of ZERO. Attack commenced – Enemy Barrage appeared to be late but strong. | |
| | | 5.45am | 2/Lts KEITH and SIMMONDS left with their teams for position. Enemy shelling heavily. | |
| | | 11am | Cpl Beat arrived from Sergt LAFFERTY with a gun that had been hit through barrel casing. This was replaced from store guns and four men also sent up to replace casualties. | |
| | | 12 noon | Message arrived from 2/Lt SIMMONDS with information that Enemy held BECK HOUSE and BORRY FARM so he had dug in with six teams in a trench near SQUARE FARM. He also reports 2/Lts KEITH and WARD both wounded. | |
| | | 3pm | Bde sent information that we were back practically on our original line, and also sent warning order for another attack at dusk on slightly modified objectives. | |
| | | 3.30pm | 2/Lt JACKSON was sent by CO to assist 2/Lt SIMMONDS. | |
| | | 9.45pm | Message received from 2/Lt JACKSON that he had arrived and also located two of 2/Lt WARDS four teams who were with A&S Highrs, but other two still missing. Terrific fire on both sides opened up at Dusk SOS being used both by us and Enemy. Enemy shelled heavily with Gas Shells. No further news received from any teams during the night. | |
| | 23.8.17 | 9am | Messages received from all teams. | |
| | | 9.30am | Two reserve teams under Sergt PRITCHARD sent to replace two teams belonging to 2/Lt SIMMONDS as the latter were required by A&S Highrs for defence in front line. | |

Army Form C. 2118.

Instructions regarding War Diaries and Intelligence Summaries are contained in F. S. Regs., Part II. and the Staff Manual respectively. Title pages will be prepared in manuscript.

# WAR DIARY
*or*
# INTELLIGENCE SUMMARY.
*(Erase heading not required.)*

| Place | Date | Hour | Summary of Events and Information | Remarks and references to Appendices |
|---|---|---|---|---|
| | 23.8.17 | 3pm. | Hqrs visited by DMGO. | |
| | | 5.30pm | C.O. attempted to visit 6 guns under 2/Lt SIMMONDS but was wrongly directed by guide and ran into heavy barrage opened up by the Enemy, and had to withdraw to Hqrs | |
| | 24.8.17 | | Quiter during morning. Runners arrived from all teams | |
| | | 10am | Message received from Bde to withdraw all guns except six which were to be left in three defensive positions and remainder with Hqrs to return to ECOLE. C.O. took this message personally to 2/Lt SIMMONDS and remainder received their orders through runners. 2/Lt JACKSON moved down to Hqrs to take over charge of six guns in the line and remainder with Hqrs left for ECOLE arriving at 2pm. | |
| | | 5pm. | Conference of C.Os at Bde Hqrs. Details instructions issued for the Capture of BECK HOUSE and BORRY FARM and GUN PITS which still held out. No Div. relief to be expected until these objectives are taken, | |
| | 25.8.17 | 9.30 a. | 2/Lt DICKINSON joined Coy from leave and went with C.O. to IBEX to see 2/Lt JACKSON to find new positions for guns for next attack. C.O. visited Bde. on return and received further instructions regarding machine Guns. | |
| | | 11pm. | ZERO HOUR for 44 Bde. who attacked GALLIPOLI FARM without success. | |
| | 26.8.17 | 2am | 2/Lt DICKINSON left to view forward positions for offensive. | |
| | | 12noon | Major KIRKPATRICK of 42nd DIV visited Hqrs and went round line with C.O. | |
| | | 5pm. | Information received that Coy Hqrs would have to move from IBEX to STABLES as IBEX was required for a Battn Hqrs. | |

Army Form C. 2118.

Instructions regarding War Diaries and Intelligence Summaries are contained in F. S. Regs., Part II. and the Staff Manual respectively. Title pages will be prepared in manuscript.

# WAR DIARY
*or*
# INTELLIGENCE SUMMARY.
*(Erase heading not required.)*

| Place | Date | Hour | Summary of Events and Information | Remarks and references to Appendices |
|---|---|---|---|---|
| | 27.8.17 | 9 am. | C.O. and 2/LT SIMMONDS visited STABLES and found them full of water and unfit for use so fixed new HQrs in a shelter in O.G.1 | |
| | | | Remainder of day spent in completing arrangements for Offensive. | |
| | | 10 pm. | Teams left for new positions in line. | |
| | | 12 midt | In heavy rain HQrs arrived in line to find only 2/LT JACKSON was in position and remaining teams and 2/LTS DICKINSON and SIMMONDS waiting for guides. Heavy rain and terrific shelling on both sides. | |
| | 28.8.17 | 3 am. | News received from Royal Scots that Offensive was postponed indefinitely. C.O. and 2/LT HENDERSON and four teams returned to HQrs. Remaining teams under 2/LTS DICKINSON and JACKSON took up defensive positions again. | |
| | | 9 am. | C.O. received orders from Bde. Major that defensive orders for Machine Guns were as before. | |
| | | 3 pm. | Orders received that Coy would be relieved of 6 defensive positions by 46 MG Coy both that we in turn should relieve Barrage Guns of 225 Coy. Lieut HAMILTON of 46 Coy visited HQrs at 5 pm and arranged relief with C.O. | |
| | 29.8.17 | 9 am. | C.O. visited C.O. of 225 Coy and arranged to relieve their Guns at 3.30 pm. | |
| | | 10 am. | CAPT NAWTON returned from leave visited HQrs. | |
| | | 3.30 pm | Four teams under 2/LTS HENDERSON and SIMMONDS relieved Barrage Guns of 225 Coy and remainder came down from line after relief by 46 Coy and also took up Barrage position | |

A5834 Wt. W4973/M687 750,000 8/16 D. D. & L. Ltd. Forms/C.2118/13.

Instructions regarding War Diaries and Intelligence Summaries are contained in F. S. Regs., Part II. and the Staff Manual respectively. Title pages will be prepared in manuscript.

# WAR DIARY
or
~~INTELLIGENCE SUMMARY.~~
(*Erase heading not required.*)

Army Form C. 2118.

| Place | Date | Hour | Summary of Events and Information | Remarks and references to Appendices |
|---|---|---|---|---|
| | 29.8.17 | 7pm | Relief Instructions received from 46 Bde. Coy to be relieved by 8 Guns of 125 MG Coy on night of 30/31st. | |
| | | 7.30pm | Bde. Major 45th Bde. rang up C.O. on telephone with reference to these orders. | |
| | 30.8.17 | 9am | C.O. went to Mill Cots and arranged with C.O. of 125 Coy to complete relief by daylight as far as possible. | |
| | | 11.30am | C.O. visited offrs. HENDERSON and SIMMONDS and gave them their relief Instructions verbally | |
| | | 8.30pm | Relief complete and duly reported to 46 Bde by B.A.B. code. | |
| | | 9.15pm | Coy marched off from ECOLE to lorries which were at ASYLUM and arrived at HAGGIS CAMP at 10.30 pm. | |
| | 31.8.17 | 10.30am | Rifle and Revolver Inspection. Remainder of morning spent in cleaning up and checking contents of limbers and Gun Kit | |
| | | 2-4pm | Packing limbers and preparing for move | |
| | | | Casualties in Operations YPRES (2nd Phase) | |
| | | | Offr. Wounded. 2 | |
| | | | O. Ranks Killed 13 Wounded 34 Missing 5 | |
| | | | J C Mawdsley [signature] O.C. 45th Machine Gun Coy | Capt. |

D. D. & L., London, E.C. (A7883) Wt W809/M1672 50,000 4/17 Sch 52a Forms/C/2118/14

Instructions regarding War Diaries and Intelligence Summaries are contained in F. S. Regs., Part II. and the Staff Manual respectively. Title pages will be prepared in manuscript.

# WAR DIARY
or
~~INTELLIGENCE SUMMARY.~~

*(Erase heading not required.)*

Army Form C. 2118.

Vol 16

| Place | Date | Hour | Summary of Events and Information | Remarks and references to Appendices |
|---|---|---|---|---|
| | | | CONFIDENTIAL | |
| | | | WAR DIARY | |
| | | | OF | |
| | | | 45th MACHINE GUN COMPANY | |
| | | | 1st to 30th September 1917 | |
| | | | VOLUMN XVI | |
| | | | [illegible] Capt. | |
| | | | O.C. 45th Machine Gun Coy | |

D. D. & L., London, E.C.
(A7853) Wt W809/M1672 50,000 4/17 Sch 52a Forms/C2118/14

Instructions regarding War Diaries and Intelligence Summaries are contained in F. S. Regs., Part II. and the Staff Manual respectively. Title pages will be prepared in manuscript.

# WAR DIARY
*or*
# INTELLIGENCE SUMMARY.
*(Erase heading not required.)*

Army Form C. 2118.

| Place | Date | Hour | Summary of Events and Information | Remarks and references to Appendices |
|---|---|---|---|---|
| HAGGIS CAMP (YPRES) | 1/9/17 | 2.15am | Reveille | |
| | | 4.15am | Coy paraded in Marching Order and proceeded to embus for WORMHOUDT Area. | |
| | | 4 am | Transport paraded to move by road and passed starting point at 4.40 am. | |
| WORMHOUDT | | 9am | Arrived at WORMHOUDT | |
| | | 7.30pm | Coy paraded with Transport and marched to ESQUERBECQ Station and entrained. | |
| | 2/9/17 | 6.30am | Arrived at AUBIGNY | |
| | | 1.30 | Marched to 'G' Huts (ETRUN) arriving 9.15am. Remainder of day spent in Cleaning Guns and settling down. | |
| ETRUN | 3/9/17 | 9-10am | Rifle and Revolver Inspection, also Inspection of Iron Rations and ammunition and Gas appliances | |
| | | 10.15am – 11.15am | Inspection by Section Officers of all Kit and Equipment | |
| | | 11.15 – 12.30pm | Belt Filling | |
| | | 2-3pm | Parade under Section Officers | |
| | 4/9/17 | 9-11.15am | Cleaning Guns and Packing Limbers | |
| | | 11.30–12.30pm | Coy paraded for Inspection by C.O. in Full Marching Order | |
| | | 9am | Lieut KNAKARNS left to visit 10th M.G. Coy in the line to ground Guns to be relieved by 45th M.G. Coy. | |

D. D. & L., London, E.C.
(A7883) Wt W809/M1672 50,000 4/17 Sch 52a Forms/C/2118/14

Instructions regarding War Diaries and Intelligence Summaries are contained in F. S. Regs., Part II. and the Staff Manual respectively. Title pages will be prepared in manuscript.

# WAR DIARY
*or*
# INTELLIGENCE SUMMARY.
*(Erase heading not required.)*

Army Form C. 2118.

| Place | Date | Hour | Summary of Events and Information | Remarks and references to Appendices |
|---|---|---|---|---|
| ETRUN | 4/9/17 | 2.30pm | Coy pay. | |
| | 5/9/17 | 10am | Coy paraded in full marching order to move to DINGWALL CAMP (BLANGY) | |
| | | 9.30am | 2/Lt JACKSON and 20R reported to OC 118 MG Coy to take over above Camp | |
| DINGWALL CAMP (BLANGY) | | 1.30pm | Arrived DINGWALL CAMP | |
| | | 3.30pm | C.O. and LIEUT H.M. BARNS left to visit 100 M.G Coy to arrange relief which was to take place next day. | |
| | 6/9/17 | 12.45pm | HQrs and 8 teams, four under 2/Lts BARNES and CANDY and four under 2/Lt DICKINSON left to relieve 8 Guns and HQrs of 100 M.G Coy in the line. | |
| | | 1am | Remainder of Coy (2 Sections) under 2/Lts SIMMONDS and BARNETT left for [illegible] as Sections in Reserve | |
| | | 2pm | Guides from 100 MG Coy picked up their relieving teams | |
| | | 10.30pm | Relief reported Complete and notified to Bde HQrs accordingly | |
| Left line | 7/9/17 | 9am | CO and 2nd i/c [illegible] left HQrs to visit guns in line. Runners from 2/Lts BARNES and DICKINSON arrived just before their departure. Gun in left sector (2/Lt DICKINSON) fired 1500 rounds. Target – main Track PLOUVAIN. Enemy Artillery quiet during night of 6/7th. | |

D. D. & L., London, E.C.
(A7883) Wt W809/M1672 350,000 4/17 Sch 52a Forms/C/2118/14

Instructions regarding War Diaries and Intelligence Summaries are contained in F. S. Regs., Part II. and the Staff Manual respectively. Title pages will be prepared in manuscript.

# WAR DIARY
*or*
# INTELLIGENCE SUMMARY.
*(Erase heading not required.)*

Army Form C. 2118.

| Place | Date | Hour | Summary of Events and Information | Remarks and references to Appendices |
|---|---|---|---|---|
| In the line | 7/9/17 | 8.30pm | C.O. left to visit Gen in ROEUX WOOD | |
| | | 9pm | Rations arrived by Rail | |
| | | 9.15pm | Issued to Ration Party who left for line about 9.30 | |
| | | 10.15pm | C.O. returned from line | |
| | | 10.30pm | Unusual activity to left of Brigade Frontage, both Artillery and Machine Guns were active lasting about half an hour. | |
| | ~~7/9/17~~ | | Enemy shelled ROEUX WOOD intermittently between hours of 10-12 noon. Also traversed and searched the area with MG fire during the night | |
| | | | Enemy MGs also active firing on CORDITE RES during the night. | |
| | 8/9/17 | 9am | C.O. left to visit teams in line to make arrangements for alteration | |
| | | 9.30am | Divl. MG Offr visited H.Qrs | |
| | | 12 noon | Reserve Section of Coy moved to cutting in Railway within 400 yards of H.Qrs. | |
| | | 2pm | 2/Lt. BARNETT moved up to CEYLON TRENCH to assist 2/Lt DICKINSON | |
| | | 10pm | Considerable activity of enemy artillery and MGs [illegible] on account of raid by 17th Div on left. Quiet after 1 hour | |
| | | | Enemy searched and traversed ROEUX WOOD with MG fire during the night. | |

D. D. & L., London, E.C.
(A7283) Wt W809/M1672 50,000 4/17 Sch 52a Forms/C/2118/14

Army Form C. 2118.

# WAR DIARY
*or*
# INTELLIGENCE SUMMARY.
(*Erase heading not required.*)

Instructions regarding War Diaries and Intelligence Summaries are contained in F. S. Regs., Part II. and the Staff Manual respectively. Title pages will be prepared in manuscript.

| Place | Date | Hour | Summary of Events and Information | Remarks and references to Appendices |
|---|---|---|---|---|
| In the Line | 9/9/17 | 8am | C.O. visited Bde HQrs and went round the line with Div M.G.O. to site new positions | |
| | | 12.30p | C.O. returned with D.M.G.O. to Coy HQrs | |
| | | 9-12am<br>2-5pm | Working party from Reserve Sections extended HQrs and strengthened main shelter | |
| | | 7pm | C.O. left for line. Staying up the line all night and visiting spots for new positions by night | |
| | | | One M.G. in ROEUX WOOD fired 1000 rounds onto Trenches and Sunken Road in I 25 1 | |
| | | | One MG at L4 fired 3000 rounds at usual Target (PLOUVAIN MAIN ST) | |
| | | | Enemy Artillery normal throughout day and night | |
| | 10/9/17 | 7am | C.O. returned from line | |
| | | 2pm | C.O. and 2/Lt BARNS visited proposed site for emplacement at I 25 d 2 2 | |
| | | 7pm | Working parties under Lt BARNS and 2/Lt SIMMONDS left HQrs to construct new emplacements after dark | |
| | | | Working parties under 2/Lt [illegible] and [illegible] out of 7 [illegible] constructed emplacements at | |
| | | | 2 i [illegible] in front of position L8. [illegible] at L2 altered. Two constructed in front of post | |
| | | | at L20. One open emplacement and [illegible] constructed at I 25 d 22 | |
| | | | Two other guns fired 1800 and 1200 rounds respectively on usual targets. | |
| | | | Enemy Artillery Normal | |

Instructions regarding War Diaries and Intelligence Summaries are contained in F. S. Regs., Part II, and the Staff Manual respectively. Title pages will be prepared in manuscript.

# WAR DIARY
*or*
# INTELLIGENCE SUMMARY.
*(Erase heading not required.)*

Army Form C. 2118.

| Place | Date | Hour | Summary of Events and Information | Remarks and references to Appendices |
|---|---|---|---|---|
| In the Line | 11/9/17 | 9am | CO left HQ to visit work done by working parties overnight | |
| | | 10am | Capt [illegible] & [illegible] WYNNE [illegible] visited HQ and were taken by Lt BARNES to [illegible] | |
| | | | WOOD to see positions of [illegible] | |
| | | 1.30pm | CO returned from [illegible] | |
| | | 2.30pm | Summary of [illegible] in the case of the WOOD taken at HQ | |
| | | 3.30pm | CO sent for by Brigadier | |
| | | 5pm | [illegible] under Sergt BLANCHARD left for new position in T[illegible] | |
| | | 7pm | CO left [illegible] | |
| | | 7.30pm | Lt [illegible] and [illegible] party [illegible] completed work started on the [illegible] | |
| | | | [illegible] on [illegible] WOOD [illegible] the place between [illegible] | |
| | | | [illegible] | |
| | 12/9/17 | 3am | Lt BARNS [illegible] TRENCH with C.O. | |
| | | 7am | Working parties under [illegible] and 2/Lt SIMMONS left for [illegible] | |
| | | | CO also left at this time to [illegible] with C.O. | |
| | | | [illegible] of [illegible] WOOD by enemy. | |
| | | | Bombardment of [illegible] TRENCH at [illegible] with Artillery and TM by Enemy | |

D. D. & L., London, E.C.
(A7283) Wt W809/M1672 50,000 4/17 Sch 52a Forms/C/2118/14

Instructions regarding War Diaries and Intelligence Summaries are contained in F. S. Regs., Part II, and the Staff Manual respectively. Title pages will be prepared in manuscript.

# WAR DIARY
*or*
# INTELLIGENCE SUMMARY.
*(Erase heading not required.)*

Army Form C. 2118.

| Place | Date | Hour | Summary of Events and Information | Remarks and references to Appendices |
|---|---|---|---|---|
| In the Line | 13/9/17 | 8.30 | C.O. went round Gun Positions with G.O.C. and [illegible] and [illegible]. | |
| | | 11pm | Work Completed on new emplacement at Trench in I 25 d. | |
| | 13/9/17 | 7.30 | C.O. sent for by G.O.C. | |
| | | 3pm | Unusual activity to the Right of Bde. frontage, in the direction of [illegible] lasting about 1 hour. | |
| | | 8.30pm | C.O. and Capt Barnett 44 MG Coy went round Gun Positions. | |
| | | | Nos of 44 MG Coy left to join teams of 45th MG Coy to be relieved on [illegible] [illegible]. | |
| | | | Enemy very quiet, a suspected relief apparently taking place. ([illegible]) | |
| | 14/9/17 | 8am | [illegible] and two teams left for Div. HQrs to proceed to ST POL [illegible] for [illegible] aircraft work. | |
| | | 10.30am | LIEUT BARNE sent for by Bde Major, C.O. being up the line. | |
| | | 2.15pm | 2/Lt. SIMMONDS left HQrs for STIRLING CAMP as a member of a F.G.C.M. assembling at HQrs. | |
| | | | 2/Lt R.L. [illegible] | |
| | | 3.30pm | 2/LT. WYNNE 44th. MG Coy arrived at HQrs. and took over all stores and shelters. | |
| | | 9.00pm | 44th. MG Coy arrived at FAMPOUX by train and picked up their guides and commenced relief at once. | |
| | 15/9/17 | 2.30am | Relief Complete, reported to Bde. HQrs. through 44th. Bde. All Company left for | |

D. D. & L., London, E.C.
(A7883) Wt W809/M1672 50,000 4/17 Sch 52a Forms/C/2118/14

Instructions regarding War Diaries and Intelligence Summaries are contained in F. S. Regs., Part II, and the Staff Manual respectively. Title pages will be prepared in manuscript.

# WAR DIARY
or
# INTELLIGENCE SUMMARY.
(*Erase heading not required.*)

Army Form C. 2118.

| Place | Date | Hour | Summary of Events and Information | Remarks and references to Appendices |
|---|---|---|---|---|
| DINGWALL CAMP | 15.9.17 | 2.30am | DINGWALL CAMP on completion of Relief | |
| | | 3.30am | Coy arrived at DINGWALL CAMP. | |
| | | 9.30am -12.30pm | Cleaning Guns and Ammunition, and Inspection of Clothing by Section Officers. Anti Aircraft Emplacement located and manned by 1 N.C.O. and 4 men from A Section. | |
| | | 12 noon | Conference of Commanding Officers at Bde. H.Qrs. at LOGAN CAMP. | |
| | | 2pm | LT. H.M. BARNS and 2/LT. H.E. BARNES reconnoitred emergency route to front system in accordance with orders received in conjunction with Bde. defence scheme. | |
| DINGWALL CAMP | 16/9/17 | 9am | Coy. paraded in Camp (A & C Sects) for points before firing. | |
| | | 10am | Coy. left for MOAT ARRAS for Range firing. | |
| | | 2.30pm | Returned to Camp. | |
| | | 10.30 am | 2/LT. SIMMONDS left to commence course at 3rd Army School | |
| | | ~~12.30pm~~ | ~~Remainder of Coy. left for Baths (Mns)~~ | |
| | 17/9/17 | 9-10.30am | Guns and Ammunition Cleaning. Belt Filling. | |
| | | 10.45am -12.30pm | Inspection of Company in full Marching Order by C.O. | |
| | | 12.30pm | Coy Paraded for Baths. | |
| " | 18/9/17 | 9-10am | Inspection of Sections in fighting order by Section Officers | |

D. D. & L., London, E.C.
(A7283) Wt W809/M1672 50,000 4/17 Sch 52a Forms/C/2118/14

Army Form C. 2118.

Instructions regarding War Diaries and Intelligence Summaries are contained in F. S. Regs., Part II, and the Staff Manual respectively. Title pages will be prepared in manuscript.

# WAR DIARY
or
# INTELLIGENCE SUMMARY.
(*Erase heading not required.*)

| Place | Date | Hour | Summary of Events and Information | Remarks and references to Appendices |
|---|---|---|---|---|
| DINGWALL CAMP. | 18/9/17 contd. | 10-15 am -12.30 pm | All NCOs paraded under C.O. for Instruction in Map Reading and use of Compass. | |
| | | | Sections paraded under Section Officers for Map reading and use of Compass. | |
| | | 2 pm | Coy Pay. | |
| " | 19/9/17 | 9-11.15 pm | Mechanism and Immediate Action. | |
| | | 11.30-12.30 pm | Instruction in Indirect Fire by Section Offrs. | |
| " | 20/9/17 | 9 am | Divl Gas NCO Inspected Gas Appliances of Coy. | |
| | | 10.30 am -12.30 pm | Coy paraded under LT. H M BARNS and proceeded to FREDS WOOD for instruction in construction of emplacements | |
| | | 11 am | C.O and 2/LT. HENDERSON left for line to visit 46 MG Coy to arrange relief etc. 2LT T PEARCE joined company from Base | |
| " | 21/9/17 | 9 am -10 am | Physical Drill | |
| | | 10.15-12.30 | Gun drill and instruction in Indirect fire | |
| | | | All company guns sent to ordnance to be overhauled. | |
| | 22.9.17 | 9-10 am | Physical Drill | |
| " | | 10.15-12.30 | Gun instruction + Immediate action | |
| " | | 4.15 pm | 12 NO 1's parade under L/c CAIRNS and proceeded to 46 MGC HQrs to go into line in positions to be taken over next day. | |

D. D. & L., London, E.C. (A7283) Wt W8c9/M1672 50,000 4/17 Sch 52a Forms/C/2118/14

Instructions regarding War Diaries and Intelligence Summaries are contained in F. S. Regs., Part II. and the Staff Manual respectively. Title pages will be prepared in manuscript.

# WAR DIARY or INTELLIGENCE SUMMARY.

(Erase heading not required.)

Army Form C. 2118.

| Place | Date | Hour | Summary of Events and Information | Remarks and references to Appendices |
|---|---|---|---|---|
| DINGWALL CAMP | 23.9.17 | 9 am | Gun cleaning and packing limbers | |
| | | 230 | Teams 6 7 8. 9 10 11.12.13 14 15 16 17 21 parade & proceeded to relieve 46 Coy in Right Sector | |
| | | 245 | Remainder of Company parade & marched to Billets in ARRAS | |
| | | | Relief complete by 7 pm | |
| | | | Following promotions made 35536 L/C DAVIES E to be A/CORPORAL 37335 L/C CROFT to be A/CORPORAL 104373 Pte COLLINS L.D. & 81468 Pte COX E.A. to be A/LANCE CORPORALS. | |
| | | | 2LT W.C. DICKINSON commenced 4 days Gas Course at AGNEZ-LE-DUISANS. | |
| | | | 2LT H. BARNETT & 2 teams of A returned from Anti Aircraft positions at ST POL | |
| | | | LT. BARNS proceeded to U.K. on leave. | |
| In the Line | 24.9.17 | 9 am | C.O. round all guns everything in order & very quiet | |
| | | 6.30 pm | C.O. visited C.O.s of Battalions in Line | |
| | | 7 pm | Headquarters shelled one shell burst in the Mess & killed Ptes WALKER STEWART & RUDGE | |
| | 25.9.17 | 9 am | C.O. round all guns | |
| | | 2 pm | C.O. visited Brigade & later burials of men killed on previous day. | |

Instructions regarding War Diaries and Intelligence Summaries are contained in F. S. Regs., Part II, and the Staff Manual respectively. Title pages will be prepared in manuscript.

# WAR DIARY
*or*
# INTELLIGENCE SUMMARY.
(*Erase heading not required.*)

Army Form C. 2118.

| Place | Date | Hour | Summary of Events and Information | Remarks and references to Appendices |
| --- | --- | --- | --- | --- |
| In the line | 25.9.17 | | Guns at positions 7. 8 & 9 carried out usual night firing | |
| " | 26.9.17 | | Co. round all guns in morning. Very quiet day. Usual night firing carried out | |
| " | 27.9.17 | | Very quiet day weather beautifully fine<br>Night firing carried out according to programme | |
| | 28.9.17 | | Co. round all guns in morning. 2 Places selected for firing on BIT LANE when wanted. Everything very quiet | |
| " | 29.9.17 | 10 am | Conference at Brigade Headquarters<br>Co. round guns in afternoon. weather fine<br>Sgt LAFFERTY awarded DCM. Sgt Beatson the Military Medal | |
| " | 30.9.17 | 10 am | Co. went to ARRAS to arrange relief for following day<br>2Lt W.C. DICKINSON was thrown from his horse & broke his arm<br>Co. round guns in evening.<br>Weather fine everything very quiet. | |

H Dawson Capt
O.C. 45th Machine Gun Company

D. D. & L., London, E.C.
(A5883) Wt W809/M1672 350,000 4/17 Sch 52a Forms/C/2118/14

Army Form C. 2118.

Instructions regarding War Diaries and Intelligence Summaries are contained in F. S. Regs., Part II, and the Staff Manual respectively. Title pages will be prepared in manuscript.

# WAR DIARY
or
# INTELLIGENCE SUMMARY.
(*Erase heading not required.*)

Vol. 17

| Place | Date | Hour | Summary of Events and Information | Remarks and references to Appendices |
|---|---|---|---|---|
| | | | CONFIDENTIAL | |
| | | | WAR DIARY | |
| | | | of | |
| | | | 45th MACHINE GUN COMPANY | |
| | | | 1st to 31st October 1917 | |
| | | | VOLUMN XVII | |
| | | | [illegible signature] | |
| | | | Capt | |
| | 31st October 1917 | | O.C. 45th Machine Gun Company | |

D. D. & L., London, E.C.
(A7883) Wt W809/M1672 50,000 4/17 Sch 52a Forms/C/2118/14

Instructions regarding War Diaries and Intelligence Summaries are contained in F. S. Regs., Part II, and the Staff Manual respectively. Title pages will be prepared in manuscript.

# WAR DIARY
or
# INTELLIGENCE SUMMARY.
(*Erase heading not required.*)

Army Form C. 2118.

| Place | Date | Hour | Summary of Events and Information | Remarks and references to Appendices |
|---|---|---|---|---|
| In the Line | 1.10.17 | 6 am | CO round guns in morning. Very quiet, weather fine | |
| | 1.10.17 | 4 pm | Company relief carried out | |
| | 2.10.17 | | C.O. round guns with Brigade Major. | |
| | 3.10.17 | | Very quiet in line. Heavy artillery & Trench Mortar activity at night especially on right of Brigade front. | |
| | 4.10.17 | | CO round guns. | |
| | | | 2Lt H J BARNETT left to join Company proceeding to EGYPT. | |
| | 5.10.17 | | CO round guns in morning. Weather rather wet and very windy. Some Trench Mortar activity in morning & emplacement No 6 in CHAIN SUPPORT blown in | |
| | 6.10.17 | 5 am | C.O. and 2/Lt JACKSON laid guns for use in Raid which was to take place later. Weather very wet all day. | |
| | 7.10.17 | 9 am | CO and Lt. H.M. BARNS went round guns returning to HQrs at 11 am | |
| | | 11.30 am | O.C. with M.G. Coy with 2/Lt. WYNNE visited HQrs to arrange forthcoming relief. Rain nearly all the day. | |
| | | 5 pm | 2/Lt CANDY left to take over the two guns for use in the Raid | |

D. D. & L., London, E.C.
(A7883) Wt W8c9/M1672 50,000 4/17 Sch 52a Forms/C/2118/14

Army Form C. 2118.

# WAR DIARY
*or*
# INTELLIGENCE SUMMARY.
*(Erase heading not required.)*

Instructions regarding War Diaries and Intelligence Summaries are contained in F. S. Regs., Part II. and the Staff Manual respectively. Title pages will be prepared in manuscript.

| Place | Date | Hour | Summary of Events and Information | Remarks and references to Appendices |
|---|---|---|---|---|
| [illegible] | 8/9/17 | 9am | C.O. left H.Qrs with Lt BARNS to go round Guns. Enemy very quiet all day | |
| | | 9.15pm | ZERO time for Raid by [illegible] A & Suth Highrs. | |
| | 9/9/17 | 10.30am | Bde Major rang up to say our guides had not arrived to meet 44th MG Coy for relief. Relief had been arranged for three o'clock but arrangements were altered by 44 Coy in accordance with Bde Relief table with notification to us. Guides sent off at once and relief proceeded at an earlier time | |
| | | 2.30pm | Relief Complete and duly reported to Bde. Teams marched independently to DINGWALL CAMP under their Officers. | |
| DINGWALL CAMP | 10.9.17 | 9.30am | Inspection of Arms Gas Appliances and Iron Rations | |
| | | 10.30am | Coy Pay | |
| | | 2.5pm | Cleaning Guns and Ammunition | |
| | 11.9.17 | 9–11.30 | Gun and Ammunition Cleaning | |
| | | 12.45pm | B & D Sects paraded under Lt H.M. BARNS and proceeded to Range at Rifle Camp. | |
| | | 2.3pm | C & A Sects ~~[illegible]~~ gun Inspection of Gas Appliances by Bde Gas N.C.O. | |
| | | 3.15pm | B & D Sects. Points after firing | |

D. D. & L., London, E.C.
(A7883) Wt W809/M1672 50,000 4/17 Sch 52a Forms/C/2118/14

Instructions regarding War Diaries and Intelligence Summaries are contained in F. S. Regs., Part II. and the Staff Manual respectively. Title pages will be prepared in manuscript.

# WAR DIARY
*or*
# INTELLIGENCE SUMMARY.
(*Erase heading not required.*)

Army Form C. 2118.

| Place | Date | Hour | Summary of Events and Information | Remarks and references to Appendices |
|---|---|---|---|---|
| DINGWALL CAMP | 12.10.17 | 9am | 11 Men paraded under Orderly Officer and proceeded to ARRAS for boot repair. | |
| | | | Box Respirators of B and D Sections inspected by Coy Gas N.C.O. | |
| | | 10am | NCOs paraded under C.O for Instruction in Indirect Overhead Fire. | |
| | | 3pm | Coy paraded and moved into Billets in Rue du [illegible] ARRAS arriving 3.45 pm | |
| ARRAS | 13.10.17 | 7.45 am | Coy paraded and marched to Baths under Orderly Officer. | |
| | | 10-10.45 am | Cleaning Clothing and Equipment. | |
| | | 10.15 am | Visited by Act. Brigadier and Bde Major, who went round Billets. | |
| | | 11am -12.15pm | Cleaning Guns and Ammunition. | |
| | | 2-3pm | Box Respirator Drill. | |
| | 14.10.17 | 9am | ~~C of E~~ Prot. Parade Service under 2/Lt JACKSON | |
| | | 10am | Parade Service for R.Cs. | |
| | | 10am | Parade Service for C of E under 2/Lt SIMMONDS | |
| | 15.10.17 | 9-10am | Physical Drill | |
| | | 10-12.30 pm | Gun Drill | |
| | | 11am | Major Genl of American Army with Brigadier inspected Coy at work. A. Sect under 2/Lt SIMMONDS demonstrating the different drill movements for Gun Drill. | |

D. D. & L., London, E.C.
(A7883) Wt W809/M1672 50,000 4/17 Sch. 52a Forms/C/2118/14

Instructions regarding War Diaries and Intelligence Summaries are contained in F. S. Regs., Part II, and the Staff Manual respectively. Title pages will be prepared in manuscript.

# WAR DIARY
*or*
# INTELLIGENCE SUMMARY.
*(Erase heading not required.)*

Army Form C. 2118.

| Place | Date | Hour | Summary of Events and Information | Remarks and references to Appendices |
|---|---|---|---|---|
| ARRAS | 15.10.17 | 2.30pm | Gun Cleaning | |
| | 16.10.17 | 9-10am | Physical Drill | |
| | | 10.15–11.30pm | Gun Drill. | |
| | | 2.15pm | Inspection of Nos. 1 and their Guns by Officer from Army Ordnance Corps | |
| | | 4.45pm | Ten Nos. 1. of teams going into line left to take up positions their teams would occupy following day. | |
| | 17.10.17 | 9am | Cleaning Guns. | |
| | | 2pm | Reserve Sections (A & D) proceeded to reserve billets in Railway Cutting. | |
| | | 4pm | Remainder of Coy moved up to relieve 10 Guns and HQrs of 46 MG Coy in the line | |
| | | 8.15pm | Relief Reported Complete. | |
| In the line | 18.10.17 | 9am | C.O. left to go round Guns | |
| | | 9.15am | D.M.G.O. called at HQrs. and went up line with LT. BARNS meeting C.O. at 10am | |
| | | 2am. | Enemy attempted to raid Division on our left without success. | |
| | | 5pm. | C.O. left HQrs. to visit Gun in ROEUX WOOD. | |
| | 19.10.17 | 9am | C.O. left to go round guns | |
| | | 7.30pm | LT. BARNS called at Right Battalion HQrs to explain position etc of Nos. Gun | |

D. D. & L., London, E.C.
(A7883) Wt W8c9/M1672 750,000 4/17 Sch. 52a Forms/C/2118/14

Instructions regarding War Diaries and Intelligence Summaries are contained in F. S. Regs., Part II, and the Staff Manual respectively. Title pages will be prepared in manuscript.

# WAR DIARY
*or*
# INTELLIGENCE SUMMARY.
*(Erase heading not required.)*

Army Form C. 2118.

| Place | Date | Hour | Summary of Events and Information | Remarks and references to Appendices |
|---|---|---|---|---|
| In the line | 19.10.17 | | Our Gun in ROEUX WOOD fired 3000 rounds as per programme | |
| | | | Enemy TMs active during afternoon otherwise very quiet day | |
| | 20.10.17 | 9am | C.O. round Guns in morning | |
| | | | Our Artillery active during afternoon firing on HAUSA and DELBAR WOODS | |
| | | | Our Gun in ROEUX WOOD fired 3000 rounds as per programme during the night | |
| | 21.10.17 | 8am | C.O. went round line with D.M.G.O | |
| | | | Very quiet until late in evening when there was unusual activity on Right Bde frontage lasting about one hour. | |
| | | 6pm | C.O. sent for by Brigade Major. | |
| | 22.10.17 | 9am | C.O. round Guns in the morning | |
| | | | Enemy TMs again active on ROEUX WOOD, enemy Artillery considerably below normal during day. | |
| | | 6.30pm | LT BARNS and 2/LT JACKSON visited No1 Gun off CHINSTRAP LANE. Met Bde. Major on the way up. | |
| | 23.10.17 | 9am | C.O. went round Guns with LT BARNS. | |
| | | | Very Quiet all day. | |
| | | 11pm | Bombardment opened by our Artillery in support of Division on our left who carried out a raid. | |

D. D. & L., London, E.C.
(A7883) Wt W809/M1672 30,000 4/17 Sch 52a Forms/C/2118/14

Army Form C. 2118.

Instructions regarding War Diaries and Intelligence Summaries are contained in F. S. Regs., Part II, and the Staff Manual respectively. Title pages will be prepared in manuscript.

# WAR DIARY
*or*
# INTELLIGENCE SUMMARY.
*(Erase heading not required.)*

| Place | Date | Hour | Summary of Events and Information | Remarks and references to Appendices |
|---|---|---|---|---|
| In the line | 24.10.17 | 9am | C.O. visited all Guns in the morning and made arrangements for two Guns which were to | |
| | | | co-operate during bombardment and raid in the afternoon | |
| | | 2.30pm | ZERO hour for Bombardment. Enemy retaliation heavy especially on CEYLON AVENUE. | |
| | | | Division on our left carried out a raid after Bombardment. | |
| | 25.10.17 | 9am | C.O. left to visit Guns. | |
| | | 5pm | Guides from teams in line arrived at Coy HQrs | |
| | | 8pm | Inter Coy relief reported complete without casualties | |
| | 26.10.17 | 9.15am | LT. BARNS went round Guns. | |
| | | 4.30pm | C.O. and Bde Major went up to ROEUX WOOD. | |
| | 27.10.17 | 9am | LT. BARNS went round Guns in morning | |
| | | 2pm | 2/Lt. TRACEY joined Coy and reported at Coy HQrs | |
| | | | Our two indirect fire Guns fired 4000 rounds on targets according to programme. | |
| | 28.10.17 | 9am | C.O. went round Guns | |
| | | | 4000 rounds fired by our Indirect Fire Guns. Enemy TMs active during day especially | |
| | | | between 9-11am. | |
| | 29.10.17 | 9am | C.O. visited Guns during the morning. | |

D. D. & L., London, E.C.
(A7883) Wt W829/M1672 50,000 4/17 Sch 52a Forms/C/2118/14

Instructions regarding War Diaries and Intelligence Summaries are contained in F. S. Regs., Part II. and the Staff Manual respectively. Title pages will be prepared in manuscript.

# WAR DIARY
*or*
# INTELLIGENCE SUMMARY.
*(Erase heading not required.)*

Army Form C. 2118.

| Place | Date | Hour | Summary of Events and Information | Remarks and references to Appendices |
|---|---|---|---|---|
| In the line | 29.10.17 | | Our Indirect fire Guns fired 4,500 rounds according to programme. Enemy MGs active during the night. | |
| | 30.10.17 | 9am. | C.O. visited Guns in the line | |
| | | | Enemy aeroplanes active all day. Several appeared to be observing for Artillery. | |
| | | | Indirect fire Guns fired 4,000 rounds according to programme. | |
| | | | AA Guns at HQrs and in line fired 500 rounds. | |
| " " | 31.10.17 | 9am. | LT BARNS left HQrs to prosecute in the Case of PT. JAMES to be tried by F.G.C.M. at RIFLE CAMP. Trial postponed as President injured by fall from his horse while proceeding to RIFLE CAMP. | |
| | | 9am. | C.O. left HQrs to visit Guns in the line. | |
| | | | Unusual Artillery activity on both sides during the day. | |
| | | | Our Indirect fire Guns fired during night according to programme. 4000 rounds expended. | |
| | | 8pm. | Warning Order of relief of Bde. by 44th Inf Bde received. | |

[signature] Capt
O.C. 45th Machine Gun Coy

D. D. & L., London, E.C.
(A7853) Wt W869/M1672 50,000 4/17 Sch 52a Forms/C/2118/14

Index........................................

# SUBJECT.

| No. | Contents. | Date. |
|---|---|---|

(41,365). Wt.9392—94. 2000. 6/19. **Gp.164.** A.&E.W.
(44,173). ,, 21,613—105. 500. 10/19. ,, ,,

Instructions regarding War Diaries and Intelligence Summaries are contained in F. S. Regs., Part II, and the Staff Manual respectively. Title pages will be prepared in manuscript.

# WAR DIARY
*or*
~~INTELLIGENCE SUMMARY.~~
*(Erase heading not required.)*

Army Form C. 2118.

Vol 18

| Place | Date | Hour | Summary of Events and Information | Remarks and references to Appendices |
|---|---|---|---|---|
| | | | CONFIDENTIAL | |
| | | | WAR DIARY | |
| | | | of | |
| | | | 45th Machine Gun Company | |
| | | | 1st to 30th November 1917 | |
| | | | VOLUMN XVIII | |

In the Field
30th November 1917

[signature] Capt
O.C. 45th Machine Gun Company

D. D. & L., London, E.C.
(A7283) Wt W809/M1672 350,000 4/17 Sch 52a Forms/C/2118/14

Army Form C. 2118.

Instructions regarding War Diaries and Intelligence Summaries are contained in F. S. Regs., Part II, and the Staff Manual respectively. Title pages will be prepared in manuscript.

# WAR DIARY
*or*
# INTELLIGENCE SUMMARY.
*(Erase heading not required.)*

| Place | Date | Hour | Summary of Events and Information | Remarks and references to Appendices |
|---|---|---|---|---|
| In the Line | 1/11/17 | 9am | C.O. left HQrs to visit guns in line | |
| | | 9.30 | Capt Barrett 44 M.G. Coy arrived at HQrs and visited Gun Positions with LT. BARNS | |
| | | | Relief arrangements completed. | |
| | | 2pm | C.O. left HQrs to visit 3 Sect to check direction of Gun in ROEUX WOOD. | |
| | 2/11/17 | 9am | C.O round guns in morning | |
| | | 5.15p | 44th M.G. Coy arrived and relief proceeded. | |
| | | 9pm | Relief Complete and duly reported to Bde Office | |
| ARRAS | 3/11/17 | 9am | Cleaning Clothing and Equipment. Inspections of Gas Appliances and Iron Rations. | |
| | | -12.30p | All Guns sent to Ordnance for Inspection | |
| | | 2-3pm | Coy Pay. | |
| | | 5.30pm | LT. BARNS went to Bde HQrs to represent Coy at meeting of Bde Sports committee. | |
| " | 4/11/17 | 9am | Coy paraded and marched to Coy Parade Ground | |
| | | 9.15-10.15 | Physical Drill. | |
| | | 10.30-11.30 | Coy. Drill | |
| | | 11.30-12.30 | Advanced Gun Drill. | |
| " | 5/11/17 | 9am | Coy Paraded and marched to Parade Ground at B 20 b 20.80 | |

D. D. & L., London, E.C.
(A7883) Wt. W809/M1672 50,000 4/17 Sch 52a Forms/C/2118/14

Instructions regarding War Diaries and Intelligence Summaries are contained in F. S. Regs., Part II, and the Staff Manual respectively. Title pages will be prepared in manuscript.

# WAR DIARY
*or*
# INTELLIGENCE SUMMARY.

*(Erase heading not required.)*

Army Form C. 2118.

| Place | Date | Hour | Summary of Events and Information | Remarks and references to Appendices |
|---|---|---|---|---|
| ARRAS | 5/11/17 | 9.15 – 10.45 | Physical Drill | |
| | | 10.30 – 11.30 | Coy Drill | |
| | | 11.30 – 12.30 | Gun Drill | |
| | 6/11/17 | 9.15 – 10.15 | Physical Drill | |
| | | 10.30 – 12.30 | Advanced Gun Drill | |
| | | 8.45 am | Practice Alarm for Bombardment of Arras. | |
| | | 2-3 pm | Inspection of Coy Gas Appliances by Divl. Gas N.C.O | |
| | 7/11/17 | 9-10 am | Physical Drill | |
| | | 10.15 – 11 am | Gas Helmet Drill | |
| | | 11 – 12.30 pm | Coy Drill | |
| | | 9 am | Attached Men from Sections paraded under 2/Lt JACKSON and SERGT SIMPSON for Gun Instruction. | |
| | 8/11/17 | 9 – 12.30 pm | Attached Mens Instructional Course continued. | |
| | | 9 am – 1.30 | C.O. went up the line with CAPT DUNN T.M.B. to arrange forthcoming relief | |
| | | 〃 | LT BARNS left to visit new range in H7d. | |
| | 9/11/17 | 9 – 12.30 | A & D Sections on MOAT RANGE under Lt BARNS | |
| | | | Remainder of Coy Company Drill and handling of Arms. | |

D. D. & L., London, E.C.
(A7883) Wt W809/M1672 750,000 4/17 Sch 52a Forms/C/2118/14

Army Form C. 2118.

Instructions regarding War Diaries and Intelligence Summaries are contained in F. S. Regs., Part II. and the Staff Manual respectively. Title pages will be prepared in manuscript.

# WAR DIARY
or
# INTELLIGENCE SUMMARY.
*(Erase heading not required.)*

| Place | Date | Hour | Summary of Events and Information | Remarks and references to Appendices |
|---|---|---|---|---|
| ARRAS. | 9/11/17 | 9.30 | C.O gave a lecture to Divl. Offrs School | |
| | | 2.40 | Remainder of Coy (B & C Sections and Attd. men) on Range at A 7d. | |
| | | 4pm | Nos 1 paraded and proceeded to trenches under Cpl. CAIRNS | |
| | 10/11/17 | | Morning spent in cleaning billets and preparing for move to line. | |
| | | 12.50 pm | Coy paraded and marched to trenches to relieve 46 MG Coy. | |
| | | 6.30 pm | Relief Complete and duly reported to Brigade | |
| | | | Fourteen Guns in the line. Remaining men and Guns left at Transport Lines. | |
| | 11/11/17 | 9 am | C.O and LT BARNS visited Guns in the morning. | |
| | | 1 pm | D.M.G.O. visited HQrs. | |
| | | 3.30 pm | C.O went to Brigade Conference. | |
| | | 4 pm | LT BARNS visited 2/LT. PEARCE'S two teams after dark as impossible to approach them by day. 6,800 rounds fired by indirect fire Guns on enemy tracks etc. | |
| | 12/11/17 | 9 am | LT. BARNS visited Guns in morning | |
| | | | C.O. visited 2/LT. PEARCE | |
| | | 1 pm | MAJOR WILSON (A & SUTH HIGHRS) visited HQrs. | |
| | | 2 pm | C.O left to go to Brigade HQrs. | |

D. D. & L., London, E.C.
(A7853) Wt W809/M1672 350,000 4/17 Sch 52a Forms/C/2118/14

Instructions regarding War Diaries and Intelligence Summaries are contained in F. S. Regs., Part II. and the Staff Manual respectively. Title pages will be prepared in manuscript.

# WAR DIARY
or
# INTELLIGENCE SUMMARY.
(*Erase heading not required.*)

Army Form C. 2118.

| Place | Date | Hour | Summary of Events and Information | Remarks and references to Appendices |
|---|---|---|---|---|
| In the line | 13/11/17 | 9am | LT. BARNS visited Guns in line during the morning | |
| | | | Indirect fire Guns fired 52,200 rounds on various targets during the night. Also | |
| | | | co-operating with TM Battery at intervals. | |
| | 14/11/17 | 9am | C.O. visited Guns in the line | |
| | | | LT. BARNS arranged with C Coy of 6/7th R.S. Fusrs for carrying party & stand rock the | |
| | | | day | |
| | | 3.pm | Carrying party of R.S. Fusrs carried 70,000 to forward positions | |
| | | | Indirect fire Guns fired 50,000 rounds during the night | |
| | 15/11/17 | 9am | C.O. round Guns in the morning | |
| | | 11am | Carrying party of R.S. Fusrs carried 120,000 rounds to forward positions. | |
| | | | Indirect fire Guns fired 46,250 rounds on various targets. | |
| | 16/11/17 | 2am | Raid by Lancashire Fusiliers of 4th Div on our Right | |
| | | 9am | C.O. round Guns in the morning | |
| | | 10am | Carrying Party of R.S. Fusrs carried 70,000 rounds to forward position | |
| | | 2pm | Carrying Party carried 36,000 rounds to forward position | |
| | | | Indirect Fire Guns fired 47,000 rounds. | |

D. D. & L., London, E.C.
(A7283) Wt W809/M1672 50,000 4/17 Sch 52a Forms/C/2118/14

Army Form C. 2118.

Instructions regarding War Diaries and Intelligence Summaries are contained in F. S. Regs., Part II. and the Staff Manual respectively. Title pages will be prepared in manuscript.

# WAR DIARY
or
# INTELLIGENCE SUMMARY.
(*Erase heading not required.*)

| Place | Date | Hour | Summary of Events and Information | Remarks and references to Appendices |
|---|---|---|---|---|
| In the line | 17-11-17 | 9am | C.O round guns in the morning | |
| | | | Preparations made for co operation in Raid by Argyll & Sutherland Highrs | |
| | | 6.30pm | ZERO hour for Raid | |
| " | # | | Indirect Fire Guns fired 44,000 on various targets, and also in conjunction with raid. | |
| | 18-11-17 | 9am | CO left HQrs to visit Guns in the line | |
| | | | Preparations made for Co-operation with raid by 13th Royal Scots | |
| | | 6pm | ZERO hour for Raid by Royal Scots | |
| | | | Indirect fire Guns fired 47,000 rounds also fired in conjunction with raid | |
| | 19-11-17 | 9.15am | C.O. round Guns in the morning | |
| | | 8.30am | Carrying party of Argyll & Suth Highrs carried 45,000 rounds to forward positions | |
| | | 7.15pm | Raid by 6th Cam. Highrs | |
| | | | Indirect fire Guns fired 49,500 rounds | |
| | 20-11-17 | 8.30am | Carrying party of Argyll & Suth Highrs carried 30,000 rounds to Coy HQrs and forward positions | |
| | | 3am | Gun Hill Bombardment | |
| | | 6am | Smoke discharge. Fighting Patrols penetrated Enemy line. Total Rounds fired by MGs 49,000 | |

D. D. & L., London, E.C.
(A7883) Wt W809/M1672 350,000 4/17 Sch 52a Forms/C/2118/14

Instructions regarding War Diaries and Intelligence Summaries are contained in F. S. Regs., Part II, and the Staff Manual respectively. Title pages will be prepared in manuscript.

# WAR DIARY
*or*
# INTELLIGENCE SUMMARY.
*(Erase heading not required.)*

Army Form C. 2118.

| Place | Date | Hour | Summary of Events and Information | Remarks and references to Appendices |
|---|---|---|---|---|
| In the line | 21/11/17 | 9am | C.O. visited Guns in the line. | |
| | | | Indirect fire Guns fired 32,900 rounds | |
| | 22/11/17 | 9.15 am | C O visited Guns in line | |
| | | | Indirect fire Guns fired 6,000 rounds on enemy tracks etc. | |
| | 23/11/17 | 6am | Enemy bombarded our trenches for twenty minutes, and was more active during the day. | |
| | | | Indirect fire Guns fired 6,000 rounds. | |
| | 24/11/17 | 10-11.30 | Enemy Artillery and Trench Mortars active during morning. | |
| | | 9.15am | CO visited Guns in morning | |
| | ~~24/11~~ | | Indirect fire Guns 6,500 rounds | |
| | 25/11/17 | 10am | Capt Barrett MC [illegible] Coy visited HQrs to arrange relief for next day. | |
| | | 3pm | Enemy shelled Coy HQrs with 5.9 intermittently until 5.30pm. | |
| | | 5.45 pm | Lt. BARNS went down to Transport lines to take over rest billets next day | |
| | 26/11/17 | 10.45 pm | Guides met relieving teams of [illegible] MG Coy and relief proceeded | |
| | | 6.30pm | Relief complete and duly reported to Brigade | |

D. D. & L., London, E.C.
(A7883) Wt W809/M1672 350,000 4/17 Sch 52a Forms/C/2118/14

Instructions regarding War Diaries and Intelligence Summaries are contained in F. S. Regs., Part II, and the Staff Manual respectively. Title pages will be prepared in manuscript.

# WAR DIARY
or
# INTELLIGENCE SUMMARY.
(*Erase heading not required.*)

Army Form C. 2118.

| Place | Date | Hour | Summary of Events and Information | Remarks and references to Appendices |
|---|---|---|---|---|
| ARRAS | 27.11.17 | 9.30 | Coy employed during morning in cleaning Guns and equipment | |
| | | 1.30pm | Warning order received from Bde. HQrs that Brigade will go into line following day the 28th Inst | |
| | | | Remainder of day preparations completed for going into line next day | |
| | 28.11.17 | 12.45 am | Operation Orders received from Bde. HQrs | |
| | | 7am | 2/Lt. CANDY and thirteen Nos. 1 of teams going into line proceeded as advance party to the line | |
| | | 3.15pm | Coy. paraded and marched to line to relieve 183 & 184. MG Coys in 61st Div. Sector | |
| | | 9.30pm | Relief Complete and duly reported to Bde. HQrs | |
| In the line | 29.11.17 | 9am | C.O and Lt BARNS went round Bde front and visited Guns in line returning to HQrs at 6pm | |
| | | | Indirect fire Guns fired 6,000 rounds during the night, enemy very active all day. | |
| | 30.11.17 | 9am | C.O met G.O.C at Bde HQrs, and went round Guns with G.O.C | |
| | | | Lt BARNS met Capt Barrett and McCoy and arranged relief for 1st line. | |
| | | 2.30 | New position in TRENT TR. taken over and team under SERGT. LAFFERTS sent to take over. | |
| 30-11-17 | | | [signature] O.C. 45th Machine Gun Co. | Capt. |

(A7883) Wt W809/M1672 350,000 4/17 Sch 52a Forms/C/2118/14

Addendum to W.D for 28.11.17.

28-11-17 Lt Colonel H.A. DUNCAN left for the Base under ADMS. orders & ceased to command the Battalion. The Battalion take this opportunity of placing on record their appreciation of the services he has rendered during the 6 months in which he has held command. His high sense of duty & his personal bravery, during the Ypres Operations, will always remain as an incentive to those who had the honour to serve under him.

G. Wilson

P.T.O.

Instructions regarding War Diaries and Intelligence Summaries are contained in F. S. Regs., Part II. and the Staff Manual respectively. Title pages will be prepared in manuscript.

# WAR DIARY
*or*
# INTELLIGENCE SUMMARY.
*(Erase heading not required.)*

1/11 Bn Argyll & Sutherland Highlanders [illegible] for November 1917

Army Form C. 2118.

| Place | Date | Hour | Summary of Events and Information | Remarks and references to Appendices |
|---|---|---|---|---|
| Front Line ~~[illegible]~~ | 2[illegible]/11/17 | | Enemy Activity quieter a day of possibilities with 1 [illegible] to be ready to | |
| Nr MONCHY | | | follow [illegible] Enemy withdrawal (2) [illegible] to hold the front line more | |
| | | | strongly in case of enemy attack (3) [illegible] to [illegible] [illegible] the front | |
| | | | line. Active Patrols only ascertained however that enemy was holding (as usual) front line | [illegible] |
| | 2[illegible]/11/17 | | The first two possibilities of yesterday became improbabilities. [illegible] | [illegible] |
| ARRAS | 2[illegible]/11/17 | | Relieved by 9th R. B.W. (44 Bde) Battalion moved to Beaudimont Barracks for 8 days in | |
| BEAUDIMONT | | | Bde Reserve. Congratulatory message received from Corps Commander Lt General Sir Charles | |
| Barracks. | | | Ferguson Bt K.C.B. M.V.O. D.S.O. on work of Division during previous fortnight. | [illegible] |
| " | 27/11/17 | | Cleaning up. Orders received (1.30 PM) that Bde will move into line on 28th inst. to take | |
| | | | over part of 61st Divisional Front (183 & 184 Bdes) from left of Corps Front (Near GAVRELLE) | |
| | | | to ARRAS-DOUAI Railway. Operation Orders received very late. | [illegible] |
| " | 28.11.17 | | Bn moved up by Train & Busses to ATHIES & took over (day light Relief) from 2/4 | |
| | | | Royal Berks Regt & part of 1/7 Worcester Regt. in Reserve to Bde Front. Relief complete | |
| | | | by 4.30 PM. Relief apparently not spotted by Enemy despite the fact that relieved | [illegible] |
| " | 29.11.17 | | troops were not too particular to conceal movement. 29/11/17. Work Parties. Considerable activity | |
| | | | on Bde Area A Coy [illegible] in, only one casualty during day, very light. | [illegible] |
| | 30.11.17 | | Work [illegible] Patrols ~~quieter~~ Loss G.S.O. 2. [illegible] Staff Officer, Killed by Shell in front line. | [illegible] |

G. L. Wilson [illegible] Major

D. D. & L., London, E.C. (A7983) Wt. W5034/M1672 350,000 4/17 Sch. 52a Forms/C/2118/14

Instructions regarding War Diaries and Intelligence Summaries are contained in F. S. Regs., Part II. and the Staff Manual respectively. Title pages will be prepared in manuscript.

# WAR DIARY
or
~~INTELLIGENCE SUMMARY.~~

(*Erase heading not required.*)

Army Form C. 2118.

Vol 19

| Place | Date | Hour | Summary of Events and Information | Remarks and references to Appendices |
|---|---|---|---|---|
| | | | CONFIDENTIAL | |
| | | | WAR DIARY | |
| | | | of | |
| | | | 45th Machine Gun Company | |
| | | | 1st to 31st December 1917. | |
| | | | VOLUME XIX | |

In the Field
31st December 1917.

[illegible]
Capt.
O.C. 45th Machine Gun Company

D. D. & L., London, E.C.
(A7885) Wt W829/M1672 50,000 1/17 Sch 52a Forms/C/2118/14

Army Form C. 2118.

# WAR DIARY
*or*
# INTELLIGENCE SUMMARY.
*(Erase heading not required.)*

Instructions regarding War Diaries and Intelligence Summaries are contained in F. S. Regs., Part II, and the Staff Manual respectively. Title pages will be prepared in manuscript.

| Place | Date | Hour | Summary of Events and Information | Remarks and references to Appendices |
|---|---|---|---|---|
| In the line | 1/12/17 | 5 pm. | 44th M.G. Coy arrived at H.Qrs and relief between companies commenced. | |
| | | | Enemy fairly quiet during the night. | |
| | | 9.15 pm | Last team to be relieved reported at Coy H.Qrs. and completion of relief duly | |
| | | | notified to Brigade H.Qrs | |
| ARRAS | 2/12/17 | 10–12.30 pm | Coy employed sorting out Guns, kit and equipment | |
| | | 5.30 pm | Coy paraded for Baths. | |
| | 3/12/17 | 9–10 am. | Cleaning Parade | |
| | | 10–10.30 pm | Inspection of Coy in full marching order by C.O. in Billets. | |
| | | | G.O.C's inspection to be held in afternoon Cancelled. | |
| | 4/12/17 | 8.30 am | Section paraded for Inspection by Section Officers | |
| | | 9 am. | Coy. paraded for inspection by G.O.C | |
| | | 7.30 am | 1 NCO and 10 men from each Section proceeded to Transport Lines to pack limbers | |
| | | 10 am | LT. BARNS attended Court-Martial as a member, Court held at H.Qrs of 1/7th R Scots Fus | |
| | 5/12/17 | 9–10 am | Physical Drill | |
| | | 10.15–12.30 pm | Advanced Gun Drill and Instruction | |
| | | 11.30 am | A & B Section points before firing 12 noon – 2 pm A & B Section on MOAT RANGE | |

D. D. & L., London, E.C.
(A7863) Wt W829/M1672 350,000 4/17 Sch 52a Forms/C/2118/14

Instructions regarding War Diaries and Intelligence Summaries are contained in F. S. Regs., Part II, and the Staff Manual respectively. Title pages will be prepared in manuscript.

# WAR DIARY
*or*
# INTELLIGENCE SUMMARY.
(*Erase heading not required.*)

Army Form C. 2118.

| Place | Date | Hour | Summary of Events and Information | Remarks and references to Appendices |
|---|---|---|---|---|
| ARRAS | 6/12/17 | 8.30am -10am | Company paraded for inspection of Gas Appliances | |
| | | 10.15 -11.30am | Physical Drill. | |
| | | 11.15 -12.30pm | A & B Sections Gun Drill. C & D Sections Coy Drill. | |
| | 7/12/17 | 9-10 am | Physical Drill. | |
| | | 10.15- 12.30 pm | A & B Sections Gun Drill | |
| | | 10.15- 11.30 | C & D Sections Gun Drill and Points before firing. | |
| | | 12 noon -2pm | C & D Sections on Range | |
| | | 2pm | Nos. 1 of Gun Teams departed for line, with PT. ROWE of Signal Section. | |
| | 8/12/17 | 9-10 am | Physical Drill | |
| | | 10.15 -12.30 pm | Gun Cleaning and Packing Limbers | |
| | | 10am | LT. H.M. BARNS a member of F.G.C.M. assembling at 45th. Field Ambulance. | |
| | | 2.30pm | Company left billets for line to relieve 46th. MG Coy. | |
| | | 8.10pm | Relief Complete and duly reported by code to Brigade HQrs. | |
| In the line | 9/12/17 | 9.30 am | C.O. and LT. BARNS visited Guns in the line returning to Coy HQrs at 1.30 pm. | |
| | | | Indirect Fire Guns fired 6,500 rounds | |
| | 10/12/17 | 1. am | Warning Order received for Bde. to 'stand to' | |

D. D. & L., London, E.C.
(A7883) Wt W8c9/M1672 250,000 4/17 Sch. 52a Forms/C/2118/14

Army Form C. 2118.

Instructions regarding War Diaries and Intelligence Summaries are contained in F. S. Regs., Part II, and the Staff Manual respectively. Title pages will be prepared in manuscript.

# WAR DIARY
*or*
# INTELLIGENCE SUMMARY.
*(Erase heading not required.)*

| Place | Date | Hour | Summary of Events and Information | Remarks and references to Appendices |
|---|---|---|---|---|
| In the Line | 10/12/17 | 9am. | C.O. went to Bde Hqrs. | |
| | | 9.30pm | C.O. returned to Coy Hqrs and went round right sector with 2/Lt. JAMES | |
| | | 10am. | LT. BARNS went to Bde Hqrs | |
| | | | Enemy very active all day. Indirect Fire Guns fired 7,000 rounds | |
| " | 11/12/17 | 9.30 am | C.O visited Hqrs. of 6/7th Royal Scots Fusrs (Right Bn) | |
| | | 10 am | Lt. BARNS visited Hqrs of 6th Cam Highrs & 11th A&S Highrs (Centre & left Bns) | |
| | | 12 noon | Capt. HAMILTON a/D.M.G.O. visited Coy Hqrs. and went round CORPS LINE with | |
| | | | CAPT NAWTON and LT. ROSHER of 46 MG Coy. | |
| | | | Indirect Fire Guns fired 7,000 rounds on enemy tracks and approaches. | |
| " | 12/12/17 | 9am. | C.O. went to Bde Hqrs to meet G.O.C. and went round the Guns in the line with G.O.C. | |
| | | 2.30pm | Summary of Evidence in the Case of Pte. CULLEN taken at Coy Hqrs | |
| | | | Indirect Fire Guns fired 6,500 rounds on selected targets during the night. | |
| " | 13/12/17 | 9.30 am. | C.O. and 2/Lt JAMES visited portions of the Corps Line of Defence. | |
| | | | Very Quiet day. Indirect Fire Guns fired 7,000 rounds during the night. | |
| " | 14/12/17 | 10am. | LT. BARNS visited Guns in left Sector of the line. C.O. and 2/LT JACKSON visited CORPS LINE. | |
| | | 4.30pm | LT. BARNS visited Guns in Right Sector (ROEUX WOOD and VILLAGE) | |

D. D. & L., London, E.C.
(A7883) Wt W809/M1672 350,000 4/17 Sch 52a Forms/C/2118/14

Army Form C. 2118.

Instructions regarding War Diaries and Intelligence Summaries are contained in F. S. Regs., Part II. and the Staff Manual respectively. Title pages will be prepared in manuscript.

# WAR DIARY
*or*
# INTELLIGENCE SUMMARY.
(*Erase heading not required.*)

| Place | Date | Hour | Summary of Events and Information | Remarks and references to Appendices |
|---|---|---|---|---|
| In the Line | 15/12/17 | 9.30 am | C.O. visited Guns in the line | |
| | | 5 pm | 2/LT. JAMES relieved 2/LT. JACKSON in ROEUX WOOD. | |
| | | | Enemy Artillery active all the afternoon. LT. STRANGE slightly wounded and remaining at duty. | |
| | | | Indirect Fire Guns fired 3,500 rounds. | |
| | 16/12/17 | 9.30 am | C.O. visited Guns in the line. | |
| | | 5 pm | Inter team relief carried out as follows: No 6 Team relieved No 15 Team at No 6 Position. | |
| | | | No 5 Team relieved No 14 Team at No 10 Position. No 7 Team relieved No 16 Team at No | |
| | | | 11 Position. | |
| | | | Enemy Artillery less active all day. | |
| | | 6.30 pm | LT. BARNS went to Brigade H.Qrs. | |
| | | | Indirect Fire Guns fired 3000 rounds during the night. | |
| | 17/12/17 | 5.30 am | LT. BARNS and 2/LT. JACKSON visited Guns of Right Sector at 'Stand To'. | |
| | | 9 am | C.O. visited Guns in Left Sector. | |
| | | 9.30 pm | C.O. and 2/LT. JACKSON visited Guns in Right Sector. | |
| | | 2.15 pm | Summary of Evidence in Case of PT. CULLEN taken for third time. | |
| | | | Indirect Fire Guns fired [illegible] rounds during the night | |

D. D. & L., London, E.C.
(A7883) Wt W809/M1672 50,000 4/17 Sch. 52a Forms/C/2118/14

Army Form C. 2118.

# WAR DIARY
*or*
# INTELLIGENCE SUMMARY.
*(Erase heading not required.)*

Instructions regarding War Diaries and Intelligence Summaries are contained in F. S. Regs., Part II, and the Staff Manual respectively. Title pages will be prepared in manuscript.

| Place | Date | Hour | Summary of Events and Information | Remarks and references to Appendices |
|---|---|---|---|---|
| In the line | 18/12/17 | 5.30 | C.O. and 2/LT. JACKSON visited guns in Right Sector at 'Stand To'. | |
| | | 9.30 am | C.O. went round guns in Right Sector with G.S.O. | |
| | | 10am | D.M.G.O. called at Coy H.Qrs and went round line with LT. BARNS | |
| | | | Artillery Activity quiet on both sides during day and night. | |
| | | | Indirect Fire Guns fired 6,000 rounds during the night. | |
| " | 19/12/17 | 9.30 am | C.O. went to Guns in K. L. & M. POSTS to site new positions for special scheme for defence of LANCER AVENUE. | |
| | | 2pm | C.O. and LT. BARNS visited CORPS LINE (TRENT TR. SECTOR) to find emplacements to be occupied while Coy is in Brigade Reserve. | |
| | | | Indirect Fire Guns fired | |
| " | 20/12/17 | 9am | C.O. went round guns in the line | |
| | | 2pm | LT. BARNS went to H.Qrs. of Royal Scots to take over. | |
| | | 6pm | H.Qrs. moved from Railway Cutting to H.Qrs. of 13th Royal Scots in CRETE TR. | |
| | | | Indirect Fire Guns fired 7,000 rounds during the night. | |
| " | 21/12/17 | 9.30 am | C.O. went round guns in the line. | |
| | | 2.30pm | Conference of Commanding Officers at Bde. H.Qrs. | |

D. D. & L., London, E.C.
(A7883) Wt W809/M1672 350,000 4/17 Sch 52a Forms/C/2118/14

Instructions regarding War Diaries and Intelligence Summaries are contained in F. S. Regs., Part II, and the Staff Manual respectively. Title pages will be prepared in manuscript.

# WAR DIARY
or
# INTELLIGENCE SUMMARY.
(*Erase heading not required.*)

Army Form C. 2118.

| Place | Date | Hour | Summary of Events and Information | Remarks and references to Appendices |
|---|---|---|---|---|
| In the line | 22/12/17 | 9.30 am | LT BARNS showed 2/LT. CANDY and LT. STRANGE round the CORPS LINE. | |
| | | " | C.O. visited Guns in the line. | |
| | | | LT BARNS took over the work of O/c CAVES and went round same in afternoon. | |
| | | | Very quiet all day. Indirect Fire Guns fired 7,000 rounds during the night. | |
| | 23/12/17 | 3pm | 44th. MG Coy arrived at Coy HQrs and relief proceeded. | |
| | | 6.10pm | Last team to be relieved reported at Coy HQrs and 'Relief Complete' duly reported to Bde | |
| | | 6.15pm | Unusual activity ~~by the~~ on the front of Division on our right, heavy shelling and trench mortar fire by Enemy. S.O.S. sent up by this Division and again repeated by 44th. Bde on our front. Artillery barrage opened out by us. Enemy reported to be raiding S. Sap. (Front of Division on our Right.) | |
| | | 8.30pm | Company arrived in Billets at ARRAS, no casualties during relief. | |
| ARRAS | 24/12/17 | 9 am | Officers took their NCOs and showed them their positions in CORPS LINE in case of attack by Enemy. | |
| | | 9-12 noon | Remainder of Coy packing fighting Limbers at Transport Lines. | |
| | | 12-2pm | Remainder of Coy on MOAT RANGE under LT. BARNS. | |
| | 25/12/17 | 10am | C of E Church Parade. No parades held during the day by Instructions received from Bde | |

D. D. & L., London, E.C. (A7833) Wt W3eg/M1672 50,000 4/17 Sch 52a Forms/C/2118/14

Instructions regarding War Diaries and Intelligence Summaries are contained in F. S. Regs., Part II, and the Staff Manual respectively. Title pages will be prepared in manuscript.

# WAR DIARY
*or*
# INTELLIGENCE SUMMARY.
*(Erase heading not required.)*

Army Form C. 2118.

| Place | Date | Hour | Summary of Events and Information | Remarks and references to Appendices |
|---|---|---|---|---|
| ARRAS | 26/12/17 | 9am | Coy paraded and marched to Transport Lines | |
| | | 9.30–10.30am | Physical Drill | |
| | | 10.45–11.30am | Cleaning Guns. A Section filled belts used on range the day previous. | |
| | | 1pm | B & C Sections paraded and proceeded to range in H 7 d. | |
| | | 5.30pm | Coy paraded for Baths. | |
| " | 27/12/17 | 9am | Inspection of Iron Rations, Clothing & Ammunition by Section Officers, followed by cleaning of Equipment. | |
| | | 11.30am | D Section proceeded to MOAT RANGE | |
| " | 28/12/17 | 9am | Coy Paraded and Marched to Transport Lines | |
| | | 9.30–10.30 | Physical Drill | |
| | | 10.45–12.30 | B & C Sections Coy Drill. Reminder Points before Firing until 11.30. | |
| | | 1pm | A & D Sections paraded and proceeded to Range in H 7 d. | |
| | | 10am | CAPT. NAWTON. LT. BARNS & 2/LT JACKSON attended Court Martial held at HQrs of the 13th Royal Scots, for various duties. | |
| " | 29/12/17 | 9.30–10.30 | Physical Drill | |
| | | 10.45–12.30 | Coy Drill (A & D Sects) Reminder Points before Firing. | |

D. D. & L., London, E.C. (A7853) Wt W809/M1672 350,000 4/17 Sch 52a Forms/C/2118/14

Army Form C. 2118.

# WAR DIARY
*or*
# INTELLIGENCE SUMMARY.
*(Erase heading not required.)*

Instructions regarding War Diaries and Intelligence Summaries are contained in F. S. Regs., Part II, and the Staff Manual respectively. Title pages will be prepared in manuscript.

| Place | Date | Hour | Summary of Events and Information | Remarks and references to Appendices |
|---|---|---|---|---|
| ARRAS | 28/12/17 | 1pm | B & C Sections proceeded to Range in H.7.d | |
| " | 30/12/17 | 9am | Coy Paraded for Testing of Box Respirators by Divl Gas Officer in Gas Chamber | |
| " | | 1.45 pm | Brigade Cross Country Run | |
| " | 31/12/17 | 9.30 – 10.30 | Inspection of Coy at Transport Lines by C.O | |
| | | | Remainder of Morning Spent by Cleaning Guns and preparing for move next day | |

H Marston
Capt.
O.C. 45th Machine Gun Coy.

D. D. & L., London, E.C.
(A7853) Wt. W8o9/M1672 50,000 4/17 Sch. 52a Forms/C/2118/14

Instructions regarding War Diaries and Intelligence Summaries are contained in F. S. Regs., Part II. and the Staff Manual respectively. Title pages will be prepared in manuscript.

# WAR DIARY
*or*
~~INTELLIGENCE SUMMARY.~~
*(Erase heading not required.)*

Army Form C. 2118.

Vol 20

| Place | Date | Hour | Summary of Events and Information | Remarks and references to Appendices |
|---|---|---|---|---|
| | | | CONFIDENTIAL. | |
| | | | WAR DIARY of 45th Machine Gun Company | |
| | | | 1st to 31st January 1918. | |
| | | | VOLUME ~~XXV~~ XX | |
| | | | H M Boon Lieut O.C. 45th Machine Gun Company. | |
| | | | In the Field. 31st January 1918. | |

D. D. & L., London, E.C. (A7883) Wt W809/M1672 750,000 1/17 Sch 52a Forms/C/2118/14

Army Form C. 2118.

# WAR DIARY
*or*
# INTELLIGENCE SUMMARY.
(*Erase heading not required.*)

Instructions regarding War Diaries and Intelligence Summaries are contained in F. S. Regs., Part II. and the Staff Manual respectively. Title pages will be prepared in manuscript.

| Place | Date | Hour | Summary of Events and Information | Remarks and references to Appendices |
|---|---|---|---|---|
| ARRAS | 1/1/18 | 9-11.45 | Cleaning Billets and preparing for move | |
| | | 2pm | Coy paraded in Full Marching order and marched to billets in WARLUS | |
| WARLUS | 2/1/18 | 9-1pm | Unpacking limbers and Sorting Equipment Gun Cleaning | |
| " | 3/1/18 | 9-10 | Physical Drill | |
| | | 10.15 -1pm | Gun Drill and Section Drill under Section Officers. | |
| | | | 2/Lt TRACEY returned from course with R F C | |
| " | 4/1/18 | 8.15am | Coy paraded and marched to Bde. Training Area for Tactical Scheme. | |
| | | 8.30am | CAPT. NANTON left for A Aircraft Course with R F C. | |
| | | | 2/Lt BARNES returned from MG School CAMIERS | |
| " | 5/1/18 | 9-10am | Physical Drill | |
| | | 10-11.30 am | Gun Drill | |
| | | 11.45-1pm | Gun Cleaning Pay in Afternoon. | |
| " | 6/1/18 | 9.15am | C of E Church Parade at BERNEVILLE | |
| | | 10.45 am | Prest. Church Parade at WANQUETIN | |
| | | 10.15am | R.C. Church Parade at BERNEVILLE | |
| " | 7/1/18 | 9.15 | Right Half Company paraded and moved to Bde Training Area. | |

D. D. & L., London, E.C.
(A7883) Wt W829/M1672 350,000 4/17 Sch 52a Forms/C/2118/14

Instructions regarding War Diaries and Intelligence Summaries are contained in F. S. Regs., Part II, and the Staff Manual respectively. Title pages will be prepared in manuscript.

# WAR DIARY
or
# INTELLIGENCE SUMMARY.
(*Erase heading not required.*)

Army Form C. 2118.

| Place | Date | Hour | Summary of Events and Information | Remarks and references to Appendices |
|---|---|---|---|---|
| WARLUS | 7/1/18 | 8.45 | HQrs and remainder of Coy paraded and Marched to Bde Training Area for Tactical Scheme | |
| | | 12 noon | CAPT. NANTON returned from A. Aircraft Course. | |
| | 8/1/18 | 9-10 am | Box Respirator Drill | |
| | | 10-11.30 am | Company Drill under LT BARNS | |
| | | 11.45-1 pm | Gun Drill under Section Officers | |
| | | 5.30 pm | All available Officers and two Senior NCOs per Section attended lecture at BERNEVILLE on 'Aircraft' | |
| | 9/1/18 | 9am | Coy Paraded in full Marching Order for Route March | |
| | | 2.45 | Coy Canteen opened | |
| | 10/1/18 | 9-10 am | Physical Drill | |
| | | 10-1 pm | Advanced Gun Drill. Schemes detailed by Section Officers and NCOs. took command of same | |
| | | 9am | Instructional Classes for attached Men (Carriers) opened under 2/LT BARNES and Sergt. | |
| | | | ANDERSON. Capt Nanton proceeded on 14 days leave to U.K. | |
| | 11/1/18 | 9-10 AM | Physical Drill. | |
| | | 10-11 AM | Judging Distances. | |
| | | 11.45-1 pm | Gun Drill | |
| | 12/1/18 | 9-10 AM | Company Drill. | |
| | | 10.15 AM | A + B Sections & Transport parade for Baths | |

D. D. & L., London, E.C.
(A7883) Wt W8o/M1672 750,000 4/17 Sch 52a Forms/C/2118/14

Instructions regarding War Diaries and Intelligence Summaries are contained in F. S. Regs., Part II, and the Staff Manual respectively. Title pages will be prepared in manuscript.

# WAR DIARY
*or*
# INTELLIGENCE SUMMARY.
*(Erase heading not required.)*

Army Form C. 2118.

| Place | Date | Hour | Summary of Events and Information | Remarks and references to Appendices |
|---|---|---|---|---|
| WARLUS | 12/1/18 | 10-11 AM | C+D Sections gun cleaning | |
| | | 11.15 AM | C+D Sections parade for Baths. | |
| | | 11.45-12.45 PM | A+B Sections gun cleaning. | |
| | | 2 P.M. | Company Pay out. | |
| | 13/1/18 | 10 AM | Church of England parade under 2/Lt Sweeney to church army hut BERNEVILLE. | |
| | | | ~~Presbyterians under 2/Lt BARNES~~ [initialled] | |
| | | 10.15 AM | Roman Catholics under Sgt LAFFERTY. | |
| | | 4 P.M. | Five N.C.Os parade & march off to attend 7 days course under the D.M.G.O. | |
| | 14/1/18 | 9-10.45 AM | Advanced gun drill | |
| | | 11-12 noon | Demonstration for all ranks by Divisional Gas Officer. | |
| | | 12-1 P.M. | Box Respirator drill. Lecture by G.O.C to Company. | |
| | 15/1/18 | 9-10 AM | Company drill. | |
| | | 10-11 AM | C+D Sections cleaning Equipment | |
| | | 10 AM | A+B Sections parade for Baths | |
| | | 11 AM | C+D Sections parade for Baths. | |
| | 16/1/18 | 8.30-9.30 AM | Inspection of Company in Battle Order by C.O. | |

D. D. & L., London, E.C. (A7883) Wt. W809/M1672 350,000 4/17 Sch. 52a Forms/C/2118/14

Army Form C. 2118.

Instructions regarding War Diaries and Intelligence Summaries are contained in F. S. Regs., Part II. and the Staff Manual respectively. Title pages will be prepared in manuscript.

# WAR DIARY
*or*
# INTELLIGENCE SUMMARY.
*(Erase heading not required.)*

| Place | Date | Hour | Summary of Events and Information | Remarks and references to Appendices |
|---|---|---|---|---|
| WARLUS. | 16/1/18 | 9-30AM | Inspection of Company in Battle Order by G.O.C. | |
| | | 11-1PM | Gun Drill under Section Officers. | |
| | 17/1/18 | 9-9.30AM | Inspection of small kit. | |
| | | 9.30-10AM | Inspection of Iron Rations, Ammunition, Box Respirators, & P.H. Helmets. | |
| | | 10.45-11.30AM | Immediate action. | |
| | | 11.30-12.30PM | Mechanism. | |
| | | | ~~2/Lt B.C. SIMMONDS & 2/Lt PEARCE visited the 17th Corps Camouflage Depot.~~ | |
| | | | ~~LIEUT H.M. BARNS attended 70th Bgde R.F.A. Vaccination scheme.~~ (Cancelled [illegible]) | |
| | 18/1/18 | 9-10AM | Physical Drill. | |
| | | 10-11.30AM | Advanced Gun Drill | |
| | | 11.45-1PM | Judging Distances. | |
| | | | Trench Boards laid in Camp. | |
| | 19/1/18 | 9 A.M. | Company Parade in full marching order for Route march. Route:- WARLUS-WANQUETIN-SIMENCOURT-BEAUMETZ- main ARRAS-DOULLENS Rd to X Rd N of D in LE-BAC-DU-NORD-BERNEVILLE-WARLUS. | |
| | | 9 A.M. | 2/Lt TRACEY and 1 N.C.O for section parade under Bgde S.M. Instructor of Physical Training. | |

D. D. & L., London, E.C.
(A7883) Wt W3891/M.672 30,000 4/17 Sch 52a Forms/C/2118/14

Instructions regarding War Diaries and Intelligence Summaries are contained in F. S. Regs., Part II. and the Staff Manual respectively. Title pages will be prepared in manuscript.

# WAR DIARY
*or*
# INTELLIGENCE SUMMARY.
*(Erase heading not required.)*

Army Form C. 2118.

| Place | Date | Hour | Summary of Events and Information | Remarks and references to Appendices |
|---|---|---|---|---|
| WARLUS | 20/1/18 | 10 A.M. | Church of England parade under 2/Lt B.C. SIMMONS, to Church Army Hut BERNEVILLE. | |
| | | 10.30 AM | Roman Catholic parade under Sgt LAFFERTY to BERNEVILLE Parish Church. | |
| | | | Remainder of Company to clean up Huts and ground in their vicinity. | |
| | 21/1/18 | 9-10 A.M. | Physical Drill. | |
| | | 10-11 AM. | Company Drill under C.S.M. | |
| | | 10.45 AM | A+B Sections parade for Baths. | |
| | | 11.15-1 P.M. | C+D Sections advanced Gun Drill (Section Officers Schemes) N.C.Os to take charge | |
| | | 1 P.M. | No 1+2s of each Section proceeded to range under one Officer per Section. | |
| | | 2 P.M. | 1 N.C.O + 4 men per Section washed Limbers. | |
| | 22/1/18 | | Brigade Boxing Competition held in Cinema Hut SIMENCOURT. | |
| | | 9-10 AM. | Physical Drill. | |
| | | 10-11 AM. | Company Drill under C.S.M. | |
| | | 10 A.M. | C+D Sections + all employed men of those Sections paraded for Baths. | |
| | | 11.15-12.15 P.M. | Combined Gun Drill. | |
| | | 12.15- | Inspection of Box Respirators. | |
| | | 5.30 P.M. | Signallers attended lecture on "Communications" at SIMENCOURT | |

D. D. & L., London, E.C.
(A7853) Wt W869/M.672 30,000 1/17 Sch 52a Forms/C/2118/14

Army Form C. 2118.

Instructions regarding War Diaries and Intelligence Summaries are contained in F. S. Regs., Part II. and the Staff Manual respectively. Title pages will be prepared in manuscript.

# WAR DIARY
*or*
# INTELLIGENCE SUMMARY.
*(Erase heading not required.)*

| Place | Date | Hour | Summary of Events and Information | Remarks and references to Appendices |
|---|---|---|---|---|
| WARLUS. | 23/1/18 | 8.30AM. | Company Tactical Scheme. | |
| | | | 2 Lt TRACEY with two teams and two guns attached to 13th Royal Scots for Battn Scheme. | |
| | | 2 PM. | Reconnaissance of ground for Bgde Tactical Scheme by C.O. + all Section officers. | |
| | | | All company blankets taken to the FODEN Disinfector and disinfected. | |
| | 24/1/18 | 8 AM. | 2/Lt Conolly + half company moved off to A.&S.H. range. | |
| | | 8.30AM | Company paraded + proceeded to range for musketry. | |
| | | | LIEUT J.R. STRANGE + 2nd LIEUT W. TRACEY [redacted] carried out reconnaissance of forward area. | |
| | 25/1/18 | 9AM. | Brigade Tactical Scheme. | |
| | 26/1/18 | 9-10AM. | Physical Drill. | |
| | | 10-11AM. | Gun Drill + gun cleaning. | |
| | | 11-12noon | Inspection of Box Respirators. | |
| | | 12-1PM. | Section Officers Scheme. | |
| | | 8 AM. | B Section with 4 guns paraded under 2nd LIEUT JAMES for 47th R.S.F. Btn scheme. | |
| | 27/1/18 | 8.15AM. | Roman Catholic Church parade under Sgt CAFFERTY | |
| | | 10 AM. | Church of England under Lt BARNES to Church Army hut BERNEVILLE. | |

D. D. & L., London, E.C.
(A7883) Wt W809/M1672 350,000 4/17 Sch 52a Forms/C/2118/14

Instructions regarding War Diaries and Intelligence Summaries are contained in F. S. Regs., Part II. and the Staff Manual respectively. Title pages will be prepared in manuscript.

# WAR DIARY
*or*
# INTELLIGENCE SUMMARY.
(*Erase heading not required.*)

Army Form C. 2118.

| Place | Date | Hour | Summary of Events and Information | Remarks and references to Appendices |
|---|---|---|---|---|
| WARLUS | 28/1/18 | 9-10 AM | Physical Drill. | |
| | | 9.45 AM | A+B Sections and Transport proceeded to Baths | |
| | | 10-10.45 AM. | C+D Sections Barrage Drill under 2nd LT H.E. BARNES, A+B Sections on return from Baths. | |
| | | 12.30-1 PM. | Inspection and cleaning of Belt Boxes and ammunition. | |
| | 29/1/18 | | Brigade Tactical Scheme | |
| | 30/1/18 | 9-10 AM. | Physical Drill. | |
| | | 10-11.30 AM. | Company Drill | |
| | | 11.45-1 PM. | Immediate action & mechanism. | |
| | | | Lecture on Barrage to all Officers by 2LT BARNES. | |
| | 31/1/18 | 8 AM. | Butt Party & Control Party under 2nd LT W.S. TRACEY moved off to 11th A+SH range | |
| | | 8.30 AM | Company parade armed with rifles & proceeded to range (Four practices fired) | |
| | | | B. Section with 4 guns under 2nd LT H.E. BARNES met Major WILSON 11th A+SH for Battn Tactical Scheme. | |
| | | | 2nd LT PEARSE takes over command of Transport Section (temporarily) | |
| | | | 2nd LT CANDY takes over command of D Section (temporarily) | |

D. D. & L., London, E.C.
(A7883) Wt W809/M1672 350,000 4/17 Sch. 52a Forms/C/2118/14

Army Form C. 2118.

Instructions regarding War Diaries and Intelligence Summaries are contained in F. S. Regs., Part II, and the Staff Manual respectively. Title pages will be prepared in manuscript.

# WAR DIARY
*or*
# INTELLIGENCE SUMMARY.
*(Erase heading not required.)*

| Place | Date | Hour | Summary of Events and Information | Remarks and references to Appendices |
|---|---|---|---|---|
| WARLUS. | 31/1/18 | | C.O. with Sgt STEVENS + Sgt BLANCHARD proceeded by lorry to forward area for reconnaissance. | |
| | [illegible] | | [illegible] | |
| | | | H M Barns Lieut<br>O.C. 45th Machine Gun Company | |

D. D. & L., London, E.C.
(A7853) Wt W809/M1672 50,000 4/17 Sch 52a Forms/C/2118/14

Instructions regarding War Diaries and Intelligence Summaries are contained in F. S. Regs., Part II, and the Staff Manual respectively. Title pages will be prepared in manuscript.

# WAR DIARY
or
# INTELLIGENCE SUMMARY.
(*Erase heading not required.*)

Army Form C. 2118.

Vol 21

| Place | Date | Hour | Summary of Events and Information | Remarks and references to Appendices |
|---|---|---|---|---|
| | | | CONFIDENTIAL. | |
| | | | WAR DIARY. | |
| | | | of | |
| | | | 45th Machine Gun Company | |
| | | | 1st to 28th February 1918. | |
| | | | VOLUME XXI | |
| In the Field, 28th February 1918. | | | H Mawdsley (?) Capt. O.C. 45th Machine Gun Company. | |

D. D. & L., London, E.C. (A7883) Wt. W809/M1672 350,000 4/17 Sch. 52a Forms/C/2118/14

Army Form C. 2118.

Instructions regarding War Diaries and Intelligence Summaries are contained in F. S. Regs., Part II. and the Staff Manual respectively. Title pages will be prepared in manuscript.

# WAR DIARY
*or*
# INTELLIGENCE SUMMARY.
*(Erase heading not required.)*

| Place | Date | Hour | Summary of Events and Information | Remarks and references to Appendices |
|---|---|---|---|---|
| WARLUS | 1-2-18 | | Brigade Tactical Scheme. | |
| | 2-2-18 | 9.30 - 10-30 am. | Physical Drill. | |
| | | 10.30 am | A & B Sections paraded for Baths | |
| | | 10.30 - 11-30 am | C & D Sections: Barrage Drill | |
| | | 12.30 pm | Remainder of Company paraded for Baths. | |
| | | 12.15 pm. to 1 pm | A & B. Sections Cleaning guns | |
| | 3-2-18 | 9.16 am | Roman Catholics paraded under Sgt Lafferty to Berneville Church. | |
| | | 9.45 am | Church of England Church parade under 2/LT. R CANDY to Church Army Hut BERNEVILLE. | |
| | 4-2-18 | 9 am | Cleaning billets and vicinity of same before leaving camp. | |
| | | 11 - am | Inspection of Camp by C.O. | |
| | | 12.30 pm. | Company paraded to march to billets in ARRAS. | |
| | 5-2-18 | 7.30 am | Company paraded under Section Officers for feet inspection and rubbing in Whale Oil preparatory to going into the line. | |
| | | 9 am. | Company paraded to entrain at Y. Dump for the purpose of relieving 10th Machine Gun Company and part of 234th Machine Gun Company. | |
| | | 1.40 pm | Relief completed and duly reported to Brigade. | |
| | | | C.O. visited gun positions | |

A5834 Wt. W4973/M687 750,000 8/16 D. D. & L. Ltd. Forms/C.2118/13.

Army Form C. 2118.

Instructions regarding War Diaries and Intelligence Summaries are contained in F. S. Regs., Part II. and the Staff Manual respectively. Title pages will be prepared in manuscript.

# WAR DIARY
*or*
# INTELLIGENCE SUMMARY.

*(Erase heading not required.)*

| Place | Date | Hour | Summary of Events and Information | Remarks and references to Appendices |
|---|---|---|---|---|
| In the line | 6-2-18 | | C.O. visited gun positions. | |
| | 7-2-18 | | Enemy artillery very active. Our machine guns fired 11.000 rounds | |
| | 8-2-18 | 9 am | C.O. visited guns in the line | |
| | | 11 am | Summary of evidence in the case of Pte Thompson | |
| | | | 46th Machine Gun Company relieved 10 guns of this Coy. Gun teams on being relieved withdrew to Coy Headquarters | |
| | 9-2-18 | | Relieved 4 guns of 44th Machine Gun Company taking over positions O.2: R.8: I.5 and I.6. | |
| | 10-2-18 | 6 am | C.O. visited the gun positions with Major NASMYTH | |
| | 11-2-18 | | C.O. visited guns in the line | |
| | 12-2-18 | | C.O. visited guns in the line | |
| | 13-2-18 | | C.O. visited guns in the line. Working party sent up to improve gun positions and make shelters for gun teams. | |
| | 14-2-18 | | 2/Lt. B.C. SIMMONDS visited guns in the line. | |

A5834 Wt. W4973/M687 750,000 8/16 D. D. & L. Ltd. Forms/C.2118/13.

Instructions regarding War Diaries and Intelligence Summaries are contained in F. S. Regs., Part II. and the Staff Manual respectively. Title pages will be prepared in manuscript.

# WAR DIARY
*or*
# INTELLIGENCE SUMMARY.
*(Erase heading not required.)*

Army Form C. 2118.

| Place | Date | Hour | Summary of Events and Information | Remarks and references to Appendices |
|---|---|---|---|---|
| In the Field | 15-2-18 | | C.O visited gun positions in the line. | |
| | 16-2-18 | | "B" Section relieved 4 guns of "C" Section at positions R.9; R.10; R.11; R12. Teams 15 and 16 of "D" Section relieved teams 13 and 14 at positions O2 and R.8. On relief C section marched to billets in ARRAS while teams 13 and 14 took up positions in shelters near Coy. Headqrs. | |
| | 17-2-18 | 9. am | C.O. visited gun positions in the line with Major Nasmith | |
| | 18-2-18 | 9 am | C.O visited gun position in the line | |
| | | 9. pm | Bombs dropped in our lines by Enemy aeroplanes. | |
| | 19-2-18 | | C.O. visited Brigade Headquarters | |
| | | 6 pm | Capt NAWTON returned from duty in U.K. & took over command of Company | |
| | 20.2.18 | 4.30 pm | C.O. went up to Company Headquarters & took over from Lieut BARNS | |
| | 21.2.18 | 9. am | C.O. round all guns, weather fine | |
| | | | Co to Brigade in afternoon. Major NASMITH came to Company H.Q. in morning | |
| | 22.2.18 | 9. am | C.O. round line | |
| | | 3 pm | Conference at Camerons H.Q. WILDERNESS CAMP. | |
| | | 4 pm | 4 teams of C relieved 4 teams of A at positions I 5.6.7.8. | |
| | 23.2.18 | 9 am | C.O. round guns. Weather dull everything quiet. | |
| | | 3.30 am | 44th Brigade raid. 6 guns fired 12.500 rounds in support | |
| | | 4.30 pm | 2 teams of D relieved 2 of B at R.9. R10 positions | |

A5834 Wt. W4973/M687 750,000 8/16 D. D. & L. Ltd. Forms/C.2118/13.

Instructions regarding War Diaries and Intelligence Summaries are contained in F. S. Regs., Part II. and the Staff Manual respectively. Title pages will be prepared in manuscript.

# WAR DIARY
or
# INTELLIGENCE SUMMARY.
(*Erase heading not required.*)

Army Form C. 2118.

| Place | Date | Hour | Summary of Events and Information | Remarks and references to Appendices |
|---|---|---|---|---|
| In the Line | 23.2.18 | | Lieut BARNS returned to Transport Lines ARRAS. 2Lt TRACE + c/pl BUDGE to | 17 Corps School |
| | 24.2.18 | 9 am | C.O. + Lieut JACKSON round line | |
| | | | Lieut STRANGE returned from leave to UNITED KINGDOM | |
| | | 3 pm | Conference at Headquarters 11th A+SH WILDERNESS CAMP | |
| | 25.2.18 | 9 am | CO round guns. Weather dull | |
| | | | 2 Lieut T. Pearce relieved 2Lt A. James at MONCHY CHATEAU | |
| | 26.2.18 | 9 am | C.O. round guns. Weather bright + cold. | |
| | | 10 am | F.G.C.M. on Pte Heggarty 6th Camerons, att'd 45 M.G.C. Accused found "Not Guilty" + discharged. | |
| | | | 2/LT. C.F. TIGUE reported for duty. | |
| | 27.2.18 | 9 am | C.O. round guns. Weather dull. | |
| | 28.2.18 | 9 am | C.O. round guns. | |
| | | 1 pm | 2/Lt G. HARBOTTLE reported to C.O. | |

[illegible]
Captn.
O.C. 45 Machine Gun Company

D. D. & L., London, E.C.
(A7853) Wt W595/M1672 50,000 4/17 Sch 52a Forms/C/2118/14

www.ingramcontent.com/pod-product-compliance
Lightning Source LLC
Chambersburg PA
CBHW080901230426
43663CB00013B/2599
*9781474509688*